T4-AHF-600

ROBERT LANSING AND AMERICAN NEUTRALITY

1914-1917

A Da Capo Press Reprint Series

THE AMERICAN SCENE
Comments and Commentators

GENERAL EDITOR: WALLACE D. FARNHAM
University of Illinois

ROBERT LANSING AND AMERICAN NEUTRALITY

1914-1917

By Daniel M. Smith

DA CAPO PRESS · NEW YORK · 1972

Library of Congress Cataloging in Publication Data

Smith, Daniel Malloy, 1922-
  Robert Lansing and American neutrality, 1914-1917.

  (The American scene: comments and commentators)
  Reprints of the 1958 ed., which was issued as v. 59 of
University of California publications in history.
  Bibliography: p.
  1. Lansing, Robert, 1864-1928. 2. United States—
Neutrality. 3. United States—Foreign relations—
1913-1921. I. Title. II. Series: California.
University. University of California publications in
history, v. 59.

E768.L32S58   1972   327'.2'0924 [B]   79-126610
ISBN 0-306-70057-3

This Da Capo Press edition of *Robert Lansing and American
Neutrality, 1914-1917,* is an unabridged republication
of the first edition published in Berkeley and Los Angeles
in 1958 as Volume LIX of the *University of California
Publications in History.*

Published by Da Capo Press, Inc.
A Subsidiary of Plenum Publishing Corporation
227 West 17th Street, New York, New York 10011

ROBERT LANSING AND AMERICAN NEUTRALITY

1914-1917

ROBERT LANSING

ROBERT LANSING
AND AMERICAN NEUTRALITY

1914-1917

BY

DANIEL M. SMITH

UNIVERSITY OF CALIFORNIA PRESS
BERKELEY AND LOS ANGELES
1958

University of California Publications in History
Editors (Berkeley): K. M. Stampp, D. M. Brown, J. F. King, R. J. Son.ag

Volume 59, pp. 1–242, frontis.

Submitted by editors April 29, 1957
Issued November 14, 1958
Price, $5.00

University of California Press
Berkeley and Los Angeles
California

◇

Cambridge University Press
London, England

PREFACE

IT IS STRANGE, indeed, that no adequate study has been made of the career of Robert Lansing, who, as counselor and as secretary of state, played so significant a role in the formulation of policy from 1914 to 1920. Of this major participant in the crucial events of America's neutrality and belligerency only one account has been written and that, by Julius W. Pratt in 1929, is hardly more than a sketch. To fill this gap in the literature of America's intervention in World War I the present work was undertaken.

A number of eminent scholars have touched upon Lansing in monographs dealing with the period of American neutrality. The most remarkable aspect of these accounts is the wide divergence in the interpretations of Lansing's contributions. One group has dismissed the secretary as a mere legal clerk who simply affixed his signature and the department's seal to decisions made by President Woodrow Wilson. The president and his peripatetic advisor, Colonel Edward Mandell House, have emerged as the real policy makers. Samuel Flagg Bemis, one of the leading writers in the field of American diplomacy, has epitomized this view when he pithily described Lansing as a "political funambulator, walking the unsteady tightwire of neutrality to the end, leaving the decisions to others."

Other historians have maintained that the secretary was by no means an errand boy for Wilson and House but that he served, rather, as an important figure in the policy-making process. There is still a third group of writers who have ascribed to Lansing a decisive influence on the formulation of American policy. Even within these latter two groups there is a difference of opinion. Edwin M. Borchard has characterized Lansing as one who "seems to have fumbled nearly every legal issue." Charles Callan Tansill has criticized the secretary savagely for having been a tool of the financial and industrial interests. Richard W. Van Alstyne, on the other hand, has portrayed Lansing as a far-sighted statesman whose conduct was impelled by the loftiest motives.

These divergencies might be attributed to a number of factors. Those writers who have assigned an inconsequential role to Lansing were probably conditioned by their views of Lansing's very modest and reticent personality vis-à-vis the more dynamic Wilson and House, and by the lack of pertinent historical materials. As more private collections and diplomatic documents became available, it was no longer possible to dismiss Lansing as of little or no consequence. However, though attributing more importance to Lansing's role, later historians have sharply disagreed in their evaluations of Lansing primarily because of their individual approaches toward the problems of neutrality and intervention.

From all these sharp disagreements in points of view there emerged the need for a new interpretation. The recent opening of a most important documentary source, the Confidential Memoranda of Robert Lansing (sometimes referred to as Diaries), enhanced the opportunity to meet the challenge. The private memoranda have revealed material which indicates that not only was Lansing's role of supreme importance but that his tenure in the Department of State has earned for him a place among the leading American secretaries of state.

It is a pleasant obligation to acknowledge the generous advice and aid I have had in the course of this study. I am indebted to Professor Armin Rappaport of the University of California at Berkeley for guidance, and to Professor John D. Hicks of the same university for his valuable criticisms. To Mr. William McCoy I am very grateful for a careful reading of the original manuscript. Professor Thomas A. Bailey of Stanford University has also read it and offered valuable suggestions. I wish to express my appreciation to the Regents of the University of California for the University Fellowship which enabled the completion of this study, and to Stanford University for helpful research and typing grants from the Dean's Fund, administered by the Institute of American History. To my wife, Aladeen, for her careful typing, proofing, and encouragement, is due my principal debt.

DANIEL M. SMITH

Boulder, Colorado
September, 1957

CONTENTS

Chapter I

ROBERT LANSING, PREWAR YEARS

Robert Lansing was born October 17, 1864, in Watertown, New York.[1] The son of John Lansing, a prominent attorney, and of Maria Lay Dodge, Lansing could claim descent from distinguished Dutch colonial forebears who had come to America in 1640. After attending local schools, he entered Amherst and graduated in 1886. In 1889 he was admitted to the bar and became a junior partner in the Watertown firm of Lansing and Lansing. His marriage the following year to Eleanor Foster, the eldest daughter of John Watson Foster, served to rescue him from ordinary legal practice which he had found rather uninteresting. John W. Foster was then a distinguished international lawyer, with an extensive private practice as consultant for foreign governments.[2] A new field in international law was thus opened to Lansing, who entered actively into Foster's practice and soon acquired a comprehensive knowledge of this highly specialized profession.

As a consequence of his international law practice, Lansing soon was called into government service. In 1892 Secretary of State James G. Blaine appointed him associate counsel for the United States at the Bering Sea Fur Seal Arbitrations. In the course of this work, he visited the Pacific coast on an evidence-gathering mission and later went to Paris for the arbitral sessions.[3] For the next twenty years he represented the government before international tribunals and as a delegate at several conferences: the Bering Sea Claims Commission in 1896, the 1903 Alaskan Boundary Tribunal's sessions in London, the North Atlantic Fisheries Arbitration at The Hague from 1908 to 1910,[4] the North Atlantic Fisheries and Fur Seals Conference in 1911, and the arbitrations held under the Special Agreement of August 18, 1910, with Great Britain.[5] During the intervals between government missions, Lansing aided Foster in his private international law practice, serving the Mexican and Chinese legations and representing private persons in the 1905 Venezuelan Asphalt disputes. These experiences gave Lansing an extensive knowledge of the complexities of international law and acquainted him with the leading figures in this field. Work had several times taken him to Europe, consequently broadening his attitudes and thought. By 1914 Lansing had served on more international arbitrations than any other living American.[6]

During these busy years, Lansing found time for other varied activi-

ties. He joined his friend, Gary M. Jones, principal of the Watertown
high school, in editing a textbook on American government.[7] He also
participated in the formation of the American Society of International
Law in 1905, which was an outgrowth of the annual Lake Mohonk conferences devoted to discussions of international arbitration. A committee of twenty-one was appointed to draw up the charter of the
organization. This committee included a good cross section of the legal
profession: John W. Foster, Chandler P. Anderson, J. W. Griggs, Oscar
S. Straus, Robert Lansing, and others.[8] The society was formally established January 12, 1906, and began publication of the *American Journal of International Law* in 1907. Lansing published his "Notes on
Sovereignty" in the first volume and thereafter served as an associate
editor and contributor until his death in 1928.[9]

The victory of the Democratic party in the 1912 election, when
Woodrow Wilson was elected president of the United States, opened
new vistas for Lansing. His career had so far been satisfactory, with
steady advancement and increasing prestige in his profession. John W.
Foster had not only introduced him into the field of international law
but also had enabled him to secure substantial legal appointments from
various Republican administrations. Nevertheless, as a Democrat, it
was problematical if Lansing could have advanced much further. Had
the Republicans been in control during World War I, use might have
been made of Lansing's talents and experience; however, it is extremely
doubtful that he would have risen to a high post in the Department of
State. The Democratic victory thus seemed to offer Lansing the opportunity to enter the State Department in a policy-making position. This
hope was buttressed by the fact that the Democrats had been long out
of power and consequently faced a shortage of experienced and politically acceptable men for positions within the department.

The problem of reorganization within the department had long interested Lansing, and he concentrated his aspirations on the post of
assistant secretary of state, then charged with administrative functions.
In December of 1912 he asked John N. Carlisle, a Watertown attorney,
to intercede on his behalf with William Jennings Bryan, the secretary-
designate in Wilson's cabinet. Lansing averred his desire to render
public service, even at a loss of income, and asserted that past Republican administrations had offered him several posts which as a loyal
Democrat he had been forced to turn down, accepting only nonpolitical
legal work. Carlisle answered favorably and assured Lansing that he
was certain that appointments would be made on the basis of merit, not

boss-indorsement.[10] Others also came to Lansing's support. James Brown
Scott interceded for Lansing with Frederic R. Coudert of Watertown,
in an effort to secure the approval of New York's Senator James A.
O'Gorman.[11] Judge Henry Purcell of Jefferson County also wrote
O'Gorman, certifying Lansing's status as a good party man.[12] On
February 17, Lansing had a satisfactory interview with the senator in
Washington, which encouraged him to hope for success. John Bassett
Moore, distinguished international lawyer and Wilson's first counselor
of the State Department, declared Lansing excellently qualified for the
post of assistant secretary. Thereupon Lansing on March 18 called on
Secretary Bryan who requested a detailed biography but made no
promises.[13]

In spite of these efforts and encouragements, Lansing failed to secure
an appointment in 1913. This failure may have been caused by Lansing's rather weak party status, and by the large number of politically
deserving candidates who descended upon Washington. Bryan was
particularly responsive to the need of rewarding the faithful. Lansing,
therefore, continued his regular duties as United States counsel at the
Anglo-American arbitration taking place under the agreement of August, 1910. These duties consisted of preparing and arguing cases, some
of which dated back to the War of 1812, and arranging schedules for
the following sessions. While engaged in these duties, Lansing closely
observed foreign policy developments and was pleased that Wilson was
gaining in popularity. He compared Wilson favorably with Theodore
Roosevelt, concluding that Wilson possessed Roosevelt's energy and
determination without his impulsiveness and brutality.[14] Lansing approved the administration's Mexican policy of "watchful waiting"
toward Huerta, which he described as constructive statesmanship and
believed that it was likely to succeed. In the meantime a vacancy occurred in the department and Lansing resumed his candidacy for an
appointment.

On March 14, 1914, the counselor of the State Department, John
Bassett Moore, resigned his position, having originally agreed to serve
only one year. In addition Moore had disagreed seriously with Wilson
and Bryan and had advocated recognition of the Huerta regime in
Mexico, an act that, although contrary to Wilson's policy of morality
and constitutionalism, was in conformity with the past American policy
of recognizing *de facto* governments. Moore furthermore was discon-
tented with the general chaos within the State Department, created
largely by Bryan's inexperience and "spoils system" policy.[15] This sud-

den development offered Lansing another opportunity for entering the upper levels of the department, and his name was taken immediately under consideration. With the possible exception of the departing counselor, Lansing was the best qualified man for the position. With the support of prominent men, which he had been securing for more than a year, all seemed clear until the old Ward claims story was revived in an attempt to block his appointment. This case involved the heirs of General Frederick T. Ward, who had served China in 1861–1862 during the Taiping Rebellion. For more than thirty years thereafter various attorneys had pressed unsuccessfully Ward's claims for his unpaid military services. In March, 1881, Secretary of State William M. Evarts had fixed the amount due, but the Chinese government refused to approve the award. John W. Foster accepted the case on a contingency basis in January, 1902, and brought Lansing in as his assistant. Representations to the State Department and to the Chinese Foreign Office were renewed. These resulted finally in agreement to allow the estate $388,236 to be taken from the American portion of the Boxer Indemnity. This was the sum originally determined by Secretary Evarts and reapproved by Secretary John Hay in 1903. Soon after the award was made, charges were raised that Foster and Lansing had abused their official connections, although neither was at that time in government service, and that the amount they received for their legal services was exorbitant. When attorneys formerly employed by the Ward estate, dissatisfied with their share of the compensation, brought the matter before Secretary Elihu Root, the case was reëxamined and the charges of excessive fees dismissed.[16]

Now, more than ten years later, when Lansing was being considered for the counselor's office, these old charges were revived. A new accusation claimed that the money used to settle the case was taken illegally from Boxer Indemnity funds which Congress had ordered returned to the Chinese government. This was speedily proved false, since Congress had not authorized the first remission of the unused part of the Indemnity until 1908, several years after the Ward case had been settled. President Wilson, upon being informed of these accusations, directed Secretary Bryan to confer with Root on the matter, and Root completely exonerated Lansing.[17] Thereupon Lansing's name was submitted to the Senate for confirmation as counselor. Bryan went before the Senate Foreign Relations Committee on March 25, explained the Ward affair, and praised Lansing's qualities. The committee was convinced of his honesty and unanimously approved his nomination.[18]

Lansing's appointment as counselor was confirmed by the Senate on March 27, 1914, and on April 1 he took the oath of office in the State Department in the presence of his wife and James Brown Scott.[19] The office of counselor was then second only to that of the secretary, and in this position Lansing was destined to have an important part in the formulation of policy.[20] He frequently was called upon to act as secretary while Bryan was absent. Under Bryan the department had become quite disorganized, partly because of the inevitable confusion attendant upon the installation of a new administration as well as those factors previously mentioned—Bryan's lack of proficiency and his excessive zeal in rewarding the politically faithful.[21] The effects had been particularly unfortunate in the foreign service which, during the long years of Republican rule, had begun to evolve gradually into a professional career service. These public servants took Lansing's appointment as a positive sign that a halt had been called in the political shake-up of the service and as presaging a return to the merit system.[22] The *Nation* also took this view and in favorable comment (in 1915) on Lansing's appointment added that Lansing, unlike the formal and unbending Moore, rendered valuable service as a "lubricator" within the department and as an extricator of Bryan from his frequent difficulties.[23] Lansing's appointment was favorably received in the limited public notice given the event, and he was launched upon his new career.[24]

When Lansing became counselor in 1914, he was fifty years old, a short, dignified man of handsome visage, graying hair, and impeccable manners, corresponding closely to the popular stereotype of a diplomat. Diffident almost to the point of painful shyness, he restricted his more intimate personal relations to a narrow circle of friends, to whom he was known as "Bert."[25] By birth, rearing, and education he was a member of the upper classes, accustomed to sufficient wealth and other attributes necessary to a comfortable, cultured life. Conservative in outlook, studious, and well informed, Lansing appeared more the scholar than the man of action.[26] In religion, he was a conservative Protestant, with emphasis on the Bible as the literal source of God's will and with complete reliance upon the doctrine of Christ's death and individual repentance as the only means to spiritual salvation. Throughout his long residence in Washington, Lansing was a member and an Elder in the Presbyterian Church.[27] Religion was a major force in Lansing's psychological make-up, and he steadfastly followed a strict course of Bible study, often reading late into the night.

Conservatism in religion and in mental outlook often is accompanied by conservatism in politics. This was true in Lansing's case. He classified himself as an "individualist," believing in as little control as possible by government over the lives of its citizens, as opposed to the "nationalists" and their desire for a larger role for government in the economic sphere. To Lansing, the latter were best defined as "lukewarm socialists."[28] He was a Democrat, but had never been in sympathy with Bryan's agrarian radical wing, with its demands for currency inflation and increased governmental regulation of business and finance; instead he subscribed to the conservative views of the Cleveland "gold" Democrats.[29] Lansing never took a large part in politics, and most of his limited activities in this field concerned only the city of Watertown and Jefferson County, New York. In 1886–1887, he served on the Jefferson County Democratic Committee, held briefly the chairmanship in 1889–1890, and thereafter retained a seat in the county executive committee. In 1902 he ran for the mayor's office in Watertown, and although he lost he did manage to reduce the usual Republican majorities from 1,200 to only 150 votes.[30] Thereafter Lansing restricted himself to the role of inside participant only, and played a part in the 1912 state convention and election where an unsuccessful attempt was made to clean up the state's politics and reduce the influence of Tammany.[31] On the whole, because of Lansing's very restricted political activities and his long record of legal service in the State Department under both Democratic and Republican administrations, he was generally considered to be nonpartisan.

Lansing's approach to foreign policy and international relations was necessarily conditioned by his long career in international law and arbitrations. Vittorio Orlando, the Italian premier during the later part of World War I, characterized Lansing (in 1919) as a person of an eminently analytical and purely realistic mind, with little play for fancy or imagination.[32] These qualities were well demonstrated in Lansing's views on the question of sovereignty among nation states. In a paper prepared for the *Proceedings of the American Political Science Association* in early 1914, he advanced a concept of sovereignty based on force alone, which he frankly admitted was a "materialistic" interpretation.[33] Lansing thought it paradoxical to talk of a superiority that was not superior or a supremacy not supreme, which he discerned in the argument advanced by his friend W. W. Willoughby and other scholars, that a sovereign state in many ways finds itself legally able to command but powerless to control. To Lansing real sovereignty meant control, not as the mere expression of will but as a physical coercive power. He found it difficult to conceive of law as a command of the sovereign state when the concept of sovereignty was itself made dependent upon the existence of law. Lansing admitted that what was termed the right of sovereignty, in the political sense, was a legal right, but he held that because all human rights stem from sovereignty, this legal right of sovereignty was merely the right to exercise political authority and pertained to "artificial sovereignty," which had its source in the real or actual sovereignty. In normal times the law, resting upon the superior might of the real sovereign, confers the legal right for its exercise upon the artificial sovereign. In times of war or crisis, however, when enacted law loses its force, the right of artificial sovereignty is dependent directly upon the will of the real sovereign, which manifests itself not by law but by physical force and superiority.

The concept of physical force as the effective instrumentality within an organized state applied particularly to the international relations of sovereign states. "Force is the great underlying actuality in all history, which, regardless of the higher intellectual and spiritual impulses affecting human conduct, must be recognized and reckoned with in international and national relationships."[34] This force, Lansing held, must be organized and coördinated to be effective, and in essence this has been the function of civilization. Social coöperation is induced by common impulses, which Lansing divided into categories of material and moral drives. Material impulses he likened to animal instincts, being essentially primitive remnants of savagery. Moral impulsion came from the intellect and was not instinctive as was the material, but instead was the product of man's slow ascent from barbarism, typified by the increasing awareness of "right" and "wrong." These moral impulses were closely akin to religion. With cultural advances and the increase of man's sensibilities, the moral forces became more clearly defined and tended increasingly to control the intrapersonal relations of a society. Lansing viewed this increasing moral control as the distinguishing line between savagery and civilization. Although some individuals were influenced by these moral drives early in history, society reacted far more slowly, since cultural development and the acquisition of knowledge are the mental acts of individuals. Historically, a rudimentary beginning at developing a moral sense was made in the Roman Empire, but this was seriously checked by barbarian inroads and the subsequent Dark Ages. The Crusades manifested a religious fanaticism closely allied to moral impulses, and this rebirth was powerfully stimulated by the intellectual awakening which followed. The most rapid progress in the development of a moral sense was under the influence of the Protestant Reformation, opening the epoch of ethical culture which characterizes modern society. Thus within a political state, law and government came increasingly under the control of moral standards. Unfortunately this had not yet been extended into the international arena, where governing impulses were still primarily materialistic and selfish, with altruism playing a very small part. Therefore to assume otherwise, to feel that the foreign policy of a nation is based on unselfish motives, is a fallacious assumption, and to base a foreign policy on it is a grave error. In essence a nation deals with its own people in a civilized manner and with other nations in a savage way, with the basic assumption underlying international relations being the presumption of violence and physical force. To Lansing, a policy which denied or repudiated facts, or which was based on an impractical theory or objective, was a menace to the best conduct of foreign affairs. "Idealism which cannot be harmonized with sound common sense is worse than useless."[35]

From this schematic, oversimplified version of history, we can draw several conclusions about Lansing's intellectual processes. He was a realist and as such did not blind himself to ugly facts merely because they contradicted his aspirations and ideals. This is a valuable quality in a statesman who must shape his policies largely by what is attainable. Furthermore, Lansing demonstrated that he was not a mere legalist, that he could clearly see the difference between domestic law, capable of enforcement, and international law which could not be enforced and which therefore represented little more than custom and expediency. In a world of sovereign nation states, each dedicated to follow in foreign relations its own interests, chief among which is self-preservation at all costs, force—not international law and morality—is the ultimate determinant of behavior. Lansing did not proceed beyond this point to the conclusion which later thinkers have reached, that the nation-state system should be replaced by a world union or government, in order to eliminate war and the selfish international use of force. Nevertheless, Lansing was not a pessimist, for he believed that the inevitable increase in moral sensibilities would eventually transform national societies and thus change profoundly international relations.

This brief exposition of Lansing's thought explains much about his career as counselor and secretary of state. His realistic approach and thorough grounding in international law were most valuable and most appreciated by President Wilson in the 1914–1917 period of American neutrality. After the United States entered the war, and particularly at the peace conference, Lansing's realism was to result in basic disagreement with Wilson's idealistic views on postwar international organization and was eventually to culminate in Lansing's forced resignation in 1920.

The four months that intervened between Lansing's appointment as counselor of the State Department and the outbreak of World War I were occupied mostly by the normal routine of foreign relations, except for the Mexican crisis. Lansing immediately assumed the position on the executive committee of the American Red Cross that was reserved for the State Department. Some demands were also made on Lansing by requests of friends and acquaintances in Watertown for political appointments, and, wherever possible, he used his influence to aid them.[36] To illustrate the range of more or less routine problems with which Lansing was concerned before the outbreak of the war, it would be well to examine several: the tariff, Panama wireless stations, Panama tolls repeal, and the Nicaraguan treaty.

Although the State Department is charged with primary responsibility for the conduct of foreign affairs, it frequently finds that other executive departments have in effect interfered in this duty. A good illustration is the tariff-bounties question which arose in 1914 with Great Britain. In 1911 the United States Treasury Department had ruled, at the request of the British embassy, that British bounties on spirits were not bounties within the meaning of the 1909 Payne-Aldrich Tariff. This ruling was reversed by the Treasury Department in 1914 and countervailing duties were invoked. Lansing received protests from the British embassy and wrote the Treasury that such reversals unduly embarrassed the State Department by creating in foreign eyes the impression that the American government was extremely unreliable in its decisions. This action was particularly unfortunate in view of pending trade negotiations with Great Britain. Nevertheless, the Treasury Department refused to reconsider its decision, stating that the 1913 tariff allowed no discretion in regard to bounties, and Lansing perforce had to agree.[37]

Latin America has long been a primary concern of American foreign policy. The nearly completed Panama Canal in 1914 accentuated concern with the security of American interests in the Caribbean area. Therefore, when in April of 1914 Lansing's opinion was requested on the Panamanian government's reluctance to grant the United States a monopoly of wireless stations, he ruled that the Canal Treaty of 1903 enabled the American government to use "due process" and eminent domain wherever required by defense needs, Panama's constitution or laws notwithstanding. Then, in complete harmony with past American arrogance in this area, he had the department's Latin American division apply sufficient pressure to secure a speedy "agreement" on wireless control with Panama.[38] This action was justified on the grounds of the strategic need to defend the canal against all eventualities.

The question of the repeal of the Panama Tolls Act was less a question of security than of national honor, in President Wilson's opinion. This act, by its preferential treatment of American coastwise shipping, apparently conflicted with the Hay-Pauncefote Treaty with Great Britain, which pledged equal treatment to all nations using the Canal. In the course of the repeal fight in Congress, Wilson secured the unexpected support of the Republican senator from New York, Elihu Root. Consequently, Lansing was assigned by Wilson to join James Brown Scott and Joseph H. Choate in the preparation of Root's repeal speech, delivered in the Senate May 21.[39] In large measure because of this support, the act was repealed and American honor, as conceived by Wilson, was upheld.

Security was the chief motive behind the Nicaraguan treaty. The Taft administration in 1913 had negotiated a treaty with Nicaragua which gave the United States an option in perpetuity on the alternate canal route and the right to establish a naval base in the Gulf of Fonseca, together with leases of the Great and Little Corn islands. In return, the United States was to pay $3,000,000, which would enable Nicaragua to straighten out her financial affairs. The incoming Wilson administration accepted this treaty, added a protectorate article allowing intervention and guaranteeing government stability and territorial integrity, and submitted the revised treaty to the Senate for ratification. Lansing drew up a memorandum for Bryan which discussed the probable objections which this treaty would meet in the Senate. He pointed out that for the sake of control of the alternate route, the United States government was assuming the burden of maintaining Nicaraguan independence and territory not only against any European threat but against any originating in the Western Hemisphere as well; the latter aspect was contrary to general American policy. The memorandum cited President Cleveland's withdrawal of a similar treaty with Nicaragua in 1885, on the grounds that he was unable to approve an agreement which involved an unlimited commitment to defend the territory of a foreign state. Lansing pointed out that opponents could argue that the Monroe Doctrine alone was sufficient to forestall any construction of a canal by a foreign power, a canal which was manifestly not the intent of the United States to construct at present. Heavy opposition was predicted in the Senate; therefore temporary postponement of the treaty was recommended. This memorandum displayed strikingly Lansing's realistic approach to foreign affairs and his awareness of the relation of policy to domestic political currents. Large numbers of Democrats, both within and out of Congress, were opposed to continuation of the protectorate policies initiated by the previous Republican administration. Lansing's memorandum was sent to Wilson, who admitted its force but held that strategic necessity allowed no delay.[40] The result was as forecast: senatorial opposition forced the renegotiation of the treaty, without the protectorate features. The verification of Lansing's analysis in this case illustrated why both Wilson and Bryan came to rely increasingly upon him for advice on policy matters.

In terms of immediate consequences, Mexico was by far the most serious problem for American foreign policy during the spring of 1914. Mexico was undergoing a profound social and economic revolution. The resultant chaos seriously affected the United States because of proximity and economic investments, and created problems which concerned the whole of Wilson's two administrations. This larger story will not be told, but to present the picture as of August, 1914, a short résumé is desirable at this point.

Since the conquest by Cortés the Mexican population had been composed of a small upper class of Spanish descent ruling the masses of mestizos and Indians. Most of the Indians lived in villages surrounded by communal lands called *ejidos*. The mid-nineteenth century regime of Benito Juárez sought to modernize Mexico on the pattern of the more advanced Western bourgeois states and instituted a program of which one aspect was to substitute small proprietorships for the communal holdings. Unfortunately, the Indian had little understanding of private property rights and soon began to lose the few acres allotted him when the *ejidos* were dissolved. The long dictatorship of Porfirio Díaz, 1876–1911, based upon the conservative interests in Mexico, continued Juárez' program but distorted its purpose completely in favor of the wealthier classes. The result was that the Indian was gradually reduced to the status of a landless agricultural laborer, usually in debt servitude to the great landlords with which Mexico abounded. Díaz also encouraged the entry of foreign capital in the exploitation of Mexico's resources, particularly minerals and petroleum. The inevitable result was that the lower classes sank lower on the economic scale, and a privileged class of domestic landholders and foreign capitalists became rich and drained Mexico's wealth at a tremendous pace. By 1910 more than 90 per cent of the communal holdings in Mexico's central plateau had been eliminated, and three million natives were held in debt peonage. Mexico had truly become the "mother of foreigners and the stepmother of Mexicans"; conditions were ripe for revolution.[41]

Francisco Madero, who led the successful revolution against Díaz, was of the upper classes himself, more interested in political than economic reforms. However, though well-meaning and sincere, he was rather indecisive and ineffectual as a popular leader. The result was the outbreak of a second wave of revolution, with General Venustiano Carranza in the north and Emiliano Zapata in the south rising against the capital. At this point the conservatives instigated a counterrevolution whereby Victoriano Huerta, Madero's general, seized power in February, 1913. The sequel was the apparently accidental killing of Madero, which many people, including Wilson, believed to have been political murder by Huerta. President Taft's expiring administration postponed the question of recognition, apparently in order to bargain for the settlement of certain disputes.[42]

The foreign interests in Mexico had prospered greatly under Díaz' conservative rule, and they tended to support Huerta as the new "strong man" capable of maintaining the order and stability requisite for the continued prosperity of business.[43] Several European countries, including Great Britain, had already recognized the Huerta government. President Wilson, however, entered office determined to produce a radical reform in policy which would assert world moral leadership and advance American ideals, instead of merely advancing financial interests as, in his view, his predecessors had done. Therefore he reversed the former policy of recognizing *de facto* governments and substituted the criterion of constitutionalism and legitimacy.[44] Huerta's regime was particularly distasteful, being tainted with Madero's death as well as with unconstitutional violence. A policy of nonrecognition and moral pressure against Huerta was inaugurated, and in August, 1913, an embargo on arms shipments to Mexico was applied. As the tension increased, "watchful waiting" began to give way to more positive intervention, and in February, 1914, the embargo was lifted to enable arms to reach the Carranza and Villa factions.[45] The stage was being set for the Tampico-Veracruz incident.

On April 9, some American sailors were arrested in Tampico by the local Huerta officials. Although the men were soon released, Admiral

Henry T. Mayo of the American squadron promptly demanded a formal apology, punishment of the offenders, and a salute to the American flag. The reluctance of Huerta to comply with these exacting and humiliating demands raised the question if force should be used to secure compliance. In a preliminary memorandum of April 14, Lansing examined the use of armed force from the standpoint of domestic and international law, and concluded that though Congress alone could declare war, the enforcement of demands by the display or use of force in peacetime could be authorized by the president without resort to Congress, since international precedent and practice had not classified that as actual war.[46] He pointed out, however, that armed reprisals could be used only after diplomatic negotiations had been exhausted, and should cease as soon as the delinquent state made the proper reparations. The United States government, on executive authority alone, had used similar measures in the Shimonoseki affair in Japan in 1863 and in the bombardment of Greytown, Nicaragua, in 1854.[47] Wilson was particularly impressed by the Greytown incident, using it in a statement of April 20 to demonstrate the effectiveness of armed reprisals.[48]

In keeping with the nonrecognition policy, Lansing advised that all diplomatic correspondence with Huerta be addressed to him as the "*de facto* government" at Mexico City. In a detailed memorandum to Bryan April 19, Lansing again supported the power of the executive to take all acts short of war, but urged caution in seeking a congressional resolution approving executive action.[49] He pointed out that a declaration of war implied recognition, which occurs only between independent nations, and that therefore any congressional resolution should be very carefully phrased. Caution in this matter was all the more necessary since the nations which had recognized Huerta would tend to view reprisals and interferences with neutral vessels in Mexican ports as factual proof of a state of war. Lansing then suggested that the congressional resolution should declare merely that the president was justified in using force, rather than authorizing specifically such an act. This would be in effect an admission by Congress of the constitutionality of unilateral executive reprisals.

On April 20, 1914, Wilson addressed Congress on the Mexican situation and requested approval of the projected armed retaliation, which he claimed was amply within the executive powers but was so grave as to require legislative consideration.[50] A resolution, which Lansing had drafted April 18 and which had been modified and approved by the Cabinet April 20, was introduced in the House of Representatives and speedily passed.[51] The Senate concurred April 22, but on the previous day American naval forces had begun the reduction of Veracruz, a decision hastened by the need to prevent the landing of a cargo of arms consigned to Huerta. On April 22, Lansing advised that relations be severed with Huerta by recalling the chargé at Mexico City.[52] This was done, amid mounting war enthusiasm in the United States. The alternatives now appeared to be withdrawal without the requisite atonement from the stubborn Huerta or full-scale intervention. Fortunately, a way out was provided when Argentina, Brazil, and Chile offered mediation, much to the relief of the harassed Wilson.[53]

Mediation was complicated by the fact that the United States had not recognized the government with which it was in conflict, an anomalous situation for a conference. Lansing defined it as an attempt to restore peace among the several Mexican factions, directed at securing guarantees conducive to the restoration of constitutional government, and not a mediation between two established states or belligerents. He discerned the real quarrel, as far as America was concerned, was with the intolerable conditions in Mexico, and not with the factions except so far as they produced those conditions. Therefore it was consistent with propriety that the United States be considered as neutral ground for the mediation conference, with American representatives to be unofficial, serving as channels of communication.[54]

Lansing's analysis pointed out the fundamental difficulty, which was more than the Tampico-Veracruz incident. The internal chaos attendant on a revolution endangered foreign lives and property within Mexico and impaired Mexican ability to perform the international duties incumbent upon a sovereign state. Great pressure for more positive intervention in Mexico was exerted by vested American interests, and the Wilson administration deserves much commendation for resisting these forces.[55] Even if Wilson's nonrecognition policy is viewed as unjustified intervention, which in itself accounted for some of the disorder in Mexico, the fact remains that the revolution would probably have continued its measured pace regardless of outside influences, and American and European interests would have been involved. In view of the internal conditions within Mexico, it is assuming much to contend that American recognition of Huerta would have enabled him to control the entire country and to have maintained order. Such order, purchased at the price of democratic virtues, would have faced the same social unrest and dissidence that had driven Díaz from power, and would have had at most a temporary stability.

Lansing recognized the underlying factors behind Mexican turbulence, which he classified as large land-ownership, debt peonage, corrupt government, and mass illiteracy. "Revolution has been the only means by which the Mexican people have ever exercised their sovereign rights, and even a revolution has been generally the result of a quarrel between the dominant class, in which the mass of the Mexicans derive no benefit, and only obtain a change of masters."[56] This insight accurately summarized the essence of previous Mexican politics and revolutions and expressed the truism of political scientists that where political rights are denied and orderly change precluded, opposition is driven underground and eventually resorts, of necessity, to violence as the only means of expression. Lansing recognized that not until extensive land reforms and educational projects were realized could the Mexican people raise their cultural level into conformity with their constitutional aspirations. The entire approach of Lansing to Mexico demonstrated not only that he was a well-informed person, but that his conservatism was of a most enlightened kind, capable of seeing the need of economic changes involving the sanctity of private property.

The elimination of Huerta, still in doubt during May, would not necessarily restore constitutionalism and order in Mexico. Lansing forecast three possibilities which might follow Huerta's removal: reorganization of Huerta's Federalists under a new leader, the triumph of Carranza's Constitutionalists, or the victory of Zapata's forces in the south. He advised the formulation of a policy designed to meet all of these potentialities, particularly since Mexico City would probably be the scene of a reign of terror during the changes—an accurate forecast as events were to demonstrate. If that happened, the United States would be blamed by many people at home and abroad, since it would have been partly responsible for the overthrow of Huerta. As Lansing saw it, the United States had only two alternatives: a reliance upon diplomatic pressure alone, or occupation of Mexico City by American forces.[57] Unfortunately his suggestions were not acted upon; Mexico City was left to its fate, and definite recognition was not extended to any of the factions until mid-1915.

The mediators met at Niagara Falls in late May, 1914, and began discussions with the Mexican factions. On June 3, Lansing wrote Wilson that, although the United States had recognized neither Huerta nor Carranza, these two groups together represented all that could be termed the *de facto* government of Mexico. Consequently the mediators should not cease making proposals because of rejection by either faction but rather should continue to offer suggestions until agreement by both groups was obtained. The proper role of the American mediators was that of intermediaries only. Lansing remarked that the mediators had erred from the beginning, had been arbitrary in manner, and had sought to dictate rather than propose. Wilson wrote Bryan on June 4 that this was an "admirable" letter and should be sent to the mediators as a guide.[58] Meanwhile the conference continued its sessions and on June 24 reached an agreement which the Carranza faction rejected. Mediation thus failed to solve Mexico's internecine strife, but it did tide over the Veracruz crisis, and Huerta's resignation in July partly met Wilson's objectives.

In this atmosphere of routine business, strained only by the Veracruz clash, the State Department faced the unexpected outbreak in August, 1914, of the European War. There were few indications in the department that anything unusual was about to occur. Summer was the time for vacations; Lansing requested his month beginning June 20, with Bryan's scheduled to follow immediately. Wilson agreed to these plans, although remarking that the Mexican crisis hardly permitted key men to be absent.[59] When the war came, it found the department lacking in both preparation and personnel for so great a crisis.

CHAPTER II

LANSING AND THE ESTABLISHMENT OF AMERICAN NEUTRALITY

AMERICA'S neutral policies were defined, in their basic elements, within the first few months of the war, and in a manner to render almost inevitable her eventual active participation.[1] On the formulation of American policy, Lansing had a decisive influence.

As a neutral, America faced a series of problems in the fall of 1914, principally centered around such matters as the Declaration of London, armed merchantmen, contraband trade, and loans to the belligerents. International law, as it related to these problems, was largely a matter of interpretation, and as counselor of the State Department, it became Lansing's responsibility to supply the requisite definitions. Lansing brought to bear on his policy decisions and recommendations his developing concept of the significance of the war to America's national interests. The resulting policy decisions, for which he bore considerable responsibility, made the American neutrality structure highly benevolent toward the Allies and strictly technical toward the Central Powers. America was closely connected with the Allies through political, economic, and emotional bonds. Hence American neutrality eventually lost most of its value for the German government; the lack of mutual interests meant that little existed either to restrain American condemnation of German war policies or to moderate the German determination of those policies.[2] In the determination of American policies, two underlying factors were significant—the American people's predisposition toward the Allies and the past relations of the United States with Great Britain and Germany.

Large numbers of German-Americans and Irish-Americans favored the Central Powers, but the preponderant mass of the American people, influenced by language and cultural bonds with England, sympathized with the Allied cause.[3] Even among pro-Allied Americans, however, there was no immediate eagerness to enter the war. Nevertheless, the general disposition toward the Allies did make possible the later intervention in the conflict. This pro-Allied sentiment increased as the war continued. Most of the war news entering the United States came over wireless and cable systems controlled by the Allies, and most American newspapers depended upon the British news services for their foreign coverage.[4] Allied propaganda, through skillful techniques of unob-

[17]

trusiveness and the services of native Americans, was able to exploit such patent facts as the German invasion of Belgium and France and, with the inevitable atrocity stories, to synthesize a unified picture of the sacredness of the Allied crusade against German brutality and militarism.[5] German attempts to counter Allied distortions were handicapped by institutional and cultural differences with the United States, which the later use of the submarine with its toll of noncombatant lives only accentuated. The general American predilection for the Allies was further increased by the economic bonds between the United States and the Entente, resulting from increased trade—a consequence of the British command of the seas and therefore of access to American industry.

Officially, Anglo-American relations had been steadily improving since the Venezuelan crisis of 1895. Great Britain, acutely aware of her comparative isolation in the face of the growing naval and military power of Germany, began a *rapprochement* with the United States. Paralleling this development, the course of German-American relations was less than cordial, largely because of economic and colonial competition between the two expanding powers, as well as the ideological conflict between Prussianism and the American democratic tradition.[6] In addition, a few Americans realized the vital interests of the United States in the European balance of power, viewing past American growth and development, unhampered by insecurity and the need to maintain large armaments, as largely due to this power structure and Britain's pivotal role therein. American isolation, therefore, was relative, dependent primarily on British naval supremacy; hence any major war threatening to alter sharply the European balance would of necessity involve American national interests. In 1913, Lewis Einstein, an experienced American diplomat, wrote an article on Anglo-German rivalry which emphasized America's stake in the European power structure.[7] He pointed out that any alteration would immediately affect the Far East and the Caribbean, that a British defeat in Europe or even a stalemated war would create far-reaching disturbances in those areas. Therefore, he concluded, the United States might find it necessary to intervene in any future European war. Lansing himself came to share this view, at least by mid-1915, recording in his private records the conviction that national interests and the political structure of the world required American intervention to prevent either an Allied defeat or a stalemated conflict.[8] This view was current among other administration officials and, with the other factors of sentiment and economics, did much to define American neutral policies and to facilitate the ultimate entry into the war.[9]

American attempts to cope with the European war during the fall of 1914 can be divided into two categories: international and domestic. On the international level, the adoption by the belligerents of the Declaration of London was sought, in order to secure a definite code of international law capable of adequately safeguarding American rights as a neutral and of forestalling serious controversy with the belligerents. The latter aspect primarily concerned Great Britain, whose command of the seas was most likely to affect American commercial interests. On the domestic level, it was necessary to establish policies on such matters as armed belligerent merchantmen, the trade in contraband, and loans to belligerents. A study of these problems and their solutions will demonstrate the basic pattern of American neutrality throughout the period 1914–1917.

* * *

Like most Americans, Lansing had been shocked at the sudden outbreak of the European war and his first reaction had been to rejoice that America was so far removed from the "... slaughter fields of poor little Belgium."[10] Nevertheless, he was definitely pro-Ally from the beginning, a feeling promoted not only by the general attitudes prevalent among prominent Easterners and by his many past contacts with English officials at international arbitrations, but even more by his grasp of the significance of the war to American interests. As the war progressed and the issues were apparently clarified, he became convinced that American interests in the balance of power, particularly as it bore upon the Caribbean and the Far East, gave the United States a stake in the war and justified intervention on the Allied side, if that proved necessary. Even during the early months of the war, he agreed with John Watson Foster and others that any American attempts at peaceful mediation would fail, for the Allies would not halt short of destroying Germany's power.[11] The war had just begun however, the Allies appeared capable of securing their own destinies, and American people apparently hoped and expected to remain out of the holocaust. As a trained lawyer and as counselor of the Department of State, Lansing sought, in conducting relations with the belligerents, to protect American rights as he viewed them and to preserve a record of formal and legal protests and reservations to acts of both belligerents transgressing those rights.

War presented the State Department with a horde of new problems, requiring departmental reorganization. Thousands of American citizens were stranded in Europe, suddenly bereft of funds as the world's finance exchange system collapsed.[12] The United States was called upon not only to rescue its own citizens but also to handle the affairs of several of the belligerents. To meet the press of events, the State Department recalled all officials on leave and vacations and hired the first of an ever-increasing wartime staff. Problems of neutrality, such as the invoking of the neutrality laws, the foreign nationals resident in America and seeking to return to Europe for military duty, and belligerent vessels in American harbors, vastly increased the work load of the counselor's office. To cope with these responsibilities, Lansing created the Joint State and Navy Neutrality Board.[13]

The board, composed of Dr. James Brown Scott of the State Department and two naval officers, Captains H. S. Knapp and James H. Oliver, served as a central clearing office for various problems of neutrality which arose, sending their findings to Lansing's office for approval and action. It was hoped that the board, besides relieving the counselor of many minor details, would prevent the confusion and delay most likely to occur, particularly since other executive agencies were also involved in the enforcement of the neutrality provisions. Under the very able chairmanship of Dr. Scott, upon whom Lansing depended heavily for advice and consultation on legal questions, the board was destined to perform a most valuable function. Later, at Lansing's suggestion, high-level collaboration was established between the State, Navy, and Treasury departments to enforce more efficiently the neutrality statutes, with special emphasis on close supervision of the sea ports.[14]

While the State Department was organizing for the tasks ahead, it became necessary to announce formally the status of the United States in relation to the European war. In keeping with precedent, President Wilson issued on August 4, 1914, the proclamation of neutrality, which Lansing had originally drafted.[15] As counselor, Lansing had primary responsibility for neutrality matters; hence he urged President Wilson to appeal publicly for individual neutrality in thought and action to match that of the government on the official level.[16] Lansing called attention to the large hyphenated population in the United States and the natural tendency of these persons to support the countries of their origin; an appeal to their common sense and duties as citizens to "preserve a strict neutrality" would not be amiss. The counselor also felt that the press especially should try to restrain itself by barring highly partisan opinions from the news columns. Secretary Bryan approved the suggestion, as he did almost any proposal which in his view might promote genuine neutrality, and sent the memorandum to Wilson. The result was Wilson's August 18 appeal for neutrality in thought and spirit.[17] Perhaps unfortunately, this wise advice was largely ignored by the population at large and even by the administration.

The status of neutral rights was the most important problem facing the United States on the international plane in the fall of 1914. American commerce to Europe was jeopardized, the cotton crop was about to enter the world market, and many shippers and manufacturers besieged the State Department for assurances of the safe continuation of their activities. Unfortunately international law was highly tenuous, lacking the enforcement provision of domestic law and depending for validity upon international comity and coöperation. Americans in particular tended to confuse international with domestic law, perhaps because of a general moralistic approach and near-worship of written contracts, leading to the false belief in the existence of an international consensus.[18] In reality, international law as it related to neutral and belligerent rights was no more than a compromise based on expediency, with belligerents usually seeking to curtail neutral activities as far as possible and checked only by the neutral's power to retaliate successfully. Consequently, maritime law had never been much more than a collection of past precedents and actions, usually contradictory and nearly always inexact in definition.

A century of relative peace in Europe, 1815 to 1914, offered opportunity to progress in the direction of codification and compromise, and there were repeated attempts to define international maritime law. Martial quiescence led many optimists to believe that mankind was moving toward a perpetual reign of peace, promoted by the blessings of free trade and modern industrialism. Even Great Britain, long the mistress of the seas and champion of the widest possible latitude of belligerent rights, began to mellow to the extent of accepting restrictions on sea warfare favoring neutrals and small-navy powers; as early as 1856 the British had ratified the Declaration of Paris, a liberal document defining the rules of blockade and contraband procedures.

At the Second Hague Conference, in 1907, the United States proposed that freedom of the seas be assured by prohibiting capture of private property, carrying to its ultimate conclusions the general contention of traditionally neutral, small-navy powers. Great Britain demurred, unwilling to lose her only offensive weapon against potential continental opponents, and the conference broke up without achieving any specific goal beyond a proposed International Prize Court.[19] The following year another conference assembled at London, from which emerged in 1909 a codification of laws regulating sea warfare, known as the Declaration of London.[20] The declaration, although allegedly a mere summary of existing rules, contained several important modifications. Besides a limited absolute- and conditional-contraband list, it gave for the first time an extensive free list of goods not subject to capture. Blockades to be legal had to be effective, and the doctrine of continuous voyage was limited to absolute contraband; conditional contraband could be seized only if destined for an enemy government or its armed forces, and not while en route to a neutral port. On the whole, the declaration was a compromise weighted in favor of the neutrals and as such represented a victory for the traditional small-navy or continental viewpoint. It proved a short-lived victory, however, for though the declaration was favored by the other signatories, the British House of Lords rejected it as throwing away all the advantages of sea power by allowing a continental opponent to import freely through contiguous neutrals.[21] Failure to ratify the declaration left maritime law in its previous chaotic state, with large areas of controversy likely to arise between belligerent and neutral upon the advent of the next war.[22]

When war came in 1914, Lansing sought adoption of the Declaration of London, not only to protect American rights but also to preserve friendly relations with Great Britain. It was obvious that a definite set of rules, such as those embodied in the declaration, would bind both belligerents and neutrals, minimize conflict over interpretation of law, and thus enable commerce to function in a nearly normal manner.[23] Adoption of the declaration would have been especially advantageous, since its free list contained many articles which the United States exported in quantity; and foodstuffs, even though conditional contraband, could have moved freely to neutral European ports. Politically, both Lansing and Wilson were conscious of the likelihood of serious controversies arising with Great Britain, which by means of its sea power rapidly asserted control of commerce to Europe. The American experiences preceding the War of 1812 offered analogies to the current situation, and because Lansing and Wilson, together with Colonel Edward M. House and other administration leaders, had a basic sympathy for Britain and the Allied cause, expediency dictated forestalling controversies by the medium of the declaration.[24] As Lansing was to suggest during the ensuing negotiations, Britain could adopt the declaration and still control German commerce, and at the same time avoid serious conflict with the United States. Furthermore, acceptance of the declaration would have bound the Central Powers also, an eventuality that perhaps would have benefited the Allies when the submarine appeared in the war arena.

It soon became apparent that Great Britain would seek to preserve the widest latitude in the use of her Navy, and that she was willing to accept a modified Declaration of London only out of deference to America. The declaration had been accepted by most of the other powers and hence had some moral force. Furthermore, the British Foreign Office realized their dependence on America for war materials. On August 6 Bryan dispatched a proposal to all the belligerents that the declaration be adopted for the duration of the war.[25] On the previous day, the American ambassador to Great Britain, Walter Hines Page, had telegraphed the first British contraband list, which, though adhering to the list within the declaration, made no reference to the free goods category.[26] Bryan's proposal was accepted promptly by the Central Powers, on condition that Great Britain would accept, and France and Russia left the matter to Britain for decision. When the British reply did arrive, it was found to be a rather evasive acceptance which substantially modified the declaration.[27] The order in council of August 20 applied the doctrine of continuous voyage to conditional contraband, and provided that destination could be inferred from sources other than the ship's papers. No reference was made to the free list, which disturbed the United States greatly, particularly when a few weeks later Britain suddenly listed unwrought copper on the conditional contraband list.[28] Despite this evidence that Britain was not going to accept the entire declaration, which meant that if modified by one side it could also be changed by the other and thus would lose all real value, the State Department persevered in its efforts.

Realism characterized Lansing's approach to foreign policy, and this was well demonstrated by the State Department's counternote to Britain's August order in council. Although sharing the general pro-Ally views held by Colonel House, Wilson's chief unofficial political adviser and foreign policy "expert," Lansing realized that amicable relations were most likely to be preserved by strong diplomatic action. Since Bryan was absent during most of September and October, Lansing acted as secretary and conducted the negotiations for the Declaration of London. Lansing and Cone Johnson, the department's solicitor, drafted a note which sharply rejected the August 20 order in council and repeated the request for an unmodified acceptance of the declaration.[29] The compromise nature of the declaration made modifications "wholly unacceptable," particularly when all the changes were made at the expense of the neutrals. The note declared that foodstuffs could not be halted except when destined for enemy military use, mere destination for an enemy port being an insufficient ground for seizure, running counter to British practices as defined by Lord Granville in 1885 and Lord Salisbury during the Boer War. Lansing on September 27 sent the note to Wilson with the comment: "I cannot but feel that the action of the British Government calls for unqualified refusal ... to acquiesce in its legality and that our objections should be clearly and firmly stated."[30] In the letter to Wilson, illustrating his deep concern to prevent another "drifting" into war with Britain, the European bastion of democracy, he drew a parallel between the current British order in council and those which did so much to stir up American animosity and resentment during the Napoleonic Wars. Lansing was in complete accord with both Wilson and House; they differed only as to means.[31]

The question of means was highly significant. Lansing felt that an honest statement of objections was best, but House and Wilson displayed an excessive sensitivity, bordering on timidity, about pressing the British government. Such fear of arousing English ill will was hardly conducive to the successful negotiation of serious controversies with a determined belligerent which had command of the seas. Colonel House made one of his periodic trips to the White House on the night of September 27 in time to witness the arrival of the Lansing-Johnson note. He immediately expressed considerable alarm to Wilson about the general tone of the note and persuaded the president to let him work out the controversy.[32] Thereupon, on the following morning, he closeted himself with Sir Cecil Spring-Rice, the British ambassador, and the two discussed the note at length. Spring-Rice had received earlier intimations that "something was up among the lawyers in the State Department," but was amazed when he saw the document.[33] He termed the draft a catastrophe which if sent would provoke a crisis unequaled since the Venezuelan imbroglio of 1895. The two statesmen then proceeded to toss aside this note and outlined an instruction to Page which was most mild in comparison.[34]

The new instructions to Page threw away a good legal case. Lansing was dissatisfied with the draft by House and Spring-Rice, commenting to Wilson that it left much unsaid that should have been brought out.[35] Nevertheless, at Wilson's orders, he prepared the draft which after a few changes was sent to Page September 28. The instructions, though expressing "grave concern" at the British modifications of the Declaration of London, made no reference to international law and the "illegality" of British actions in regard to continuous voyage. Instead, the factor of American public opinion was emphasized, which, it was said, would probably react very adversely when British practices became publicly known. After pointing out that President Wilson desired if possible to avoid a formal protest, the note besought the British to reconsider their modified acceptance of the declaration.[36] The legal case, developed at length in the rejected note, was being sacrificed for the sake of British good will, and since this was to be the first of many controversies with Great Britain, it was unfortunate that such unorthodox diplomacy as the House session with Spring-Rice should have taken place.[37] As Lansing later remarked, referring to Page, the strong presentation of legitimate American views and protests would have done more to forestall controversy and thus facilitate good relations than all the misguided efforts of amateur diplomats and Anglophiles.[38]

In a mood of growing concern for public opinion, the administration continued the negotiations for the acceptance of the entire declaration. Discontent among American shippers and farmers was increasing, and a congressional election was near at hand. On the night of September 28, at Wilson's request, Lansing entered into informal negotiations with Spring-Rice.[39] He called the attention of the British ambassador to an editorial in the Washington *Post* which critically examined the August 20 order in council. Spring-Rice appreciated the significance of such criticism and agreed to aid Lansing in securing the modification or retraction of the order. In discussing foodstuffs, which Britain had made almost absolute contraband, Spring-Rice asserted that though this was contrary to American and British practices, it was necessitated by heavy German imports through Rotterdam, used to supply her armies operating in Belgium. Lansing thereupon suggested that this source could be cut off more efficiently and still remain within the declaration by the negotiation of a nonexportation agreement with the Netherlands government.[40] He also agreed, though unofficially, that adding copper, petroleum, and Swedish iron to the absolute contraband list would be a reasonable exchange for the repeal of the obnoxious order. Lansing reiterated official concern for American public opinion, and Spring-Rice agreed to forward his suggestions to London. Immediately after the conference Lansing issued a press statement to the effect that Britain could be trusted to deal fairly with America, and therefore no cause for uneasiness existed.[41] Still desiring adoption of the declaration, Lansing had been forced by the collaboration of House and Spring-Rice to shift from legal to political arguments and even to indulge in some questionable diplomacy, from the standpoint of neutrality, in an effort to attain the larger goal. The changes to which he informally assented in the contraband lists were practically inevitable in any protracted war and would be compensated by the free list and other provisions of the declaration.

Negotiations were also under way in London, which, though unsuccessful in relation to the declaration, did lay the basis for a working agreement on commerce. Sir Edward Grey, the British foreign secretary, informed Page and the department that the Allies sought only to deny Germany access to war materials; otherwise, no obstacles would be placed in the way of neutral trade.[42] Page, ardently pro-Ally and with little comprehension of neutral rights, did little to secure the adoption of the declaration. He even went so far as to assure Grey that America did not seek to trade with Germany, ignoring a neutral's right to trade with all belligerents, even in absolute contraband.[43] The department soon realized that Page could not be depended upon for any measure that apparently ran counter to British interests. Nevertheless, the Page-Grey conversations did lead to one practical result—establishing a basis for informal arrangements between the British government and American shippers, which, through advance clearances, freed much American commerce to the European neutrals.

The immediate obstacle to British acceptance of the declaration was the application of continuous voyage to conditional contraband. Lansing now sought a circuitous solution which at least strained the spirit, if not the letter, of the declaration. Continuing his previous conversations with Spring-Rice, he suggested that under Articles 23 and 25 of the declaration a belligerent could add to the absolute contraband list all goods used "exclusively for war," since a common-sense interpretation based on modern war conditions would allow the necessary latitude.[44] In this way Britain could enlarge the contraband lists and reach nonexportation agreements with European neutrals within the framework of the declaration. Lansing obviously sought to save the free list at the expense of the right to trade with Germany in conditional contraband, which under his rule would have been moved rapidly into the absolute category. Spring-Rice forwarded the proposal to Grey, but unfortunately Grey was also conscious of the free list and desired to preserve as much freedom as possible in curtailing neutral commerce with Germany.[45] He did intimate a possible accord when on October 4 he promised a new proclamation repealing the August order in council.[46]

Grey's proposed order in council was speedily rejected by the State Department. It was sent to Washington for consideration as a tentative proclamation on October 9 and was immediately termed a disappointment.[47] Although ostensibly repealing the earlier order, the new proposal contained even more objectionable features, particularly in reference to continuous voyage. Several items on the declaration's free list—iron ore, copper, and minerals—were placed on the conditional contraband list; continuous voyage was applied to this category of goods which were to be subject to seizure if consigned to the enemy government or if the ship's papers failed to disclose a consignee. In addition, the order advanced a principle new in international law, announcing that at the discretion of the British government a neutral country could be classified as partaking of an enemy character and therefore subject to the rules governing belligerent trade in contraband. The State-Navy Neutrality Board condemned unqualifiedly this principle, and on October 15 Lansing sent Wilson a draft note terming the order "more objectionable" than the previous one.[48] The draft thoroughly analyzed the proposed order, concluding with the observation that Britain was seeking all the advantages of belligerency without declaring war in the treatment of neutrals allegedly serving as a German entrepôt for war materials. After minor alterations in phraseology, the note was dispatched to Page on the following day, with the notation that he should use also the much-disputed September 26 instructions.[49]

In spite of the British government's reluctance to go beyond a modified declaration, Lansing made one more attempt to secure an unqualified acceptance. After studying the several British objections, he concluded that Britain could accept the declaration without change and then follow up with a separate proclamation, of which the United States needed no advanced notification, adding articles to the contraband lists and reserving the right to ascribe an enemy character to neutrals that refused to sign nonexportation agreements. The United States would not seriously protest these actions, which Britain could defend on the grounds of unusual and exceptional cases beyond the scope of the declaration. Lansing's scheme repeated in essence the contents of the tentative order in council but kept them within the declaration. His persistent efforts have been severely criticized as being pro-Ally and full of duplicity, as well as beyond reconciliation with the true spirit of the declaration.[50] In part, these criticisms were justified. He was pro-Ally, and he did seek to preserve Anglo-American amicability, which he felt would best be promoted by a definite code minimizing opportunities for controversies about trade. By accepting the entire declaration, Britain would have bound Germany as well, since the latter had already accepted on a reciprocal basis. However, the anomaly of Lansing's actions was more apparent than real; it was almost inevitable that, as the war continued and belligerent necessities increased, the contraband lists would be substantially enlarged. Even an emasculated declaration would have offered some protection to American trade and would have preserved at least the majority of the free list. In addition, Lansing and the administration apparently were concerned with public opinion in America, particularly in view of the forthcoming elections. A mixture of pro-Ally sentiment, political expediency, and genuine concern for America's economic interests motivated the proposal which Lansing sent to Page on October 16.[51]

Ambassador Page hampered greatly the negotiations for the Declaration of London. A close friend of Wilson's, he was strongly attached to the British cause and most reluctant to embarrass the Allied prosecution of the war, so much so that he either failed to present the American case or did it in an ineffective manner.[52] Lansing, sharing Page's larger concept of the war and its significance for America, nevertheless condemned him for his dereliction of duty. His failure to present the American case did more harm than good. He wrote later that Page's inaction encouraged the British to continue actions hotly resented by many Americans, which but for German blunders could have had most serious results.[53] Page probably would have been recalled from his post if it had not been for his close relations with Wilson and the administration's reluctance to take any action encouraging Germany. Page had become increasingly distressed by Lansing's continued efforts to secure full adoption of the declaration, which he termed an "ugly academic dispute," which by antagonizing Britain might prevent the United States from being "of some service to civilization and to the peace of the world."[54] Wilson was compelled to admonish Page not to regard the American case as merely academic but to utilize to the utmost his offices in advancing Lansing's proposals.[55] Unhappily, Page was not impressed. He regarded Lansing's suggestion that he present to Grey as his own the proposal for a British acceptance of the declaration, followed by announced changes, as essentially dishonorable.[56] Page could only con-

clude that Lansing was strained by overwork: "I can hardly believe
that such a subterfuge or misrepresentation of the real facts is necessary
between ... large minded and perfectly frank and truthful representatives of two great and friendly nations. My relations with Sir Edward
have not been built on this basis. . . ."[57] Page threatened to resign if the
subject of the declaration was brought up again.[58]

The protracted negotiations ended in failure, and America was forced
to fall back upon the inadequate rules of existing international law.
The British Foreign Office refused Lansing's October 16 proposal, arguing that not only had the House of Lords earlier rejected the entire
document but furthermore it was not flexible enough to permit addi-
tions to the contraband lists.[59] Grey instead proposed to withdraw
previous proclamations and issue a new one, accepting the declaration
with modifications which added articles to the contraband lists and
reserved the right to halt neutral cargoes evidently intended for the
enemy. No request was made for American approval, but hope was
expressed that it would not be necessary to protest the new order in
council. Page added his plea to that of Grey's, advocating acceptance
of the proposal as a working arrangement removing most of the causes
of American complaint.[60] The real explanation for British obduracy
appears to have been a reluctance to bind their future actions in any
way, in keeping with the long-range goal of completely isolating Germany. Nothing remained for the State Department but to give up the
struggle for the declaration, reserving all rights under existing law.[61]
Page and the British Foreign Office were overjoyed by the withdrawal,
which was viewed as a victory, and within forty-eight hours large numbers of detained American vessels and cargoes were released.[62]

The failure to secure full adoption of the Declaration of London
boded ill for American neutrality. The State Department had put up a
determined effort, which perhaps only the threat of an arms embargo
could have brought to a successful conclusion. This weapon had been
thrown away by the October 15 circular officially accepting the arms
trade.[63] Even that might not have succeeded, as the Allies were not yet
fully dependent on the American supply, still in the formative stage.
In any case, some gains resulted from the negotiations. Britain had
become acquainted with American views, and the development of her
policy toward neutral commerce was at least restrained for the time
being. A working arrangement was in formation which relieved some
of the uncertainties of commerce and thereby partly reduced public
criticism and dissatisfaction in America. These gains were more than

offset by the losses, however. Failure to secure the declaration meant
that reliance had to be placed on the inadequate existing rules of maritime warfare. No restraints, of a closely defined legal nature, remained
either to moderate British sea practices or to prevent German retaliation. Britain was free to develop her system of extra-legal blockades
and tight control of neutral commerce. This naturally meant that Germany was also free to act, to offset blockade and economic strangulation policies with ruthless submarine warfare dedicated to starving out
Great Britain.

Lansing's role was also of paramount importance in establishing the
essentials of American domestic neutrality. As counselor of the State
Department, he supplied much of the substance for the indefinite
policies of "national honor," to which the idealistic Wilson had dedicated his administration. To his interpretations of international law,
Lansing did more than bring to bear his legal training; more important,
he brought into play his conception of America's interest in an Allied
victory. In the negotiations for the Declaration of London, he had
worked for a solution capable of protecting American interests and
preserving Anglo-American good relations; domestically he strove for
the same goals. Policies were laid down on armed belligerent merchantmen, contraband trade, and loans to the belligerents, which, with the
factor of sentiment, so bound the United States to the Allies that American neutrality lost most of its appeal to Gemany and came to offer no
effective restraint against future German actions.

The British practice of arming merchant vessels presented the State
Department with a problem destined to plague America during the
entire period of its official neutrality. The matter appeared merely routine at first, involving primarily the neutral duty of preventing its
ports from serving as bases of belligerent naval operations. Under the
generally accepted rules of international law, a belligerent merchantman had the right to arm defensively without acquiring the status of a
man-of-war.[64] It was an archaic practice dating back to the days of
wooden ships, pirates, and privateers. The only justification for its
retention was the need, in British and American eyes, to protect far-
flung commerce against enemy raiders, usually converted merchantmen; certainly the lightly armed merchantman could hardly have defended itself against any regular type of modern warship. Therefore,
when the British vessel *Francisco* arrived in New York harbor August
13, 1914, armed with two 4.7" guns mounted aft but allegedly without
ammunition, an apparently routine policy decision was required. The

British embassy asserted that the armament was purely defensive and offered written assurances which Lansing and the Joint State-Navy Neutrality Board accepted as adequate.[65] The entry of additional British armed vessels in early September, however, coupled with German protests that these were really warships and subject to the rules governing them in neutral ports, caused the State Department to contemplate a policy statement on the subject.[66]

Lansing's September circular on armed ships launched a policy which was unfortunate in its long-term results. He submitted to Bryan a memorandum recognizing the right of belligerent merchantmen to arm and attempted to establish criteria differentiating between offensive and defensive armament.[67] To overcome the presumption of offensive purposes, an armed ship should carry only a few guns of less than six-inch caliber, mounted aft, and should also meet certain other tests, as the plying of normal trade routes, the carrying of noncombatant passengers, and the presence of the regular prewar crew. Wilson approved the policy, and it was issued as a formal circular, together with another one September 19, 1914, governing the provisioning of warships by merchantmen operating from American ports.[68] Shortly thereafter Germany protested this ruling, asserting that Britain was arming ships to resist illegally German armed cruisers.[69] Lansing rejected this particular protest, but the real issue arose only with the advent of submarine warfare in 1915.

The submarine was a fragile craft, easily damaged by small caliber guns, and therefore at a serious disadvantage when it attempted to exercise the belligerent right of visit and search. Although a defensively armed merchantman had the right to resist attack if fired upon by an enemy, resistance to visit and search automatically forfeited its peaceful character. Germany was to argue that the mere presence of armament precluded the submarine from exercising cruiser rules of warfare and therefore made attack without warning mandatory. In conjunction with American insistence on the right of its citizens to travel on belligerent vessels, partly explained by the smallness of the American merchant marine, the failure to bar armed ships from American ports made probable a clash with Germany on the submarine.

The United States could have solved the problem, as had the Netherlands, by excluding all armed ships from its ports.[70] Britain was largely dependent upon America for war materials, and a ban on armed ships would have been obeyed. Lansing and the administration, however, seem to have been merely following precedent, which was entirely reasonable in view of the existing situation. The submarine was not then a problem; its use as a commerce destroyer was hardly anticipated. But even in 1914, Lansing had doubts about the practicability of distinguishing between defensive and offensive armaments, and resorted to an unsatisfactory evasion for a temporary solution. Instead of applying the September circular, he secured from the British government an informal promise to keep armaments off ships entering the United States. This agreement was kept until September, 1915, when British vessels, in an attempt to prevent challenge by German submarines, once more began to arrive in American ports carrying armaments.[71] Lansing then attempted to rectify his earlier mistake and proposed a *modus vivendi* to both belligerents. It was then too late; Britain refused to comply; the contraband trade was too important to risk its loss through the exclusion of armed vessels; and the September circular in any case prevented a complete reversal of policy.

Contraband trade was even more important than the policy on armed ships in determining the nature of American neutrality. The historic American position had been an insistence on the right of its citizens to manufacture and export munitions of war.[72] No domestic laws precluded contraband trade, which seldom had been restricted in any way. The few exceptions related mostly to Latin America, where for reasons of expediency embargoes had been invoked to help suppress revolutionary turmoil. International law and practice permitted neutral trade to belligerents in munitions of war. Thomas Jefferson in 1793 clearly enunciated this right, unrestricted as long as the neutral government took no part in these activities, with the duty of preventing the traffic devolving not on the neutral but upon the contending belligerent.[73] Therefore, upon the outbreak of World War I, American firms began to engage on a large scale in the manufacture and exportation of munitions and arms, which, because of the efficiency of the British blockade, meant a one-sided trade with the Allies.[74]

On the philosophical level, Lansing was convinced not only that the munitions trade was perfectly neutral but also that it was the duty of a peace-loving, nonaggressive state to permit the free exportation of arms and munitions. In a memorandum late in 1914, he recorded the conviction that an aggressor state, stock-piling war materials in peacetime, would alone be benefited by neutral embargoes on arms exports. Peace-loving states, such as the United States, normally were unprepared for war and consequently when hostilities broke out were dependent upon neutral imports for defensive purposes. An arms embargo would not harm the aggressor but it would seriously damage the defendant state. With permanent embargoes, designed for peacetime as well as for war, the only probable result would be a universal arms race, since all nations would then have to depend solely upon their own resources in the advent of war. Hence an embargo in any form would "put a premium on aggression."[75] There can be little doubt of the sincerity of Lansing's views, although it could be noted that none of these convictions were very relevant to the paramount problem of preserving a genuine neutrality in the particular war at hand. Undoubtedly, such convictions lent weight to the primary factor of the inescapable economic pressure to approve an already established arms traffic. In any case, Lansing recommended that a public statement be issued which would formally announce the legality of the trade.[76] Wilson agreed, presumably because he, too, viewed the munitions trade as legitimate and economically necessary.[77] The contraband circular was issued October 15, 1914; it announced that a neutral government was ". . . not compelled by international law, by treaty, or by statute to prevent . . . sales to a belligerent . . ." and that the American executive possessed no authority to interfere with the arms traffic.[78]

Domestic political and economic considerations were the principal factors behind the official circular on the arms trade. The immediate motivation for Lansing's proposed public statement had resulted from a conversation with Senator William J. Stone, chairman of the Senate Foreign Relations Committee, who reported to Lansing the criticism of the arms trade by his St. Louis constituency, composed of many German-Americans.[79] In view of the approaching congressional elections, it was expedient to refute the unneutrality charges and defend the government's position. At the same time, an announcement of official acceptance of the contraband trade would please pro-Ally Americans generally. The American economy had been depressed for some time before the war, and the demands of the European belligerents for all types of war materials provided a great stimulus, destined soon to produce an unparalleled prosperity. An embargo in 1914 would close this major avenue to economic recovery. Neither the administration nor the American people, considered as a whole, desired neutrality at the price of economic well-being.[80]

The October circular on contraband trade laid the basis for closer economic ties with the Allies. The administration subsequently defended its refusal to contemplate an arms embargo on the ground that a change in rules while the war was in progress would be an unneutral act, depriving one of the belligerents of the fruits of naval victory. This was a rationalization, overlooking the undoubted right of a neutral to use an embargo or to make any desired changes in its rules, so long as the changes applied impartially to all the belligerents.[81] In announcing the government's policy on the munition's trade, a valuable weapon, capable of coercing Britain, was lost.[82] Furthermore, the arms trade was just beginning in 1914, whereas a year later it had reached such proportions that an embargo would have been economically crippling. The result was that America rapidly became the workshop of the Allies, their major source of practically all the tools needed to wage a modern war.[83] The resultant economic ties with the Allies strengthened pro-Ally sentiment in America, while embittering the German people and giving their government little reason to esteem American neutrality.

In the matter of loans and credits to the belligerents, closely connected with the munitions traffic, America at first followed an incongruous policy. In view of the contraband trade by American citizens with the belligerents, which the government was soon to accept officially, it was logical to permit private bankers to finance the foreign powers purchasing these war materials. Lansing took the position that floating belligerent loans and credits in the United States was legal and compatible with neutrality, having many precedents in international practice.[84] Bryan, with an insight into the spirit of true neutrality, argued that money was the worst of all contraband since it could command the other forms.[85] In the course of several discussions, Lansing apparently was influenced by Bryan's views to the point of disregarding temporarily his own contentions in order to buttress those of the secretary. Lansing commented that since the government was discouraging citizens from enlisting in foreign armies and withdrawing its protection from those defying the prohibition, it should also discourage the export of money intended to help wage a foreign war. He also noted that a prohibition might be a step in the direction of peace, by depriving the belligerents of finances and thus restraining their war ambitions.[86] When representatives of J. P. Morgan and Company approached the State Department for an opinion on a projected loan to the French government, Bryan immediately consulted Wilson and the two agreed to ban all belligerent loans.[87] Consequently, Morgan was informed on August 15 that though loans could be made to neutrals, the government considered loans to belligerents to be "inconsistent with the true spirit of neutrality."[88]

Bryan's loan policy began to disintegrate shortly after its formulation. America under the impact of increasing belligerent purchasing began to experience a financial revolution transforming the country from a debtor into a creditor nation. The heavy buying required money and, even this early in the war, the Allies began to exhaust their liquid resources. The ban against loans could not long continue without clogging the channels of war trade.[89] Pressure for a relaxation of the prohibition began in early October, 1914, when agents of the larger New York banking houses approached Lansing, Bryan, and other administration officials.[90] The Bryan letter to Morgan in August was not binding legally, since the executive was unauthorized by Congress to control foreign exchange, but financiers hesitated to pursue a policy definitely opposed by the administration. Foreign pressure also began to be applied against the ban, as exemplified by Sir George Parish's discussion of finances with Wilson on October 9.[91] Russia proposed the negotiation of a new commercial agreement with the United States, on the informal understanding that a loan could then be arranged.[92] Willard Straight, agent for Morgan, requested Lansing's opinion on the acceptance by American banks of short-term French treasury notes, and George Bakhmeteff, the Russian ambassador, made a similar request for acceptance of Russian treasury certificates. Bakhmeteff argued that this would be no more than a temporary credit arrangement, entailed by a shortage of funds in the United States, and would greatly stimulate both American and Russian manufactures.[93]

By October, Lansing apparently agreed with the advocates of credit that it was advisable to permit private credit arrangements to be made with the belligerent powers. He understood that credits through the medium of short-term treasury notes really amounted in practice to loans.[94] He had originally viewed loans as legal, and now was being informed that America's economic prosperity would be damaged if some action were not taken to relieve the financial crisis. The vice-president of the National City Bank of New York, Samuel McRoberts, told him on the morning of October 23 that if short-term credits were not granted, America would suffer economically.[95] Lansing thereupon sent Wilson a memorandum summing up the bankers' contentions, which contained their statement that these credits would not take the form of public loans.[96] Lansing then conferred with Wilson, after which he drew up a memorandum of the president's views which informally approved the use of short-term credit.[97] The rationalization was that though loans related to the actual financing of the war, credits were merely a means of facilitating a legal trade, made necessary by the clumsiness of international finance. Lansing then orally informed Straight and R. L. Farnham, of the National City Bank, that the government, having stated its position on loans, should not be consulted about credit arrangements of a purely commercial nature. A press announcement of this partial reversal of policy was not made until March 31, 1915, and then only after the circulation of many exaggerated rumors.[98]

In the evasive, almost clandestine, reversal of the Bryan loan policy, Wilson and Lansing were swayed more by their immediate concern for the American economy than by pro-Ally sympathies. The prewar depression was just beginning to relax its grip before the torrent of war orders, and in 1914 few could predict how long the war might last. It therefore behooved America to take the greatest possible advantage of the opportunity offered. Even Bryan was influenced by this factor and, although absent from Washington when the decision for credits was made, he appears to have acquiesced in the departure from the August ban.[99] The approval of credits signaled the approaching end of the loan policy. Any distinction between credits and loans was illusory; the foreign treasury notes, although ostensibly short-term notes, were renewed repeatedly and in effect amounted to long-term bankers' loans. In the following year, when this expedient had run its course, it became necessary to revoke the loan ban entirely. Nothing then remained to restrain an ever-increasing financial tie with the Allies, which went hand in hand with the economic involvement through the trade in war materials and supplies.

The administration's neutral policies did not emerge unscathed by criticism. Opposition was soon manifested to the trade in contraband and the financing of Allied purchases, which, in conjunction with the failure to achieve the Declaration of London and the apparent acquiescence of the government to British maritime measures, culminated in charges that America was unneutral and partial to the Allies. Discontent was particularly current in the German-American segment of the population.[100] Professor Hugo Münsterberg, a German national teaching at Harvard University, summed up the unneutrality charges in a long letter to the president. Wilson was sufficiently impressed with the plausibility of the criticisms to send the letter to Lansing for analysis and refutation.[101] Lansing reacted adversely, viewing German propaganda activities, such as those by Münsterberg and Dr. Bernhard Dernburg, as nefarious attempts to subvert German-Americans from their primary allegiance to America, in order to weld them into a bloc capable of coercing the government into policies favoring Germany. To Lansing, these efforts of German agents were all the more improper since they invoked the protection of American constitutional guarantees of freedom of speech and press for acts, which if they had occurred in Germany, would have been summarily repressed.[102]

Lansing refuted the Münsterberg accusations in a masterfully organized and reasoned paper.[103] His memorandum served as the administration's definitive rationalization of its neutrality policies. Two major arguments permeated his defense. The first applied to contraband trade and sought to demonstrate that since neutrality was based on the presumptive equality of the belligerents, a neutral could not take into account the actual results of the performance of its neutral policies. Thus the United States had exercised the legal right to trade in contraband and munitions with both belligerents, and the fact that one of the belligerents had deprived the other, through military preponderance, of access to the American market was completely irrelevant. For the government to change its rules during wartime, in an attempt to equalize the opportunities of the belligerents, would be an unneutral act, depriving one of the belligerents of the fruits of victory. The second theme dealt with the charge of American acquiescence in British violations of international law, principally by unwarranted extension of the contraband lists. Lansing here pointed out that the American record was inconsistent, the United States as a neutral having stood for a narrow contraband list although as a belligerent during the Civil War it had contended for a most liberal interpretation. He also emphasized that the United States during the Civil War had invoked the doctrine of continuous voyage and ultimate destination, which the Supreme Court had upheld, and therefore it was not in a position to protest the British use of those techniques.

The Lansing memorandum can be questioned on both major themes. The first argument, centering on the presumptive equality of belligerents and the unneutralness of rule changes during war, failed to apply its own logic to the question of an embargo on the arms traffic. An arms embargo need not have been invoked to equalize the belligerents but rather to preserve a strict neutrality through avoidance of contact with either belligerent. An excellent motivation could have been deduced from the entirely sane desire of pacifists that a neutral state do nothing to feed the flames of the European war. An embargo applying to both belligerents would have been legal and neutral, since it would have continued the presumption of the equality of the warring powers; the United States need not have inquired into the practical efforts thereof.

The Allies would have protested vigorously and would have raised charges of unneutrality, but no truly neutral reason existed to heed their charges any more than the actual complaints of Germany. On the second argument, that the American record was contradictory on contraband rules and had sanctioned the doctrine of continuous voyage, Lansing's reasoning was on sounder ground. It was a matter of historical record that during the Civil War the United States had in large degree reversed its traditional policies on neutral rights.[104] Contraband lists had been expanded liberally, "paper" blockades instituted, and continuous voyage invoked against ostensibly neutral to neutral commerce. Lansing failed to mention that the Supreme Court, in the Peterhof case, had upheld continuous voyage only for absolute contraband intended to enter the blockaded area, and had denied the right to blockade a neutral port.[105] In Lansing's defense, it must be remembered that the court's decisions on these matters were made in reference to the port of Matamoras, Mexico, which, because of the then existing situation, hardly permitted any considerable entry of goods into the Confederacy. In World War I, modern transportation and the contiguous neutrals around Germany made conditions quite different. Lansing was citing American precedents in an effort to silence domestic criticism; unfortunately, he brought up arguments which Britain could and did use effectively in the diplomatic exchanges arising from her maritime practices. The most serious criticism of Lansing's memorandum lies, however, in his avoidance of any discussion of the economic and political considerations behind the neutrality policies.

Wilson's doubts of the correctness of the American course were not completely satisfied by Lansing's analysis of the Münsterberg letter. The winter of 1914 was a period of increasing criticism and opposition by highly vocal minorities within the United States, which reached a climax when the Congress reassembled in December to face a series of arms embargo resolutions and bills.[106] Although these moves were eventually defeated, Wilson apparently needed reassurances of the genuineness of American neutrality. Lansing hastened to supply the requisite rationalizations. Wilson received a telegram from three prominent individuals, which protested that any congressional alteration of neutrality laws during a war would be a violation of neutrality, and he immediately sent the message to Lansing for comment.[107] Lansing replied on the same date, agreeing entirely with the argument contained in the telegram and stating that any change in the laws by Congress would *ipso facto* benefit one or the other of the belligerents and thus allow the injured party to charge that the legislation was for the benefit of his opponent.[108] The counselor buttressed this opinion by citing the concurrence of the Argentine ambassador, which had resulted from a discussion before the Pan American Union's governing board of a scheme to neutralize sea zones around the Americas. Lansing then concluded his letter with a neat though highly satisfying stratagem—a reference to the laxity of the enforcement provisions of the neutrality laws, which Congress could needfully concern itself with remedying. Wilson's doubts were overcome, and he expressed to Lansing his warm thanks, averring that he now felt "fully fortified in the matter."[109]

Lansing recommended repeatedly that a public answer be made silencing the critics of the administration's neutrality measures.[110] The counselor feared that the wide circulation of charges of unneutrality was costing the Democratic party the support of many German-Americans. Political expediency therefore, if no other reason, demanded an official defense. While Congress was considering embargo legislation, a note arrived from the German ambassador, Count Johann von Bernstorff, which greatly strengthened the administration's position. In a memorandum to Bryan, Bernstorff admitted the legality of the munitions trade. He coupled this with the assertion that since this trade benefited only the Allies, the United States should permit the supplying from its ports of German warships at sea, as long as no one vessel made repeated trips.[111] This rather amazing statement was promptly seized upon by Bryan and Lansing as the crushing counter to German-American critics, and Wilson approved its publication.[112] Meanwhile, Lansing renewed the request for a general public statement and early in January, 1915, recommended that perhaps the most effective means would be an inquiry from the chairman of the Senate Foreign Relations Committee about the policy of the government.[113] Lansing listed twenty categories of questions to be answered, running the entire gamut of neutrality from the censorship of wireless messages to the alleged unfriendliness of the government toward Germany. After Wilson's approval of the method, Senator Stone was persuaded to write the desired inquiry, dated January 8.

Bryan's reply to Senator Stone on January 20 was Lansing's work, based on his previous analysis of the Münsterberg letter and following his suggested outline of January 1.[114] The key parts of the letter endeavored to justify the munitions and general contraband trade, admitted by Germany to be legal, and with which the executive could not interfere since it lacked legislative authorization. To explain the lack of congressional action, which the administration opposed, the un-neutrality of changes in the rules during a war was cited. In general, the same arguments were advanced that Lansing had first formulated in the Münsterberg memorandum. The only addition to the letter of any great interest was the evasion of charges that Bryan's ban on loans had been reversed: "This Government has not been advised that any general loans have been made...." Thus was passed over, in eloquent silence, the October, 1914, relaxation of the ban in favor of "credits" to the Allies.[115]

CHAPTER III

THE DIE IS CAST FOR WAR

*"... Germany must not be permitted to win this war and
to break even, though to prevent it this country is forced
to take an active part."*—Robert Lansing[1]

IN THE SPRING of 1915 the United States moved rapidly toward active
involvement in the European War. American neutrality had been
shaped in 1914 with a strong orientation toward the Allies. Now the
American government was to assume an unequal attitude toward the
British blockade and German submarine warfare.

Enmeshed with the Allied Powers by bonds of sympathy and by economic and political interests, the United States was compelled to acquiesce in the British war measures directed at the Central Powers.
Through the official policies toward armed belligerent merchantmen,
the munitions trade and credits to the belligerents, the United States
had established a neutrality favorably inclined toward the Allies.
Therefore, when Great Britain early in 1915 undertook to perfect her
control of neutral commerce and embarked upon an illegal blockade of
Germany, America lacked the desire to restrain British actions. The
United States contented herself with official protests and private ac-
commodations; only a façade of neutrality remained.[2]

In contradistinction, the policy of the United States toward Germany
became one of severity and refusal to compromise. When the exigencies
of war led Germany to retaliate against alleged Allied violations of
international law, the American government refused to acquiesce. Instead, Germany was requested to comply fully with the established rules
of warfare; "strict accountability" was invoked against use of the submarine. Not only did the United States assert the right of its vessels to
traverse the high seas regardless of war zones, but declared, in emphatic
terms, the full right of American citizens to travel in safety on Allied
merchant and passenger vessels. Germany previously had little reason
to esteem American neutrality; its continuance now became even less
valuable in Teutonic eyes. In the absence of mutual interests between
the United States and Germany, the American attitude toward the submarine rendered hostilities inevitable.

For Lansing the first half of 1915 was to be the period of his greatest
achievements. His role in the shaping of the policy of strict accountability was a large one, perhaps more significant than that of any other

[41]

American official. His opinions gradually evolved from a pro-Ally senti-ment to the conviction that America's interests, relative to national safety and the world balance of power, were closely connected with the military fortunes of the Allied Powers. Lansing had had an important part in the formulation of official policy toward the munitions trade and credits to the Allies, both for the benefit of American national in-terests and for the immediate economic needs of the nation. A realistic appraiser of events, he soon recognized that American neutrality was of little value to Germany, who could gain more freedom of action by American entry into the war. Lansing, furthermore, became convinced that America, for her own interests, would probably have to participate in the war. He tended, therefore, to view the submarine issue as the necessary precipitant of hostilities.

To secure adoption of his "severe" policy on the submarine, Lansing found it necessary to cope with President Wilson's indecision and Secre-tary Bryan's opposition. He succeeded in the former by supplying Wilson with acceptable rationalizations. Because Wilson was a strange mixture of pacifist inclinations, strong British sympathies, and a stern, moralist concept of honor and duty, Lansing's recommendations were peculiarly suited to the president's needs. The policy of strict account-ability, by appealing to national honor and the rights and dictates of humanity in a manner compounded of righteousness and inevitability, satisfied the dominant elements of Wilson's emotional structure. At the same time, the policy helped create an issue capable of unifying public opinion, thus making possible the eventual entry into war.

* * *

The failure in the fall of 1914 to secure adoption of the unmodified Declaration of London left Great Britain free to develop the commer-cial blockade of Germany. In the absence of definite legal restraints, the various aspects of Allied economic warfare proceeded apace, restricted only by the time needed to perfect control machinery and the demands of expediency toward the neutrals.

Great Britain exploited her command of the seas to the fullest extent, and ignored the rules and practices of international law wherever pos-sible.[3] Geographical features, principally adjoining neutrals and the semiclosed nature of the Baltic Sea, prevented an effective blockade of Germany. Great Britain solved that problem by the institution of long-range "blockades" on the high seas enforced by naval squadrons sta-tioned off the shores of important neutrals, and by the use of embargoes and nonexportation agreements, forced upon the neutrals through the British control of the seas. The system has been aptly termed blockade by sovereign right, rather than by belligerent right.[4] Through the use of devices falling within the sphere of domestic sovereignty and legislation, as the withholding of bunker supplies, denial of cargo insurance, closing of cable and wireless systems, blacklisting of neutral firms, and prohibitions on the exportation of vital raw materials, England was able to mold the neutrals to her will. These measures resulted in a control of commerce far more efficient and less troublesome than the more formal methods of a legal blockade. In considerable part, most of the devices lay beyond the scope of international law and could be checked only by threats of neutral retaliation. This the United States government refused to contemplate. Instead, America followed a policy of acquiescence, lodging protests and reservations of right on the diplomatic level, while privately aiding working arrangements and systems of advance clearance of cargoes between American exporters and the British government.

It was not difficult for Lansing to rationalize Great Britain's departure from the narrow path prescribed by international law. The mechanism was provided by his theory of belligerent necessity, the validity of which he was thoroughly convinced. In a speech to the alumni of Amherst College, in February, 1915, Lansing discussed the new weapons of warfare and the problems they created for neutrality; he concluded, "We have to abandon the time-honored refuge of jurists and diplomats, precedents, and lay hold of the bedrock of principle. Diplomacy today is wrestling with novel problems, to which it must apply natural justice and practical common sense."[5] Lansing here referred to his concept of the nature of international relations and warfare. He considered force to be the dominant element in human society and its use in international relations essentially brutal. It followed that the phrase "humane warfare" was a contradiction in terms. Though an individual might sacrifice his interests, and even his life for honor, nations, having primary responsibility to ensure the survival of their peoples, were insensitive to such concepts. National safety and self-preservation justified any measure, no matter how inhumane or unethical.[6] A neutral, therefore, could expect little consideration from the belligerents, and unless willing to apply force to support its position, should content itself with patient protests and reservations of rights for postwar settlement.[7]

Lansing judged the actions of Great Britain and Germany within the concept of belligerent necessity. He held that though belligerent needs justified departures from the rules of law and morality, these departures should not be wanton acts without military significance. In addition, he believed that an invader had less excuse for atrocities and violations than had the invaded country, which was the more immediately concerned with survival. Lansing used this procedure when he criticized German conduct in the bombardment of Antwerp as "wanton."[8] He was sufficiently realistic, however, to penetrate propaganda assertions that Great Britain had entered the war solely because of the German violation of Belgium, writing Bryan in January of 1915, "The fact should not be ignored, however, that her [Great Britain's] political interest coincides with her conception of international morality in this case. If it were otherwise, I am not convinced that righteousness alone would have induced the British Government to declare war."[9] Apparently he felt that Great Britain was on the defensive and consequently deserved more consideration than did Germany. As far as the submarine was concerned, Lansing deplored the loss of noncombatant lives on passenger vessels as acts largely without military significance. He was willing, however, to accept the submarine, subjected to restrictions and adapted to more human usage through modifications of international law, as a legitimate weapon. His opposition to Germany did not come from the submarine per se, but instead resulted primarily from his considerations of American interests.

Lansing, in the spring of 1915, embarked upon a policy of conciliation toward Great Britain. He designed his diplomatic notes to protect, as far as possible, American commercial rights, without at the same time leading to a crisis threatening good relations with the British government.[10] The American notes to Great Britain were intended to prolong the discussions interminably, and yet, by their apparent harshness, to satisfy the demands of Americans enraged by Allied acts.[11] When Lansing later perceived that the Allies were not winning the war, but perhaps losing it, he concluded that America would have to enter in order to protect her interests. At that point, another reason existed for avoiding sharp notes to England; America might eventually have to adopt some of the measures she was currently protesting. As a result, "Everything was submerged in verbosity" and the way left open for future developments.[12]

The principal American difficulty with Great Britain centered around the contraband lists. During the negotiations for the Declaration of London, Lansing had protested informally the British order in council, issued October 29, 1914.[13] After the promulgation of the order, no formal protest was made. Instead, Lansing concentrated his efforts on specific items arising from the order, and he sought especially to protect American cotton and copper interests. American cotton growers and exporters were becoming increasingly disturbed by the Allied interferences with neutral trade and began to exert pressure upon the State Department for action. Lansing thereupon requested clarification from the British Foreign Office and asserted the right of Americans to export cotton directly to Germany.[14] The foreign secretary, Sir Edward Grey, was placed in a most difficult position, needing to placate American demands on the one hand, and, on the other, to satisfy the war requirements as determined by Great Britain's military and naval leaders. Fearing that drastic action might strain unduly American good will and possibly lead to forcible measures, Grey temporized and delayed placing cotton on the contraband list.[15] He assured Ambassador Page that cotton was not contraband and would remain on the free list so far as the British government was concerned.[16] This assurance, destined to last one year, offered Lansing the opportunity for a small diplomatic triumph. In a maneuver designed to prevent a sudden British reversal, he sought, and obtained, a German classification of cotton as noncontraband.[17] The counselor followed this with further moves intended to aid distressed Southern interests; Great Britain, upon request, agreed not to interfere with shipments of turpentine and resin.[18]

These were ephemeral gains. It soon became apparent that Great Britain could not be prevented, at least by mere protests, from extensively revising the contraband lists. The economic isolation of Germany was proceeding rapidly and required further measures if maximum efficiency was to be obtained. Consequently, when Lansing sought assurances on American copper exports, he met with signal failure; the cargoes were seized, although compensation was paid.[19] Oil shipments were also detained by the Allies, pending the conclusion of nonexportation agreements with the European neutrals.[20] In December, 1914, new contraband lists were issued which, among other things, retracted Grey's previous assurances and placed naval stores in the absolute category.[21] Lansing protested these actions but privately rationalized the matter, concluding that the dictates of modern warfare destroyed the differences between conditional and absolute contraband and thus made a single list preferable.[22] Certainly new conditions of war did involve goods never before considered as war materials. Probably nothing short of coercive measures, never seriously entertained, could have prevented enlargement of the contraband lists.[23] It was obvious, however, that American trade was suffering from the uncertainties of the situation, and some more practical solution than diplomatic protests was required.

The practical solution achieved was one that compromised American neutrality. Working arrangements were reached between private American firms and the British government. The origins of the system are obscure, but to Lansing has been attributed credit for its original proposal.[24] Lansing had earlier suggested, during the negotiations over the Declaration of London, a similar solution to the contraband problem through Allied agreements with the neutrals. At any rate, Page formally transmitted the scheme to Secretary Bryan in December, 1914, proposing that in return for the American government's promise not to support diplomatically copper exports consigned to order, Great Britain would allow American importation of rubber, hides, manganese, and other materials from the British Empire.[25] This tacit agreement formed the basis for even less formal arrangements. Various unofficial combines were established in America, similar to the Netherlands Overseas Trust, which coöperated with the British government in preventing goods from reaching Germany. Some of the more important groups were the Textile Alliance, the Rubber Association of America, the Wheat Exporting Company (an Allied purchasing agency "coördinating" the industry), and a copper producers' group based on the American Smelting and Refining Company.[26] In addition to these organizations, American shippers generally sought assurances against Allied interferences by securing licenses and clearances from British consular officials within the United States. American businesses profited from such arrangements, escaping thereby costly seizures and detentions in Allied ports. Yet the results for American neutrality were less praiseworthy. Although the State Department maintained the fiction of disassociation with the working arrangements, it tacitly condoned them.[27] American trade thus was effectively controlled by the Allies, becoming one more instrument—a vastly important one—in both the Allied war effort and the economic strangulation of Germany.

The State Department did not neglect its formal duties. While the private working arrangements were being perfected, a comprehensive protest was dispatched to Great Britain and France on December 26, 1914. Lansing intended the note primarily to satisfy American domestic discontent, rather than to secure real concessions from the British government.[28] The note was drafted by Cone Johnson, the solicitor of the department, and revised by both Lansing and Bryan. Even after this toning-down process, Wilson felt that the note was too abrupt, and Lansing had to redraft it before it was forwarded to Page in London.[29] Despite excited public comment that an ultimatum was being given to Great Britain,[30] the note actually was long, inconclusive, and without threat of any kind. Although expressing "growing concern" with Allied violations of international law in contraband matters and the searching of vessels in port instead of the legal visit and search at sea, the note made no direct reference to America's right to trade with Germany, even in the noncontraband categories. The most striking part of the protest reflected Lansing's concept of international relations in asserting that Great Britain had exceeded ". . . the manifest necessity of a belligerent . . ." by restrictions on neutral trade which were unjustified by the ". . . principle of self-preservation."[31] Lansing, of course, meant these references to indicate that although America was not unmindful of belligerent needs, British survival was really compatible with a more generous treatment of American trading interests. Nevertheless, it soon was to be regretted that such sentiments were expressed in a formal diplomatic note. Sir Edward Grey was not slow in utilizing for the British cause such a damaging rationalization, and since it was manifestly open to question as to who was to determine precisely where belligerent necessity began, Grey was able to utilize this defense in subsequent exchanges.[32]

The British reply to the American note was equally inconclusive. In the preliminary answer of January 7, 1915, Grey justified the protested measures as necessary to prevent contraband from entering Germany, and asserted that, in any case, American trade was prospering through increased exports to the European neutrals.[33] Lansing characterized the reply as conciliatory in tone but ". . . transparently illogical in many particulars."[34] He pointed out in a lengthy memorandum to Bryan that though Grey was correct in claiming that American trade was growing, the increases were due to the closure of normal sources of supply to the European neutrals, and as far as America was concerned, the improvements were spotty, leaving the general economy of the nation still seriously dislocated by British trade interferences. The cotton industry was an especially suitable example, continuing in a demoralized status because of the vacillation in Allied policies on contraband. Lansing was concerned with American trade and industrial interests, but in spite of his realization of the increasing entanglements resulting from British control measures, he made no suggestions for an effective remedy beyond suggesting another diplomatic protest. President Wilson reacted adversely to the counselor's analysis and recommendations, terming it "not worth while" to debate details with the British government.[35] Instead, failing to appreciate the true nature of affairs and believing that the two governments were near an agreement on principles, he recommended settling the controversy on a practical basis. The formal British reply of February 10 merely enlarged upon the previous arguments in greater detail, and there the matter remained for the time.[36]

One possible solution for part of America's troubles with Great Britain was the Ship Purchasing bill. The American merchant marine was small, and shippers were forced to rely heavily upon British vessels. This reliance afforded an additional instrument whereby Great Britain could control American trade to Europe. Upon the initiative of Secretary of the Treasury William Gibbs McAdoo, a bill was introduced in Congress to charter a government shipping corporation, authorized to build, purchase, and operate merchant vessels.[37] A principal source of the contemplated increase in shipping consisted of the 500,000 tons of German vessels trapped in American ports.

The proposed purchase of the German ships raised the problem of transfer. The transfer of a vessel from one flag to another, particularly when this also involved transfer of ownership, had always been a delicate subject in wartime. Belligerents, afraid that their opponents might conceal their vessels under neutral registry and thus escape the consequences of hostilities, regarded such transfers with suspicion.

The question of transfer of vessels first arose in October, 1914, when the Bureau of War Risk Insurance requested Lansing's opinion on insuring vessels transferred from belligerent registry.[38] Lansing approved the insuring of such vessels, holding that since the transfer was merely one of flag, the ships in question having been previously owned by an American corporation, no adverse reaction from the Allies was likely. As for transfer of ownership, Lansing advised that purchases of belligerent vessels were legal, if bona fide in the sense of an unencumbered sale and if the vessel were to be used, after purchase, solely in neutral trade.[39] When President Wilson requested information, relative to his forthcoming annual address to Congress, on the matter of purchasing the interned German vessels, Lansing was unable to give any definite assurances.[40] He repeated his views that such purchases were legal, but added that France was vociferously denouncing the

The Die Is Cast for War

scheme, alleging that purchase would be an unneutral act, relieving Germany of part of the burdens of warfare and destroying one of the fruits of Allied naval supremacy.[41] Lansing could only state that Great Britain seemed to be inclined to accept the government's purchase and operation of the vessels, but that she would probably first test the matter in Prize Court proceedings. Consequently, Wilson in his annual message avoided direct reference to the German ships.[42] Nevertheless, the shipping bill ran into determined Republican opposition, on the grounds of the questionable neutrality of the proposed purchase and, more importantly, Republican distaste for any measure placing the government in the field of private business. The bill was filibustered to death, and America was forced to continue its dependence upon Allied vessels for transport.[43]

The stage was set by early 1915 for German retaliation. Germany, unable to view with equanimity the increasingly effective Allied economic blockade, opened intensified submarine warfare in an attempt to break the stalemated war in Western Europe and sought to force Great Britain into submission by a counterblockade. Submarine warfare was to present American policy makers with the choice of acquiescence, which had been given to Allied actions, or of the assumption of a position making hostilities with Germany most probable.

The British declaration of a military zone in the North Sea presaged the launching of intensive submarine warfare. In October, 1914, a German naval auxiliary cruiser, the *Berlin*, evaded the British patrols and laid mines off the west coast of Ireland.[44] Great Britain, concerned with perfecting her control of neutral commerce, perceived a great opportunity in this event. Claiming that Germany was indiscriminately mining the waters north of Scotland, Great Britain on November 3, 1914, proclaimed the entire North Sea a military area within which enemy mining and Allied countermining required neutral vessels to proceed at their own peril.[45] Neutral vessels desiring to traverse the area were warned to stop at British ports for the latest Admiralty sailing directions. Naturally Great Britain used these "forced" visits to search, thoroughly and at leisure, the neutral shipping entering northern European water. The United States never formally protested the military zone, contenting itself with protests aimed at specific acts arising thereunder (e.g., the searching of ships in port instead of on the high seas). The military zone not only facilitated the Allied blockade of Germany; it also provided the rationalization for German countermeasures.

The German answer was the proclamation on February 4, 1915, of a war zone embracing the waters around the British Isles.[46] Defending the measure as a justifiable retaliation to Allied violations of international law, Germany announced that all enemy shipping within the area would be subject to attack without warning. Neutral vessels were also warned to keep out of the zone, for the alleged British misuse of neutral flags and ramming techniques precluded the submarine from surfacing and challenging in the normal manner.

The American reply to Germany's action was encompassed in the phrase strict accountability, a policy largely conceived by Lansing. As Secretary Bryan was absent at the time on a tour, Lansing sent the notification of the German war zone to Wilson on February 5, commenting that it was a "delicate situation" requiring careful treatment.[47] On the following day, after conference with the president, the counselor drafted a sharp note which expressed grave concern at the war zone proclamation and warned that the United States would hold Germany to a strict accountability if any American vessels or citizens were destroyed by submarine attacks.[48] Germany was to be notified that belligerents should conform closely to the established rules of visit and search, and that no neutral vessel should be destroyed on mere suspicion alone. Wilson approved the draft protest, making several changes in phraseology but retaining the strict accountability clause.[49] The note was apparently ready for dispatch, but Lansing was then seized with doubts, for it appeared that Germany was pleading the same "belligerent necessity" principle which he was willing to grant the Allies. Relying upon a press résumé of the German explanatory memorandum, designed to accompany the war zone proclamation, he wrote Wilson on February 7 that he was greatly impressed by the German defense and therefore wondered if any protest should be sent.[50] The German memorandum justified the war zone proclamation on the grounds of numerous British violations of international law, including the military zone and the illegal food blockade imposed upon the Central Powers.[51] Since the neutrals had acquiesced in the British actions by failing to take strong action to halt them, Germany requested the same consideration for her own retaliations.

Lansing's indecision was only temporary. Further consideration apparently reënforced his original view that the German action was contrary to American rights and interests. He decided that the note should be sent, and seeing the opportunity for a gesture of impartiality, always pleasing to some elements of the American population, he secured the approval of Wilson to couple the note to Germany with one to Great Britain regarding the misuse of neutral flags.[52] The two notes were therefore dispatched February 10, 1915.[53]

Obviously the notes were not equal in importance or severity of demand. Germany was requested to abandon her illegal methods of warfare; Great Britain, though left free to continue unabated the practices allegedly responsible for the submarine retaliation, was asked merely to give up the improper use of neutral flags. Nevertheless, the British reply of February 19 rejected completely the American note and defended the use of neutral flags as a *ruse de guerre*, necessitated by Germany's ruthless use of the submarine.[54]

The simultaneous protests, although perhaps gratifying American public opinion, had done nothing to alter the nature of the warfare at sea. What had been accomplished was the assumption of a position from which retreat would be most difficult. The note to Germany had applied primarily to American ships. Reference had been made, however, to the loss of American lives from unannounced submarine attacks, with the inference that strict accountability covered United States citizens traveling on belligerent vessels. This aspect was soon to be raised when British vessels were torpedoed with Americans on board, and Lansing was then to assert that the American note covered the loss of these nationals. He then claimed that it was too late to warn Americans against travel on belligerent vessels, that the government, by its failure to act earlier, had tacitly assured its citizens of full protection of their rights to travel the high seas. In this way, America was to adopt a course which amounted to a partial immunization of Allied vessels from submarine attack.

The German reply of February 16 seemed to offer a slight hope for compromise settlement. The note, after reviewing the record of British violations and commenting on the one-sided nature of the munitions trade, intimated that if Germany were allowed to import foodstuffs and raw materials, the war zone proclamation might be withdrawn.[55] Lansing, however, suspected a ruse. Perceiving that Great Britain was far more dependent upon food imports than was Germany, he concluded that Germany would not offer to forego the advantages of submarine warfare unless she confidently expected a British rejection of the proposed compromise.[56] He realized that the submarine was not aimed at the munitions trade alone, but rather was intended to sever all trade to Great Britain and thus reduce the mistress of the seas to capitulation—a process which, unlike the Allied measures, would inflict heavy economic damage on America as well. Nevertheless, Lansing agreed with Bryan that the United States government should make every possible attempt to bring about retraction of the war zone proclamation. The two officials, therefore, proposed a *modus vivendi* under which the Allies would allow food importations for civilian use, in return for German promises to use the submarine in accordance with the cruiser rules of warfare and to abandon mine laying.[57] Lansing saw in the situation a good opportunity for another impartial gesture—a protest to both belligerents against the indiscriminate use of mines.[58] President Wilson welcomed the food proposal, but agreed only with reluctance to the protest on mines, feeling that it was a little late to protest acts that had been going on since the early months of the war.[59] The food proposal was then dispatched to both belligerents.[60] Colonel House, then on another European "peace" mission, lent his efforts to the scheme.[61] All these efforts failed, however. As Lansing had foreseen, neither belligerent really desired the *modus vivendi*. Germany insisted upon the admission of raw materials as well as foodstuffs, and refused to give up the use of offensive mines.[62] Similarly, Great Britain rejected the proposal, preferring to continue unabated the economic blockade of Germany.[63] The United States was thus left in its original position, still facing the problem of the submarine.

Lansing predicted war with Germany over the submarine issue. As early as February, before the campaign was fully under way, he came to the conclusion that Germany had much to gain and little to lose by hostilities with America.[64] Lansing summed up the situation as one where the United States, although trading freely with the Allies in war materials, was exporting very little to Germany. War with the United States would have no deleterious effects on the commercial fortunes of the Central Powers, but it might, through the resultant war effort and domestic civil strife expected by Berlin from the German-Americans within the United States, disrupt the American flow of goods to the Allies. Militarily, the American Navy would add little to the Allied mastery of the seas, and Lansing (falsely, it proved) believed that America would be unable to send large armies to Europe. Consequently, war with America would cost Germany very little beyond the loss of the interned vessels and the cessation of American attempts to ameliorate the Allied maritime measures, and Germany would gain freedom of action to prosecute to the maximum the submarine warfare against Great Britain.

Lansing's analysis of the submarine controversy was prophetic;

within two years, war was to result from the issue. He did not delude himself into believing that economics was not a factor. He recognized that the munitions and contraband trade was a vital element tending to strain relations with Germany. The counselor simply did not question the existence of the trade, being convinced that it was legal and of great value to the American economy. No serious thought, therefore, could be given the possibility of an arms embargo, although such an act probably would have greatly improved American relations with the Central Powers. In essence, Lansing was clearly conscious of the fact that American neutrality was nearly valueless to Germany. Thus the recent exchange about the submarine had seen the American government demand of Germany alone the fullest compliance with international law and practices. Germany eventually was to conclude that America was in effect already a member of the Entente.

While the German-American situation was thus severely strained, the Allies seized advantage of the war zone declaration to proclaim a complete blockade of Germany. In the order in council of March 11, 1915, Great Britain announced that all commerce with Germany would be stopped, with compensation for the neutral goods seized in the process of enforcement.[65] In effect, a pseudo blockade was established, since it was manifest that Germany, because of neighboring neutrals and the Baltic Sea, could not be effectively blockaded under established international law. In the absence of a legal blockade, neutrals were entitled to trade in conditional and noncontraband goods with Germany. The Allied declaration circumvented the demands of legality by terming the blockade a reprisal against the illegal German submarine warfare. All distinction between different types of contraband was wiped out; the declaration made absolute contraband of all goods.[66]

The Allies had now completed their control of European commerce; neutrals, as well as the Central Powers, were blockaded. Furthermore, the partiality of American neutrality was soon demonstrated by the official reaction to the blockade. Whereas the German war zone had been vigorously opposed, the British reprisal, equally threatening to the fabric of neutral rights, though applying to property and not to lives, was to receive merely a long, but relatively mild, protest.

Lansing's initial reaction set the pace for the resulting diplomatic exchanges. Although questioning the legality of the British methods, he felt the matter should be studied carefully in order to determine ". . . what is proper and right for belligerents to do and to what extent the previous rules should be modified."[67] He therefore drafted an inquiry requesting a full British statement of the precise Allied aims and goals. Wilson felt that the inquiry was too abrupt.[68] Consequently the more moderate letter by Lansing to Bryan on March 2 was recast by Wilson and sent to Page to use in informal talks with Grey.[69] A formal protest awaited the arrival of the British memorandum accompanying the order in council.

The preliminary discussions within the State Department, preceding the protest of March 30, markedly displayed Lansing's characteristics of legalism and tenacity of purpose. As a specialist in international law, Lansing naturally sought to attack the British order in council at its weakest point, its inconsistency with international practice and past British declarations. His purpose was to lodge a strong legal reservation of rights, which would benefit America at the inevitable postwar settlement, and to protect American trade to the neutrals. The counselor was beginning to suspect that some of the British war measures were designed to further British commercial interests rather than advancing what should have been the primary goal, the economic isolation of Germany.[70] When the British explanatory note arrived on March 20, Lansing drew up a memorandum emphasizing the inconsistencies of the British position.[71] He pointed out that though the order in council carefully eschewed the term "blockade," instead, designating the measures against Germany as "reprisals," the accompanying memorandum referred to the order as establishing a blockade. Since Great Britain had accepted the modified Declaration of London, in particular Articles 1, 18, and 19, her present course in establishing a blockade of neutral ports was contradictory. Lansing concluded that the American government should not let itself be led into the trap of admitting the existence of a legal blockade.

President Wilson, although impressed with Lansing's legal analysis, decided that it was useless to debate the inconsistency with the British government.[72] Instead, he urged sending a note, which he had drafted on March 19, that expressed confidence that Britain would assume the responsibility for any violations of American rights under international law.[73] It was plain that Wilson was not too greatly concerned about the matter, believing that Great Britain's intentions were honorable, but that because of the archaic nature of international law the British government was forced to adopt innovations not in strict conformity with precedent.[74] Furthermore, as Ambassador Page wrote from London, most American commerce had previously been denied access to Germany, whereas "... trade with the Allies is ... increasing rapidly and will grow by leaps until the war ends."[75]

Lansing was less willing to trust British generosity. Although as anxious as Wilson or Page not to interfere unduly with the Allied war effort, he felt that, within that context, American trade to the European neutrals should not be needlessly curtailed. The counselor therefore concluded that Wilson's draft note was faulty and incomplete, and, with some hesitation, submitted an entirely different draft emphasizing British inconsistencies.[76] The draft asserted that though retaliatory measures applying against other belligerents were not contested in themselves, condemnation and protest were mandatory when such retaliations sought to use the neutral both as the agent and as the victim. In a following letter to Bryan, Lansing called attention to the fact that the Baltic Sea could not be blockaded and therefore the Allied blockade would operate unevenly on the neutrals.[77] Although willing to accept the British contentions that conditions of modern warfare required the maintenance of a blockade by long-range patrols, the counselor recommended that Great Britain not be permitted to block non-contraband trade with European neutrals, even if partly intended for Germany.

The counselor's persistence apparently began to irritate Wilson. Writing Bryan that debate with Great Britain was futile and that in any case there was little trade left with Germany to protect, Wilson expressed hope that "... Mr. Lansing will be kind enough to try his hand at a note such as I have indicated...."[78] Nevertheless, Lansing made one more effort to secure his objective. In another memorandum, he developed at length the reasons why a full protest should be sent to Great Britain.[79] Only a complete defense would satisfy American public opinion and remove doubts of the impartiality of the government's neutral policies; America should reserve all legal rights, both to protect its case at the postwar settlement and to exercise the American role as the world spokesman for neutral rights everywhere. A caveat would accomplish these purposes, he felt, and yet permit the Allies to continue the illegal practices necessary to their success in the war.

Lansing's efforts for a full protest were only partly successful. The note sent to Page on March 30 followed Wilson's outlines, but it did record a full reservation of legal rights. Lansing then joined Bryan in adding "a little sweetening" to the note, in the form of a postscript reiterating the friendly relations existing between the United States

and Great Britain.[80] The note accomplished little; Great Britain delayed a formal reply until late June, perhaps deliberately waiting
until the submarine controversy concentrated American attention on
more important matters.[81] America had again failed, signally, to take
any step capable of alleviating Allied exactions.

The first major crisis with Germany was precipitated when the
British vessel *Falaba* was torpedoed March 28, 1915. The *Falaba* was
sunk in the Irish Sea with the loss of 104 lives, including one American
citizen, William C. Thrasher.[82] In the ensuing diplomatic controversy,
the first really serious clash between the United States and Germany,
Lansing, more than any other individual, largely determined the policy
of the full assertion of the right of American nationals to travel the
high seas on belligerent vessels.[83]

The *Falaba* case presented a sharp issue requiring immediate decision. The American government faced two alternatives: either to
warn its citizens off belligerent vessels and thus, in effect, abandon much
of the Allied war trade to the submarine (trade routes to the European
neutrals were left open by Germany), and, as well, to abdicate the traditional right of neutrals to protect their citizens; or to assert the American right to travel freely the high seas, subject only to the normal rules
of visit and search, and thereby in effect to safeguard Allied vessels
from ruthless submarine attack. To pursue the latter course, especially
in conjunction with the benevolence of American neutrality toward the
Allies and the failure of America to alleviate in any significant way the
illegal British blockade, meant that war with Germany was probable.
As Lansing had realized earlier, Germany would then have little to
lose and much to gain from war with the United States. Therefore, the
interpretation by Lansing of strict accountability as meaning immediate reparations, disavowals, apologies, and assurances against repetition from the German government and Wilson's acceptance of that
policy were decisive in their consequences.

Convinced that the legitimate interests of the nation and an aroused
public opinion made compromise impossible, Lansing strongly cham-
pioned a flat challenge to the German submarine warfare. He asserted
as an unquestioned neutral right that American citizens could travel
on belligerent vessels in safety. It was therefore Germany's duty, if she
felt it necessary to stop the British importation of war materials, to
challenge in the normal manner belligerent vessels with Americans on
board and, if it were necessary to destroy these vessels, to remove the
crew and passengers to safety.[84] Lansing's position in essence extended

the February strict accountability clause beyond American ships so that the mere presence of Americans on board sufficed to protect Allied merchant vessels from submarine attacks without warning. This position has been criticized as totally unwarranted, on the grounds that persons on British vessels could look only to the British government for protection, but in view of the general rules of international law and the American reliance upon the British merchant marine, Lansing's premises had some justification.[85]

America, however, had tacitly acquiesced in Allied violations on the ground of modern conditions of warfare, and Germany perhaps warranted the same consideration. If the American government had prohibited its nationals from travel on belligerent vessels, the restriction of right would have affected at the most only a comparative handful of the population. At the least, the government could have changed its policy on defensively armed merchantmen and thus have helped make it possible for the submarine to observe cruiser rules of warfare. Allied ramming techniques would probably have continued, but an agreement on the aspect of armament possibly could have been extended to other phases of naval tactics as well.

In the establishment of American policy concerning the *Falaba* sinking, Lansing faced Bryan's opposition and Wilson's indecision. Lansing's eventual triumph was finally to cause Bryan to resign from the State Department. On April 2, a few days after the news of the *Falaba* disaster, Lansing sent Bryan a memorandum calling for an immediate policy decision, terming the sinking a clear violation of American rights.[86] The counselor stated that the position he was advocating would amount to a denunciation of the German war zone. Bryan's reaction was against Lansing's proposed strong policy because the secretary apparently feared that hostilities with Germany would result.[87] He felt that an American citizen traveling on a British vessel, knowing the submarine threat in advance, contributed by negligence to his own destruction. Bryan, however, sent to the president Lansing's earlier memorandum of February 15 on the probabilities of war with Germany. Wilson was impressed with the counselor's predictions, but refused to seek a softer policy in order to reduce the contingency of hostilities. The *Falaba* affair nevertheless was causing him great concern, and he expressed his eager desire for Lansing's views on the course to be adopted.[88] He depended heavily upon Lansing for advice on matters of international law, and when the counselor recommended a given policy, couched in moral terms, Wilson tended to be readily convinced.[89] Had

Lansing supported Bryan's contentions at this time, later American policy probably would have been quite different.[90]

Lansing was convinced that the United States had to challenge flatly the German intensified submarine warfare. Therefore he drafted a harsh note on the *Falaba* case which termed the sinking a wanton act, contrary to the rules of "civilized warfare."[91] The draft note asserted that Germany had violated the rules of visit and search, denied the German claim to suspend the rules within a given area of the high seas, demanded disavowal of the act and punishment of the guilty officials, and requested reparations for Thrasher's death. In a letter to Bryan accompanying the proposed note, Lansing admitted that the note was severe but he claimed that a weaker or more conciliatory note would be worse than none.[92] Only a sharp demand, fully asserting American neutral rights, would be capable of modifying German actions in the future, and nothing less would satisfy the demands of American public opinion. Although war might well follow the dispatch of the note, the counselor felt that he could advise no other course.

The strong policy toward the submarine war zone was finally adopted, but only after Lansing first overcame the doubts and opposition of Bryan and Wilson. Secretary Bryan was becoming increasingly agitated by the situation. He wrote Wilson on April 6 that he questioned the right of any American citizen, placing his own selfish interests above that of the nation, to involve the country unnecessarily in international disputes.[93] Even Wilson began to entertain doubts on the matter, inquiring if the arming of merchantmen in any way justified the sinking of the *Falaba*.[94] This question led Bryan to question further the sending of a strong note.[95] At this point, Lansing hastened to quiet these waverings, and he sent to the White House a memorandum from the Joint State-Navy Neutrality Board which upheld his view that the *Falaba* sinking was inhumane and incapable of justification.[96] Shortly thereafter, a dispatch arrived from Consul-General Robert P. Skinner in England, revealing that the vessel had been torpedoed after the passengers and crew had been allowed only ten minutes to abandon ship. This proved to Lansing that the question of armament or resistance to challenge had not entered into the affair.[97] President Wilson's indecisions were largely removed, and, brushing aside as inopportune Bryan's suggestion that a peace appeal to the belligerents be used as an alternative, he ordered Lansing to prepare a draft note to Germany.[98]

While a decision on the *Falaba* case was being considered, a German diplomatic blunder intervened. In an ill-timed move, Ambassador

Bernstorff delivered a memorandum on April 4 that complained bitterly of American acquiescence to the British blockade and criticized the arms traffic with the Allies as essentially unneutral.[99] The memorandum pointed out that though the American position accorded with the letter of neutrality, it nevertheless violated the spirit. An entirely novel situation had been established whereby the United States, the only large neutral in the war, had created an almost entirely new arms industry devoted to supplying one side with the tools of warfare. The German government therefore suggested that a true neutrality of purpose would either halt the one-sided munitions trade or else take effective measures to ensure legitimate trade with the Central Powers. Lansing termed the communication "unpardonable in insinuations," made doubly distasteful by Bernstorff's premature release of the protest to the American press. The counselor recommended a curt reply, contending that any more moderate statement would ". . . displease the American people who are jealous of our national dignity. . . ."[100] The counselor even considered requesting the recall of Ambassador Bernstorff, claiming that his conduct was as improper as that of the Turkish ambassador, Rustem Bey, in September, 1914.[101] It soon became apparent, however, that Bernstorff had acted upon instructions,[102] and since relations with Germany were already strained, Lansing's suggestion of recall was dropped. The American reply, drafted by Wilson and retouched by Lansing, rejected the German charges of unneutrality and reiterated the legality of the munitions trade.[103]

While the *Falaba* note was being prepared, further complications arose. On April 29, the American vessel *Cushing* was attacked by a German airplane, and, on May 1, the German embassy in Washington caused a press announcement to be run in American newspapers, warning Americans not to enter the war zone on Allied vessels. Lansing became convinced that Germany was insolently trying to force a rupture of diplomatic relations.[104] When news arrived that the American steamer *Gulflight* had also been torpedoed, on May 1, Lansing was positive that America was being forced, by deliberate German actions, to the breaking point. Consequently he recommended either the immediate dispatch of the *Falaba* protest, which could then be followed by a peremptory note on the American vessels, or, failing that, the drafting of a new protest incorporating all three cases.[105] Thoroughly in the mood for decisive action, Lansing bombarded Bryan and Wilson with still another memorandum, analyzing the February strict accountability note as leaving no alternative but the use of force if

Germany continued her violations on the high seas.[106] While matters were in this tense state, an even greater crisis confronted the American government, the sinking of the *Lusitania*. The *Falaba* case had determined American policy. It was only necessary to apply that policy, with slight alterations, to the *Lusitania*.

The *Lusitania* crisis removed Lansing's remaining doubts of the proper course for the United States. He had been sympathetic toward the Allies since the beginning of the war. This sympathy had not been decreased by his realization of the economic benefits flowing to America from the Entente war purchases. More important, however, he understood America's stake in the world, which the defeat of Great Britain would affect profoundly. As the war progressed and optimistic expectations of Allied victory faded, particularly when Germany demonstrated the usefulness of the submarine as a weapon, Lansing came to the conclusion that the United States would probably have to take a more positive role. In February, 1915, he saw war as the most likely result of the submarine threat.[107] The *Lusitania* sinking merely highlighted this menace. In a private memorandum of July 11, 1915, Lansing recorded his ideas on the war:

> I have come to the conclusion that the German Government is utterly hostile to all nations with democratic institutions because those who compose it see in democracy a menace to absolutism and the defeat of the German ambition for world domination. . . .
>
> The remedy seems to me to be plain. It is that Germany must not be permitted to win this war and to break even, though to prevent it this country is forced to take an active part. This ultimate necessity must be constantly in our minds in all our controversies with the belligerents. American public opinion must be prepared for the time, which may come, when we will have to cast aside our neutrality and become one of the champions of democracy.
>
> We must in fact risk everything rather than leave the way open for a new combination of powers, stronger and more dangerous to liberty than the Central Powers are today.[108]

Lansing's memorandum indicated that he was concerned primarily with the problem of national security, which depended upon a favorable balance of power. He did not fear an immediate assault on the United States by a triumphant Germany, one of the cardinal points of Allied propaganda.[109] Lansing was more farsighted; he anticipated, if Germany won the war, a future power alignment of Germany, Russia, and Japan which would threaten America on all sides. In his thinking Lansing mixed national interests in a favorable world power structure with ideology, for Germany menaced the United States in a direct power-political manner and as an aggressive autocracy threatened democracy everywhere. Democracy was for him the one great hope of universal progress and peace, and German absolutism was the principal danger. Germany, therefore, was a threat to the national security, both as an aggressive nation disturbing the world power structure and threatening dangerous combinations and extensions of influence, and as an ideology threatening democratic institutions and values generally.

To meet this threat, Lansing's memorandum concluded that American public opinion required education about the German menace. The horror aroused by the *Lusitania* case[110] and by submarine warfare generally offered the means. Speaking of the issue in terms of democracy against autocracy, Lansing concluded that the probable American entry into the war could not take place until the public could be aroused to the proper pitch.[111] Lansing later described this process as a ". . . slow and irritating period of education and enlightenment as to German aims and the meaning of the great European conflict."[112] The *Lusitania* marked the beginning of the educational phase.

The sinking of the British Cunard liner *Lusitania* on May 7, 1915, with the loss of 1,198 lives, including 128 American nationals, brought into sharp focus the question of protecting the right of American citizens to travel on belligerent vessels. Lansing continued to advocate a full assertion and defense of this right and succeeded in winning the support of President Wilson, thus overcoming Bryan's resistance.[113] Bryan was, of course, thoroughly opposed to the assumption of a position which rendered war probable.[114] When the *Falaba* had been under consideration, he had raised the question of whether American citizens should be permitted to involve the government unnecessarily in difficulties with Germany, and had proposed as an alternative that the government notify Americans traveling on belligerent vessels that they did so at their own risk. After the *Lusitania* was sunk, Lansing promptly moved to close this escape avenue by writing Bryan on May 9 that for the government now to warn citizens that they traveled at their own risk would indicate an official dereliction of duty and raise the embarrassing question of why the warning had not been issued earlier. The counselor maintained that the strict accountability note of February and the subsequent silence of the government entitled the public to assume that the right to travel on belligerent vessels would be maintained. Wilson accepted Lansing's arguments as "unanswerable."[115] The basic policy of the government was thus established, although Bryan continued his search for a peaceful way out of the controversy.

The next task was to examine the propriety of passenger vessels carrying munitions of war. Bryan was inclined to feel that there was some validity to German claims that the *Lusitania,* by carrying contraband, had laid herself open to attack without warning.[116] Dudley Field Malone, collector of the Port of New York, reported that the *Lusitania* carried a cargo consisting almost entirely of contraband goods, including ammunition and shrapnel.[117] Malone stated, however, that there was no evidence that the vessel carried guns of any type, although the *Lusitania* had been built with provisions for armament.[118] In anticipation of probable German defenses of the sinking, Lansing drafted a memorandum on May 10 that denied that the vessel was armed, rejected the advanced press warning as relieving Germany of responsibility, and asserted that, regardless of the munitions in the cargo, the ship should not have been sunk without warning and without providing for the safety of those on board.[119] Lansing then forwarded the memorandum to Bryan with the recommendation that Germany be required to disavow the act, render apologies and reparations, and give ample reassurances that such acts would not recur.[120] The counselor added that a break in relations might follow, but that such a state would not necessarily mean war. Perhaps seeking to reassure Wilson and Bryan, he suggested that the *Lusitania* protest could be coupled with an identic note to Great Britain and Germany, in which all the neutrals could join, protesting general violations of international law. Bryan was especially interested in the idea of a joint protest, for he favored any tension-relieving gesture of American impartiality toward the belligerents.

The first *Lusitania* note was based on Lansing's memorandum of May 10. Wilson, using the counselor's recommendations as his guide, drafted the note and sent it to the State Department for revision. Bryan, with a "heavy heart," turned the draft over to Lansing.[121] The draft note covered the *Falaba, Cushing,* and *Gulflight* cases, in addition to that of the *Lusitania.* It asserted the unqualified right of American citizens to travel on belligerent vessels without being subjected to unannounced submarine attacks and questioned the use of the submarine under any conditions as a lawful weapon of warfare. The German government was then requested to repudiate the act, make reparations, and give assurances against recurrence. To the sentence expressing the intent of the United States government to protect fully the rights of its citizens, Lansing added the clause "... nor omit any act necessary to the performance of its sacred duty...."[122] The only item of importance that he objected to in Wilson's draft was the term "unarmed vessel"; Lansing desired to substitute "unresisting," hoping thereby to preclude a German claim that if the *Lusitania* were armed, it was legitimately subject to attack. His advice on this point unfortunately was ignored, for the German reply raised the question. In this form, the note was dispatched to Ambassador Gerard on May 13, 1915.[123]

While the note was being coded for transmission, Bryan made another attempt to reduce the severity of the protest. He suggested to Wilson that a press statement be issued, which would indicate that strict accountability did not necessarily mean an immediate settlement, but that the case might well be settled by investigation or similar means.[124] Wilson allowed himself to be persuaded temporarily by Bryan's importunities and agreed to release a press "tip."[125] Lansing was told by Bryan of this development and, seeing his labors for a firm position thus threatened, he very anxiously contacted Tumulty and the secretary of war, Lindley M. Garrison. Pressure was then brought to bear on Wilson, with the result that the "tip" was withdrawn.[126] Wilson wrote Bryan that he had "heard something" from the German embassy which indicated that all chance to secure results from the note would be lost if the press statement were made.[127] Still persevering, Bryan then suggested that at least the note should conclude with the usual reiteration of friendly relations between the two countries. Lansing, however, opposed this as unnecessary and Wilson agreed.[128]

Bryan then resorted to still another device. On the day after the dispatch of the *Lusitania* note, Bryan referred to Lansing's offhand suggestion of May 10 that a general protest could be sent to Great Britain. The secretary hoped that such a protest, together with a press announcement warning Americans not to use belligerent vessels pending settlement of the *Lusitania* case, would strike the proper note of official impartiality and thereby persuade Germany to meet the government's demands. Lansing objected once more to any move depriving American citizens of their travel rights, claiming that such a course would arouse public condemnation by coming after, instead of before, the loss of American lives.[129] Wilson agreed, adding that a warning would also falsely encourage Germany not to meet the American demands.[130] Lansing did, however, draft a note to Great Britain, which protested the blockade and intimated more positive action if the illegal practices were not halted.[131]

While these matters were being considered in Washington, Colonel House was in London attempting to work out a *modus vivendi* between the belligerents. It was proposed that Germany abandon ruthless submarine warfare and the use of poison gas, in return for which the Allies would lift the blockade on foodstuffs.[182] In view of such a possible solution, President Wilson decided not to send the proposed note to Great Britain, feeling that nothing should be done before the *Lusitania* case was settled.[183] Lansing also took part in the attempted remedy. In an interview with Spring-Rice on May 27, he persuaded the ambassador to admit that, since Germany was not yet suffering from a food shortage but was using the food blockade as an excuse for unrestricted submarine warfare, Great Britain should seize advantage of the opportunity to place Germany in a difficult position. If the Allies would allow free importations of foodstuffs, Germany would either have to surrender the submarine blockade or else bear alone the onus of using cruel methods of warfare. Lansing stressed particularly the sensitivity of the American people to a policy apparently directed at starving innocent women and children.[184] Clearly, Lansing on his part intended the proposed note to Great Britain and the food *modus vivendi* as a means of placating American public opinion generally, without greatly altering relations with Germany. Regardless of such motivations and suggestions, the proposed working arrangement failed, neither belligerent desiring to alter his mode of warfare.

One week before Germany replied to the American note on the *Lusitania,* Bryan allowed his pacifist sentiments to lead him into a diplomatic blunder. In a conversation with the Austrian ambassador, Constantin Theodor Dumba, Bryan evidently intimated that the *Lusitania* note was intended primarily for domestic public opinion and should not be taken as threatening war. This was the construction placed upon the Dumba report in Berlin, although when confronted by Bryan, Dumba denied having reported any such remark.[185] It was possible that the German Foreign Office twisted Dumba's report to suit its own purposes. Nonetheless, Lansing believed that Bryan had made some such remark, feeling that Dumba was too clever a diplomat to have invented the story without some kind of basis.[186] Dumba naturally had to deny the affair, regardless of the question of validity, for otherwise his recall would have been demanded by the angered Bryan.[187]

The German reply of May 28 to the *Lusitania* protest was most unsatisfactory to the United States government. The note promised satisfaction for the attacks on the two American vessels, *Cushing* and *Gulflight,* but defended the *Falaba* sinking as justified by the approach of suspicious vessels and raised several questions of fact about the *Lusitania*. The German government asserted that the *Lusitania* was armed, and thus in effect a naval auxiliary, and that the vessel was also carrying munitions and Canadian troops. These alleged facts, together with secret British instructions to merchantmen ordering the ramming and firing upon submarines, were held to relieve Germany of the need to observe the usual rules of warfare.[138]

Lansing totally rejected the German arguments. He termed the note an attempt to avoid the principles of the case by drawing the United States into a debate on the facts surrounding the *Lusitania*. He therefore recommended that the American reply should refuse to discuss any details until Germany first acknowledged the principles of neutral travel on belligerent vessels, recognized the applicability of the rules of visit and search to submarines, and gave assurances against similar violations in the future.[139] In two successive memoranda, forwarded to the White House at Wilson's request, the counselor gave a detailed criticism of the German defense.[140] He pointed out the earlier mistake of using the term "unarmed" instead of "unresisting," since Germany now was taking advantage of this opening to allege that the *Lusitania* was an armed vessel and hence subject to attack without warning. Lansing averred that the question of armament was irrelevant, since the American circular of September, 1914, had recognized defensive armament. Therefore Germany should be informed that mere armament alone did not justify attacks without warning. As for the German reference to ramming, Lansing commented that a vessel the size of the *Lusitania* could not possibly ram a "small swift moving craft like a submarine."[141] In essence, Lansing held that regardless of what the *Lusitania* carried, whether Canadian troops or munitions of war, Germany was not entitled to sink the vessel without warning and without making provisions for the safety of crew and passengers. Lapsing into moralistic phrases, perhaps unconsciously, the counselor wrote to a friend that it was "a question of American lives, not of American property."[142]

Fearing that a repetition of the first *Lusitania* note would lead to war with Germany, Secretary Bryan continued to search for a way out of the dilemma. At the Cabinet session of June 1, when Wilson presented his ideas of the form the American reply should take, Bryan argued for sending a strong note to Great Britain simultaneously with the one to Berlin. Upon rejection by the other Cabinet officials, Bryan apparently lost control of his emotions and hotly accused them of being unneutral—a remark which prompted a sharp rebuke from Wilson.[143] Bryan was in fundamental disagreement with Lansing on the nature of the German reply. In a long letter to Wilson on June 2, he challenged

Lansing's opinion on armed merchantmen, holding that Germany was entitled to treat armed vessels as military ships.[144] Bryan also felt that the American reply should cover all the points raised by Germany, instead of insisting only on the prior acknowledgment of the principles for which the United States contended. On the following day, Bryan renewed his efforts with an appeal to the spirit of the "cooling-off" treaties, and once more suggested warning Americans against travel on belligerent ships pending settlement of the controversy. The secretary also felt that action should be taken to preclude the carrying of both passengers and munitions on the same vessel.[145] Convinced that Germany was looking for a way out of the crisis, Bryan thus sought to provide the means through some American concessions and perhaps even through arbitration.

All of Bryan's efforts failed. The second *Lusitania* note represented a complete victory for Lansing's contentions, and consequently led to Bryan's resignation from the State Department. Lansing was clearly the man of the hour. On June 4 he attended the Cabinet session at which the forthcoming note to Germany was discussed.[146] On the following day, he received Wilson's draft note and began the work of revision and final polishing.[147] Wilson agreed with Lansing's major suggestions as to the proper nature of the reply—no debating details with Germany and an insistence upon recognition of the relevant principles of international law. In his redraft of the note, Lansing incorporated his contention that nothing except actual resistance to challenge justified submarine attacks without providing for the safety of those on board.[148] This thesis, retained in the final note, placed America squarely in opposition to the continuation of intensive submarine warfare. The last desperate efforts by Bryan to modify the note in any way possible were rejected by Wilson.[149] Although turning down the proposal for a protest to Great Britain, Wilson was moved by Bryan's devotion to peace, and he wrote the secretary on June 5, and again June 7, that he sincerely wished it were possible to defend American rights and at the same time do nothing that might lead to war.[150]

Secretary Bryan saw no other course consistent with his principles except resignation. He formally tendered his resignation June 8, effective the following day. Despite the disagreements on policy existing between Bryan and Lansing, the retiring secretary harbored no bitterness. Lansing tried to dissuade Bryan from resigning, pointing out the public condemnation that would surely follow.[151] Bryan remained adamant, convinced that peace was worth the sacrifice of his own personal reputation. Years after the war, Lansing commented on the resignation: "No one who knew the high-mindedness of Mr. Bryan and his earnestness of purpose ever questioned for a moment the sincerity of his course of action or blamed him for refusing to be a party to a policy which he felt convinced would plunge this country into the terrible European conflict."[152] Although many individuals reacted charitably to Bryan's resignation, most Americans greeted it with sharp criticism, accusing the ex-secretary of weakening his government during the crisis with Germany. Strangely enough, both the English and German press drew comfort from the event, although for different reasons.[153] Contrary to some expectations, Bryan's resignation had no immediate results. Lansing as counselor had actually performed the functions belonging to the secretary's office; now he was able to continue his work unhampered by an immediate superior within the department.

On June 9, the effective date of Bryan's resignation, the second *Lusitania* note was dispatched over the signature of Robert Lansing, secretary of state ad interim.[154]

Chapter IV

LANSING ENTERS THE CABINET

The RESIGNATION of Secretary of State Bryan on June 9, 1915, offered Lansing an exceptional and unanticipated opportunity for advancement. Through a series of fortuitous circumstances, Lansing succeeded Bryan as head of the Department of State.

Cabinet posts were normally occupied by individuals selected on the basis of political expediency. The American political system of divided powers and responsibilities made almost mandatory the appointment of high executive officials with political influence sufficient to facilitate the attainment of desired legislation from Congress. As a consequence, the requisite qualifications for cabinet secretaries usually consisted of political power; it was merely adventitious when a given appointee combined political strength with the qualities of aptitude and experience. The State Department was no exception to the general rule. Large numbers of American secretaries of state have qualified for office solely by reason of their political utility. Ordinarily, persons of Lansing's type, possessing great ability and experience in diplomacy but lacking in political influence, were predestined to subordinate positions within the State Department or in foreign service.

Lansing, however, was most fortunate. The resignation of Bryan came after the congressional elections and well in advance of the next presidential campaign and thus reduced political considerations to a minimum. In addition, the government was experiencing a crisis in its relations with Germany, hovering on the precipice of armed hostilities. Experienced and fully acquainted with the work of the department, Lansing was able to achieve the dream of most career diplomats: he was selected to succeed the Great Commoner, thereby becoming one of the few nonpolitical secretaries of state in American history.

* * *

The official relationship between Secretary Bryan and his counselor, Lansing, was an anomalous one. Bryan had been appointed by President Wilson in 1913 primarily because of his large following within the Democratic party. As secretary of state, he was a well-intentioned and sincere person, but without professional qualifications for his high position. Devoid of experience, lacking familiarity with problems of foreign policy, and with only limited comprehension of the factors of national interests and world politics, Bryan entered office with a two-point program—the rewarding of faithful political laborers and the negotiation of "cooling-off" treaties. To compensate for the secretary's deficiencies, John Bassett Moore had been brought into the department as counselor. Moore soon resigned, having failed to protect properly the secretary from his own ignorant blunders and, as well, having opposed Wilson's policy toward Mexico. Thereupon Lansing took over the counselor's duties and succeeded admirably in all respects, especially at the task of compensating for Bryan's paucity of experience. With the outbreak of the European War, Lansing in effect became the actual head of the State Department. He oversaw its functions and supplied Wilson with advice on international law and on the formulation of foreign policies. The president came to depend heavily on the counselor, and was almost constantly in communication with him about the various aspects of American neutrality.[1] Bryan remained the titular chief of the State Department, but Lansing was its functional director.

Some tension and resentment resulted from this situation. Although the correct forms were preserved, it was widely known that the secretary's function was largely nominal. Even the press commented on the situation, noting that Lansing actually drafted the diplomatic notes and was usually consulted by the president when policies were determined.[2] The counselor became embarrassed by the lavish praise he received, realizing that some of the press laudations were primarily political shafts directed at Bryan. In November, 1914, Lansing wrote several friends that though he appreciated kind remarks such as were made in a recent issue of the New York *Sun*, the manner in which they appeared, especially the critical remarks about Bryan, were proving embarrassing.[3] Bryan was conscious of the unfavorable newspaper comments, and he well realized the unconventionality of his situation.[4] The situation was aggravated by the reliance of Wilson on Colonel Edward M. House, who was actually the president's chief adviser on foreign affairs. Bryan finally gave vent to his long-restrained feelings of neglect and abuse. When he tendered his resignation to the president, Bryan stated, with a quiver in his voice, that he had never been the real secretary of state nor had he possessed Wilson's full confidence.[5]

Despite such strains, Bryan and Lansing usually worked together amicably. Lansing was careful to observe the proprieties and, in keeping with his general behavior, was courteous and respectful toward the secretary. Bryan, on his part, was always willing to recognize Lansing's qualities and probably was glad to allow the counselor to direct many of the activities of the department. Bryan never failed to forward Lansing's suggestions to Wilson, even when he disagreed with them, and he always gave the counselor due credit for his contributions. When Bryan resigned, the two parted on a friendly basis. Lansing was quite affected by Bryan's spiritual travail during his last two weeks in office and tried unsuccessfully to persuade Bryan to reconsider his decision to resign. One of Bryan's last official acts was to commend the counselor's services, to which Lansing replied with expressions of regret at the ending of their official relations.[6] Upon Lansing's appointment as secretary, Bryan extended his congratulations. He also requested Lansing to make some provision for his former office employees, a request to which Lansing gladly responded.[7] Bryan thereafter from time to time congratulated Lansing on various official notes, and the two remained on friendly terms until Bryan's death.

In his usual deliberate manner, Wilson took several weeks to decide on Bryan's successor. It soon became apparent that there was a distinct shortage of individuals qualified by both political influence and diplomatic experience. In a period of acute crisis in the nation's foreign relations, the criterion of experience seemed to outweigh all other considerations. Furthermore, Wilson desired someone whose ideas would correspond closely to his own and who would be prepared to accept close presidential supervision in the performance of the duties of the State Department. The earlier experience with Counselor Moore, who had opposed the nonrecognition policy toward Huerta, and the difficulties which had ensued from Bryan's incumbency, convinced the president that he should not appoint any one having either strong convictions or political power. Colonel House, who probably could have had the position, preferred his unofficial role and eliminated himself from consideration.[8] Among the remaining possibilities, Wilson began to consider seriously Lansing's appointment as the most expedient course.[9] As counselor, Lansing had rendered competent services and Wilson had come to rely upon him increasingly for advice. Lansing was one of the nation's best-qualified persons in the field of international law, was thoroughly familiar with the work of the department, and understood fully the Wilsonian approach to foreign policy. Lansing was reticent, unpretentious, and lacked political influence, and therefore would be unlikely, in Wilson's view, either to oppose the presidential will or to involve the administration in political disputes and other forms of unfavorable publicity. In addition, the press, pleased with the counselor's firm attitude toward Bryan over the *Lusitania* notes, tended to favor the appointment of Lansing.[10] An editorial in the influential New York *Times* emphasized the confidence of the general public in the abilities of the counselor and commented that a nonpolitical appointment, especially in view of the crisis with Germany, would be highly satisfactory to most Americans.[11] Although not easily affected by indications of public opinion, particularly when contrary to his own convictions, Wilson probably was aided in his decision by such manifestations of approval.

Colonel House was the principal supporter of Lansing's candidacy.[12] While still undecided, Wilson sent Secretary of the Treasury William Gibbs McAdoo to confer with House in New York City and to inform him that Thomas Jones, a Chicago lawyer and a former classmate of the president, and David F. Houston, the secretary of agriculture, were under consideration. House advised the appointment of Lansing, rejecting Houston as too difficult to work with and unqualified by lack of both tact and experience.[13] As revealed by his Diary, House was most anxious to ensure that Bryan's successor would understand thoroughly that the colonel was Wilson's chief adviser and the unofficial secretary of state. As Lansing had been in the Department for some time and also because he lacked political stature, House anticipated no difficulty from that source. The colonel could continue his discharge of the "real" business of diplomacy and Lansing would remain content with the trappings of office, busily occupied with the routine functions of the department.[14] House therefore followed up the McAdoo interview with a letter to Wilson urging the appointment of Lansing. House wrote:

... the most important thing is to get a man with not too many ideas of his own, and one that will be entirely guided by you without unnecessary argument, and this, it seems to me, you would find in Lansing. I only met him once and then for a few minutes only, and while his mentality did not impress me unduly, at the same time, I hope that you have found him able enough to answer the purpose indicated.[15]

The approval of Colonel House apparently decided Wilson to appoint Lansing. He was compelled, however, to handle the Cabinet with great finesse. Almost every member, it seemed, cherished a desire for the secretaryship of state, the premier cabinet post, which was weighted with tradition and enveloped by prestige and glamour. McAdoo and Houston particularly seem to have been consumed with ambition for the office. Wilson avoided consulting the Cabinet formally but instead discussed the vacancy with several members individually, thus tactfully keeping their ambitions under control.[16] In conversations with McAdoo and Houston, Wilson made disparaging remarks about Lansing but confessed that he knew no one better qualified for the position. This was especially true, he commented, since he needed only a clerk to polish diplomatic notes, for he intended to continue acting as his own foreign secretary.[17] This approach reduced the ardor of the hopefuls and left Wilson free to appoint Lansing without producing a Cabinet revolt.

Lansing naturally had some hopes for the position of secretary of state. Understandably, he probably desired to emulate his father-in-law, John W. Foster, who had received a nonpolitical appointment from President Benjamin Harrison in 1893. The press speculations, frequently referring to the counselor as the logical choice, further increased his expectations. Yet as a realist, Lansing recognized that in view of his lack of political influence his appointment was unlikely. Therefore, when Wilson summoned him to the White House on June 23, a few hours before the president's departure on a vacation, and without preliminaries offered him the post, Lansing was practically overwhelmed. Lansing expressed his doubts of the political expediency of the selection, pointing out that he could add little political strength to the administration. Wilson brushed all objections aside with the remark that the current foreign situation reduced the importance of political considerations, and expressed his conviction that he and Lansing "were of the same mind concerning international policies."[18] Lansing therefore accepted, and the letter of appointment was issued on the same day. Since Congress was not in session, confirmation by the Senate was not made until December 13, 1915.[19] Meanwhile, Lansing had embarked upon his career as secretary of state, a position in which he was to serve with considerable distinction for the next four and one-half years.[20]

The new secretary of state was well received generally by the Washington diplomatic corps.[21] Lansing personified the attributes of the ideal minister of foreign affairs. Although small in physical stature, he was distinguished in appearance, punctiliously correct in behavior and in the observance of diplomatic proprieties, and courteous and considerate in his official relations with the foreign representatives accredited to the American government.

Outwardly withdrawn and unemotional, Lansing actually was an acutely sensitive observer and participant in affairs. He was most discriminating in his estimates of the diplomatic representatives with whom he was associated and, as a person of sincerity and integrity, he disliked intensely the sham and duplicity often found in diplomatic circles. Lansing especially mistrusted the representatives of the two principal Central Powers because of the arrogance and Machiavellian techniques apparently characterizing the Austrian and German foreign services. He also regarded several of the Allied diplomats as less than desirable. Regardless of such personal reactions and sympathies, Lansing and the State Department strove to maintain the most correct attitude toward both belligerent groups, providing separate official social functions for each.[22]

Among the representatives of the Allied Powers, and probably among all the diplomats at the capital, Lansing admired most the French ambassador, Jean Jules Jusserand.[23] The *doyen* of the diplomatic corps, Jusserand was a highly accomplished person with a broad background in art and literature. Lansing was impressed with nearly every aspect of Jusserand's personality, noting that he possessed no faults beyond the small one of an invariable tardiness for appointments. Jusserand reciprocated the secretary's admiration, later describing Lansing as a thoroughly competent person, honest and sound of heart.[24] Lansing was undoubtedly influenced by Jusserand, who was an ardent and effective propagandist for the Allied cause.[25] The ambassador, highly emotional in a controlled manner, was constantly informing the secretary of Teutonic outrages and horrors committed in northern France. In addition, Jusserand was almost a professional exponent of Franco-American traditional friendship and never missed an opportunity to recall the glorious days of the friendship and close collaboration between the two countries during the American Revolution. Jusserand was convinced that most Americans were pro-Ally only because the historical Franco-American amity was able to overcome traditional hostility toward England. Lansing enjoyed contact with the ambassador and continued the friendly intercourse after he left the State Department. When Jusserand resigned in 1924, after twenty years of service in America, Lansing wrote with genuine regret that France had never sent a more "useful and acceptable" representative to the United States.[26]

To Lansing, it was one of the great misfortunes of the war that Great Britain and the United States should have exchanged two such representatives as Sir Cecil Spring-Rice and Walter Hines Page. The secretary, as well as President Wilson and Colonel House, found the British ambassador extremely difficult to work with. Lansing dismissed Spring-Rice as a mediocre person, one of the predictable products of a foreign service that emphasized promotion on the basis of seniority rather than ability.[27] Spring-Rice was an excitable, nervous individual, constantly annoying the State Department with repeated tales of German plots against American neutrality. The ambassador evidently suffered nightmares from fear that the interned German vessels might somehow escape to sea and wreck the British war effort by refueling German warships or perhaps be converted into merchant cruisers. Lansing's patience was often strained by late night calls from Spring-Rice, always reporting still another rumor that the German ships were momentarily about to escape.[28] The secretary concluded that it was almost useless to attempt negotiations with the British ambassador, whom he believed was ignored even by his own foreign office. In despair, Lansing sought the recall of Spring-Rice and suggested that he might well be replaced by the previous British representative, Lord Bryce.[29] This proved impossible, although Colonel House intimated the desirability of a change to Sir Edward Grey. As Grey was the protector and patron of Spring-Rice, the administration naturally hesitated to press the matter and attempted to solve the problem by conducting requisite negotiations through the American embassy in London.

It was therefore most unfortunate for the State Department that Walter Hines Page was accredited to the Court of St. James. Always anxious to placate the British government and unwilling to press American complaints and protests which might, somehow, embarrass the Allied war effort, Page was even less useful than Spring-Rice. Lansing was convinced that Anglo-American relations and the Allied cause generally would be better promoted through the elimination of controversies and frictions, and he therefore viewed Page's failure to present properly the American case as a positive detriment to good relations. The only corrective appeared to be to bring Page home on leave in the hope that, by exposure to domestic opinions, he might become "Americanized."[30] But in spite of a leave at home, Page remained thoroughly convinced of the correctness of his attitudes. His visit in the summer of 1916 coincided with a period of increased tension and resentment in America at the British maritime excesses, and Lansing believed that Page, by his blindly partisan utterances, increased Wilson's mounting anger at the British government.[31] Before his return, Page left the secretary a memorandum on the British attitude toward America. The memorandum, which Page requested not be placed in the department's files, was an apology for British acts and an indictment of the administration for its failure to understand the war necessities of the Allies, particularly emphasizing the embarrassment caused by the numerous American protests.[32] Page even proposed that he be given discretionary powers to settle all outstanding differences with the British government—a request that neither Wilson nor Lansing could consider seriously. The ambassador evidently felt that his mission was to convert the administration to the proper attitude toward the war and, failing, he became very bitter toward Lansing, whom he correctly divined to have ignored him deliberately.[33] The failure either to reform or to replace Page forced the State Department to rely increasingly upon the consul general at London, Robert P. Skinner, for serious negotiations with the British government.

As for the lesser Allied diplomats in Washington, Lansing preferred the Italian ambassador to the representative of the Russian Empire. The secretary found Count Macchi di Cellere to be quite likable and capable despite a rather foppish exterior.[34] The only objection that Lansing had to the Italian ambassador, and one which he considered minor but yet disturbing to a fastidious person, was the count's irritating habit of taking notes of conversations on the white cuffs of his shirt sleeves.

The Russian ambassador, George Bakhmeteff, impressed Lansing as "... Mongol in appearance, in thought and utterance, and ... in temper."[35] Lansing considered Bakhmeteff to be crude, vulgar, and deliberately offensive, occupying his time in endless scandal mongering. In addition to his shallowness of mind, Lansing found the ambassador's callousness toward the mass slaughter of the war most shocking. In a conversation about the current heavy casualties, Bakhmeteff remarked to the secretary, "What are a hundred thousand or a million [Russian lives] for that matter. There are more where they came from. Russian women are good breeders."[36] Lansing found it rather difficult to maintain courteous relations, but in comparison to the German and Austrian ambassadors, found even Bakhmeteff's company more tolerable and preferable.

The German ambassador, Count Johann von Bernstorff, was an accomplished diplomat. Perhaps for this reason, Lansing and Wilson profoundly distrusted him, although Colonel House accepted him as earnest and sincere.[37] To Lansing, Bernstorff was an "affable though dangerous antagonist," with whom he felt that he had to be constantly on guard lest some small indiscretion be exploited by a diplomatic trick.[38] Bernstorff, however, did not reciprocate Lansing's hostility, portraying the secretary as an able person with whom his relations were cordial.[39]

A large part of Lansing's criticism resulted from Bernstorff's propaganda activities within the United States, undertaken because of the peculiar conditions of a war in which the embassy was one of the few channels for direct news from Germany. Although critical of Bernstorff, Lansing had no objections to the extensive Allied propaganda in America nor, for example, did he consider improper the many "lecture" tours undertaken by Jusserand. The secretary did, however, suspect Bernstorff of complicity in the subversive activities allegedly carried on by German agents against the munitions industries supplying the Allied Powers. In addition, Lansing believed, perhaps rightly, that Bernstorff sought his dismissal by Wilson, presumably motivated by a desire to eliminate the pro-Ally secretary of state. Lansing especially blamed the Zwiedinek cable incident on Bernstorff's desire to wreck his career.[40] In spite of such criticisms, Lansing was compelled to recognize the ambassador's abilities. The secretary knew that Bernstorff had repeatedly warned the German Foreign Office of the gravity of the submarine controversy, and he especially credited the ambassador with preventing hostilities over the *Arabic* crisis in 1915. Lansing, however, was unwilling to admit that such actions were the results of patriotism or even of statesmanship, attributing them instead to a desire by Bernstorff to promote his own selfish ends.

Lansing mistrusted Bernstorff, but he positively disliked Dr. Constantin Theodor Dumba, the Austrian ambassador.[41] Lansing and Dumba were entirely different personalities, with the latter personifying characteristics most distasteful to the sensitive and uncompromising standards of the secretary. Dumba's circuitous approach, his allegedly insincere pretense of frankness, and his devious attempts to involve the unwary caused Lansing great uneasiness in official relations with the ambassador. Lansing felt that caution was mandatory, and therefore he adopted a noncommittal attitude toward anything spoken or offered by Dumba. While still counselor of the department, Lansing warned Bryan of the Austrian's duplicity, fearing that the genial, trusting Bryan was inviting exploitation by the unscrupulous ambassador. When shortly thereafter Bryan was quoted in a Dumba report to Berlin and Vienna as stating that the *Lusitania* note was not intended seriously, Lansing became convinced of Dumba's undesirability. The ambassador finally violated the diplomatic proprieties, in the famed Archibald case, and thereby gave Lansing an eagerly awaited opportunity.[42] With considerable pleasure, he forced Dumba's recall, going to great trouble in the process to prevent the ambassador from a prestige-saving departure on leave. The secretary rationalized the rather painful episode as a necessary punishment which should give an object lesson to the other members of the diplomatic corps. Lansing's outward mildness was deceptive; he was quite capable of determined righteousness, bordering on the vindictive, and the Dumba incident offered a great opportunity to strike a blow for the "New Diplomacy." The secretary therefore welcomed Dumba's departure, especially since he found the Austrian chargé, Baron Erich Zwiedinek, far more pleasant in official relations.[43]

The relationship of Lansing with President Wilson has been called a conflict of the legal with the political mind.[44] A more accurate explanation perhaps would be that the realistic approach of Lansing to matters of foreign policy was not readily compatible with the idealistic and intuitive mental processes of Woodrow Wilson. Such radically different personalities, both tending toward obstinacy, were almost certain to clash.

Wilson had a deep antipathy for lawyers. This prejudice arose not only from his type of mind, idealistic and often impractical, but probably was partly because of his unfortunate experiences in the legal profession.[45] Intensely earnest, harshly moralistic, and uncompromising, believing that his life was dedicated to the inculcation of righteousness in the benighted world of politics, Wilson found it difficult to tolerate contrary views and principles or to submit his ideas to logical analysis and criticism.[46] As a result, the president tended to view any criticism of his policies as a personal affront. Consequently he preferred advisers who would supply not only the necessary factual information on political problems, but who would accept without question the presidential view on the principles involved.

Lansing's contacts as counselor with Wilson had been agreeable on the whole, since his recommendations on most neutrality problems, especially that of the submarine, had appealed to Wilsonian idealism. Wilson, nevertheless, had become annoyed by several of Lansing's "legalistic" memoranda, particularly when the counselor sought to debate questions of logical consistency with the British government over the pseudo blockade. In the appointment of Lansing as secretary of state, Wilson labored under the delusion that he was his own foreign minister and therefore needed only a law clerk to polish the diplomatic notes and to attend to the routine concerns of the department. Wilson apparently never realized the extent of his dependence upon others, nor did he sense that the very manner in which Lansing presented memoranda helped to determine policy decisions. This was especially true in view of Wilson's ignorance of international law and the complicated nature of most problems of neutrality.

The president, in appointing Lansing in the belief that he would unquestioningly follow the presidential lead, grossly underestimated Lansing. After an initial period of amazement and incredulity that he had been elevated to so exalted a position, Lansing became accustomed to his office and began to question Wilsonian premises and programs in the field of foreign affairs. The new secretary was fundamentally conservative in outlook, and his practical mind questioned such Wilsonian terms as "freedom of the seas" and later, "self-determination." Lansing also resented the curt treatment sometimes meted out by Wilson, particularly when the president undertook diplomatic measures, usually in the form of a peace move, without prior consultation with the secretary.

Although Lansing exerted his greatest influence in the period before American participation in the war, during which time his relations with Wilson were generally amicable, the president still found occasion to regret Lansing's appointment. Early in 1916, Lansing proposed a *modus vivendi* to the belligerents, intended to solve the armed-ship problem by the abolition of armaments on merchant vessels and by compliance by submarines with cruiser rules of warfare. Wilson had approved the scheme, but when Germany attempted to use it for her own purposes, the resultant torrent of Allied criticisms and the objections of Colonel House caused Wilson to view Lansing's suggestion with some disfavor. The president thereupon restated the American position in a letter to Senator William J. Stone, chairman of the Senate Foreign Relations Committee. Lansing was not consulted on the letter, first learning of it through the press, and he naturally felt bitter about being completely ignored. Colonel House relayed this reaction to the president who replied, according to House, that Lansing must realize that the president conducted foreign affairs and would follow the course he felt was right.[47] When Lansing opposed Wilson's mediation schemes of December, 1916, questioning their probable results, and followed this attitude with a press statement intimating that war was imminent with Germany, Wilson decided that a new secretary was needed. The president early in 1917 informed Colonel House of his intention to replace Lansing with Newton D. Baker. House, who was content with the *status quo*, felt that only his intercession saved Lansing from a forced resignation.[48] In the period after the American entry into the war, the Lansing-Wilson clashes became sharper. Lansing questioned the practicality of the world peace schemes advanced by the League to Enforce Peace, and both before and during the Paris Peace Conference he made clear his dislike of Wilson's plans for a League of Nations.[49] The eventual result was the request for Lansing's resignation in February, 1920. In general, Lansing's realistic and practical approach and his candor of expression made his relations with Wilson extremely tenuous.[50] The most remarkable aspect of the relationship was that it lasted so long.

In spite of the differences in outlook with the president, Lansing sought to keep Wilson's mediation objectives in view.[51] Nevertheless, the secretary was opposed to such peace moves. He believed that an Allied victory was essential and that probably the United States would have to intervene in order to promote that end. Consequently, he opposed formal mediation offers, especially at a time when the military situation favored Germany, realizing as well that the Allies would not seriously entertain any such proposal.[52] Instead, Lansing and House preferred private peace negotiations.[53] Neither desired peace on terms unsuitable to the Allies, and therefore supported informal overtures which, though satisfying in part the demands of the pacifist president, could be terminated easily without embarrassment to the Allied Powers.

Wilson and Lansing both agreed that controversies with the Allies should not be pressed to the breaking point. The main point of difference was Lansing's conviction that America should take an active part in the war. Wilson, torn between his pacifist sentiments and his concepts of America's moral duties, found it difficult to bring himself to the point of accepting war. At various stages of the submarine controversy the secretary urged a strong course with Germany, justifying it on the grounds of morality and the democratic struggle against autocracy. With the parallel efforts of Colonel House, Lansing did much to reduce Wilson's vacillation and resistance, and thus made possible the actual entry into the war in 1917.

At the beginning of his contacts with the president, Lansing was greatly impressed with Wilson's stature as an inspired leader. Prolonged exposure began to reduce his admiration, however, and he soon revised his original estimate. The secretary always appreciated Wilson's interest in the details of foreign problems and the care he gave diplomatic correspondence.[54] On most matters he found Wilson a receptive listener, willing to hear full details and to discuss freely the courses to be adopted. However, he soon realized that Wilson was very reluctant to receive criticisms that rested on principles contrary to his own, and this was especially true of matters relating to the postwar settlement and the League of Nations. Writing in 1921 and probably influenced in part by his recent painful break with the president, Lansing described Wilson as the possessor of a "feminist mind."[55] By this term he meant a nonlogical mind, one that arrived at conclusions through intuition rather than by the processes of logical reasoning based on factual knowledge. Lansing believed that only thus could be explained Wilson's resistance to argument—"When reason clashed with his intuition, reason had to give way."[56] This form of egotism, he believed, led to Wilson's attempts at isolation from others, seeking to avoid influences that might interfere with his independence of judgment, and resulting in his assumption of infallibility. Lansing and Colonel House, at a conference in October, 1920, agreed that Wilson had no creative genius, lacked imagination, and depended upon others for his ideas.[57] Although both men then shared a resentment of Wilson, who had also broken with House, their opinions were partly held by others, including Franklin K. Lane, Wilson's secretary of the interior.[58] In a sense, however, there were two different Wilsons, the more reasonable and tolerant Wilson of the pre-1917 years and the Wilson of the Paris Peace Conference and after; the criticism of his former advisers applied more fully to Wilson's later phase.

Lansing's work as secretary of state was complicated by Wilson's reliance upon personal and unofficial agents in the diplomatic field.[59] Chief among these was Colonel House of Texas. The colonel rendered invaluable services to the president on the domestic political level, but with the outbreak of the European War, he shifted his interests to foreign policy and soon came to regard himself as the president's unofficial secretary of state. A series of missions to the European belligerents followed, which accomplished little in relation to the primary goal of mediation but did clothe the colonel in an aura of mystery and international intrigue. House apparently enjoyed immensely his secretive role, but his achievements have been exaggerated. His peace missions were failures, although his role in shaping the basic American neutral policies was considerable. It would appear, however, that House's major contributions in the neutrality period lay in his joining forces with Lansing to persuade the president that war was necessary on the submarine issue.

In supporting the appointment of Lansing originally, House had been motivated by the belief that Lansing would accept without protest the colonel's peculiar role in American foreign affairs. Shortly after Lansing took office, Wilson visited House and assured him that the new secretary thoroughly understood the situation.[60] After stating that he intended to be his own foreign minister, the president advised House to inform Lansing of his European work only to the extent necessary for harmony. House's fears were thus laid at rest, and thereafter he concentrated on keeping Lansing conciliated and in office, opposing any change that might alter or endanger his unofficial position.[61]

Soon after his appointment, Lansing and his wife joined House at his summer home, and there the two statesmen rapidly agreed on the essentials of American foreign policy.[62] House followed the visit with a letter to Lansing, stressing the fact that the good will of Germany already had been lost and that as a consequence America should preserve good relations with the Allies, especially by not pressing issues of neutral rights too far.[63] House felt that although England would grant any concession before risking a break in American relations, the government should pursue a most liberal policy toward Allied war measures. Lansing was in agreement on the necessity of preserving Allied friendship but felt that protests, sufficiently strong to remove doubts of the impartiality of the government, had to be delivered for the sake of American public opinion.[64] This was the position Lansing had taken during the negotiations on the Declaration of London—that the greatest service to the Allied cause would be obtained by protests securing some concessions to American interests. Although thus differing as to the question of means, both Lansing and House believed that the Entente cause was America's and that ultimate participation in the war might well be necessary.

Colonel House took great pains to remain in contact with the activities of the State Department. In July, 1915, he and Lansing joined forces to select a new counselor, and after much consultation, finally settled on Frank L. Polk, corporation counsel for New York City.[65] Lansing found Polk an efficient counselor and a reliable acting secretary for the department during his infrequent absences.[66] Nevertheless, Polk was an appointee of House and kept the colonel informed of the state of affairs, particularly the secretary's reactions to House. House also utilized other subordinates in the department as sources of information, notably Breckinridge Long, who later became third assistant secretary of state.[67] With these anchors to windward, House expressed his satisfaction with Lansing, whom he described as not a great man but nevertheless experienced and sensible in his approach to matters of state.[68] House, however, continued to fear that Lansing would soon become accustomed to high office and perhaps would then take a less tolerant attitude toward the colonel's interference in the business of the State Department.[69] Indications soon began to arrive that the expected was taking place. Polk informed House early in 1916 that the secretary was rather disgruntled at the state of affairs.[70] Action was required to prevent a revolt, and House proved equal to the occasion, using flattery and tact to overcome the secretary's frustrations. When Lansing suffered a temporary breakdown in health in May, 1916, House sent him a letter replete with sympathy and heavy in praise of his services.[71]

In general, Lansing and House managed to achieve a fairly amicable relationship. Throughout his period as secretary, Lansing kept his contacts with House comparatively limited, corresponding infrequently and conferring only at widely spaced intervals. Since House exerted most of his influence directly upon the president, Lansing was able to escape too close an intimacy. The greatest strain on their relations did not occur until the Paris Peace Conference, when Wilson made painfully clear his dependence upon House to the virtual exclusion of Lansing from all official counsels. The secretary, however, blamed such slights upon the president alone and held little resentment toward House. When Lansing's death in 1928 terminated their relationship, House wrote, "The country owes Lansing much and some day I hope appreciation may be shown for his services. . . ."[72]

CHAPTER V

THE "EDUCATION" OF THE AMERICAN PEOPLE: THE LUSITANIA AND THE ARABIC CRISES

"If we get into this war, and it seems to me that we will have to in the end, we can only go in effectively as a united people."—Robert Lansing[1]

BY JUNE, 1915, America was benevolently oriented toward the Allies, the consequence of economic involvement and tacit acquiescence in the Allied war measures. Lansing, cognizant of America's stake in the war, by early 1915 began to conclude that only an Allied victory would protect America's political, economic, and ideological interests. Soon he decided that America should actively intervene, and even Wilson and House began to contemplate mediation-intervention. A representative democracy, however, with long traditions of neutrality and isolation could not possibly intervene unless its people were united around a major issue.

The submarine controversy with Germany provided the issue. The loss of noncombatant and neutral lives in the intensified submarine warfare carried the emotional impact needed to jolt the American people from their isolationist and semidetached attitude toward the war. Although considerations of national political and economic interests were perhaps capable of motivating some Americans, the masses of the people needed more emotional stimuli, and submarine warfare enabled the visualization of Germany as a brutal and almost inhuman menace to America and the world at large. As one spectacular sinking of a passenger vessel followed another, it became easier to envisage the Allies as waging a holy crusade, in the name of humanity and democracy, against the Prussian hordes.

Delay became the deliberate policy of Lansing; time was needed to bring the educational process to completion. Shortly after his elevation to the position of secretary of state, Lansing concluded that although American interests demanded entry into the war, a result which the submarine controversy threatened to precipitate at any moment, the American people were still badly divided on the issue and not yet ready to participate actively.[2] He realized, as he later noted, the danger of too hasty action, and feared that if the administration were then to request a declaration of war against Germany, it would meet either a congressional refusal or at least a very passive response from the Congress and the nation at large. Lansing estimated that the eastern section of the nation was ready but felt that the other areas, particularly the middle and far western states, were not yet sufficiently "enlightened." Fortunately, it seemed to Lansing, German blunders and stupidity provided the answer, and, through prolonging the controversies, facilitated the unification of the American people. As Lansing later noted, "It was a long slow process, the process of enlightenment."[4]

In accordance with these convictions, Lansing in July, 1915, outlined the program which he intended to promote as secretary of state.[4] All eight points which he enumerated centered around Germany as a threat to American security. The secretary placed foremost among his policies the need to delay the submarine crisis with Germany. His second concern was with the elimination of German sabotage and espionage within the United States, which Lansing was convinced was quite extensive. After these problems, the secretary was most concerned with Latin America, which he believed to be especially vulnerable to German intrigue and penetration, both economically and politically. Mexico required particular attention because of revolutionary strife and the intense dislike which many Mexicans held for citizens of the United States.[5] Lansing deemed the Caribbean area of vital concern because of the Panama Canal; the Danish West Indies, he believed, should be purchased to block a possible German lodgment.[6] Finally, Lansing concluded that if the Allies began to lose the war, America probably would have to intervene actively and immediately. At all costs the United States would have to safeguard its interests; the Allies could not be allowed to fail. These were reasonable policies, given Lansing's frame of reference, although he perhaps exaggerated the danger of German subversive activities within the United States. To a considerable degree, his goals were realized during his occupancy within the State Department. The Danish West Indies were purchased, German activity in Latin America was exposed, possible German penetration in Haiti and Santo Domingo was forestalled through American occupation, some progress was made toward a new Pan-American pact and, most important, eventual American participation in the war was accomplished.

In the first four months of Lansing's tenure as secretary of state, the vital elements of the policies which he had listed upon entering office were achieved. This was a period of increasing entanglement for the United States, for not only did the continuance of the *Lusitania* controversy and the advent of the *Arabic* crisis greatly sharpen the submarine issue with Germany, but relations with the Central Powers were embittered further by the exchange of notes with Austria on the munitions trade, the end of the Bryan ban on loans to belligerents, and the public exposure of the activities undertaken by several of the diplomatic representatives of Austria and Germany. All these events contributed to the unification of American public opinion toward the war.

* * *

A period of deceptive quiescence followed the dispatch on June 9, 1915, of the second American note to Germany on the *Lusitania* sinking. The issue had been clearly drawn. The United States had asserted the full right of its citizens to travel in safety on belligerent merchant vessels, and had demanded that Germany conduct submarine warfare in conformity with the established rules of naval war, including the provision of safety for crew and passengers. The American government had interposed demands which, if accepted, precluded the most efficacious utilization of the submarine weapon. In two successive notes, the United States had thus defined its position. The controversy could not continue much longer without either a capitulation by one of the contenders or a resort to force as the final arbiter. The exigencies of the situation prevented retraction or submission by either party to the dispute, and only the relative shortage of German submarines prevented the severance of diplomatic relations and the commencement of hostilities in 1915.[7]

The German government appreciated the significance of the situation but sought to delay the crisis by a temporary compromise. Ambassador Bernstorff reported to the Foreign Office that the tide of anti-German feeling in America was still strong, although he felt that the people as a whole did not desire war.[8] Utilizing this information, the Foreign Office decided that prudence required delaying the reply to the American note, while a search was made for some solution that would be acceptable to America and which would, at the same time, preserve freedom of action for the intensified submarine warfare. This cautious attitude was manifested by the absence of any major sinkings during the months of June and July. Finally, the German government decided to offer a compromise, guaranteeing the safety of American passenger vessels traveling through the submarine war zone. Ambassador Gerard was thus informed, and he conveyed the unofficial information to the State Department.[9]

Lansing, on his own initiative, notified Gerard that the principles advanced in the American note of June 9 were not proper subjects for preliminary negotiations.[10] The secretary then wrote President Wilson, on vacation at Cornish, New Hampshire, informing him of this development and recommending that Gerard not be given discretion to engage in informal conversations on the issue.[11] Lansing advised that negotiations for settlement of the *Lusitania* case be initiated only when Germany fully accepted the American contentions. Wilson agreed with the secretary and suggested that Gerard be instructed to intimate to Berlin that only then would the United States offer its good offices toward securing a general agreement among the belligerents on the nature of the war at sea.[12] Although Gerard was informed immediately of the American government's attitude, it was too late to forestall the German note of July 8, which contained the already rejected compromise offer.[13]

The second German note on the *Lusitania* therefore failed signally to meet the American demands. In large part, the note reiterated justifications, previously advanced, for sinking the vessel, and asserted again that Allied violations made retaliation mandatory.[14] After detailing the several excuses, the note formally proposed a compromise similar to the one reported by Gerard, which would safeguard neutrals traveling to Great Britain and yet permit continuance of intensive submarine warfare. American passenger vessels, if they were clearly identified and if the German government were notified in advance of the sailing schedule, would be allowed safe passage through the war zone. If American vessels were insufficient for passenger needs, Germany offered to allow neutral steamers, and even four Allied vessels, to operate in the trans-Atlantic service under the American flag. The only restriction was that such vessels were to be certified by the American government as innocent of contraband cargo. The note then summed up the crux of the controversy: "In particular the Imperial Government is unable to admit that American citizens can protect an enemy ship through the mere fact of their presence on board."[15]

The submarine controversy was thus spurred by the German note. Lansing cabled to Gerard his judgment that the note was a "general disappointment" which made "adjustment by compromise practically impossible."[16] Germany not only had failed to recognize the principles for which America contended, but she had coupled this omission with an almost insulting offer in regard to trans-Atlantic passenger service. Although a special conference between Wilson and Lansing was rumored, it did not occur because of the fear that a sudden move might fan the flames of disquietude within the country.[17] Consequently, Lansing refrained from joining the president and remained in Washington where he began the task of analyzing the German note. Personal conferences were not vitally necessary in any case, since both the president and the secretary were agreed that the German note of July 8 should be rejected.

Yet the spirit of Bryan had not completely left the State Department. Although the Great Commoner had departed, his friend Cone Johnson still remained as solicitor for the department. Unlike Lansing and most of his aides,[18] Johnson regarded the German note on the *Lusitania* as offering a reasonable compromise. In two successive memoranda, the solicitor questioned the right of American citizens to immunize Allied vessels by their presence, particularly as many of these vessels carried contraband and munitions of war.[19] It seemed to Johnson that the German proposal would adequately meet American passenger transportation needs, thereby obviating any necessity to resort to Allied vessels. In any case, Johnson felt that America should not consider war with Germany, if for no other reason than the lack of military preparation. His recommendations were sound from the standpoint of a genuine neutrality, especially since, as he pointed out, America had recognized or accepted Allied acts based on the changed circumstances of modern warfare. The solicitor's recommendations, however, considered only the passenger needs of America and ignored the larger problem which was Lansing's basic concern, that is, the long-range interests of the United States. Lansing rejected the solicitor's advice.

Lansing sought to solve the dilemma facing the American government by reiterating the stern policy previously assumed toward Germany. The secretary realized that the American people were not prepared for war. Lansing concluded that the public apparently wanted a strong policy toward Germany, but yet did not desire to risk hostilities. This divided state of opinion placed the government in an awkward position. The American notes to Germany had stated clearly the right of American nationals to travel in safety on belligerent vessels and had intimated that force would be used if Germany refused to respect that right. Yet after two exchanges of notes on the *Lusitania* case, Germany had failed to comply with the demands for disavowal of the sinking and for reassurances against recurrences. An impasse had been reached. Therefore, although willing to excuse partly the German note of July 8 as designed for "home consumption," Lansing concluded that American opinion required a reiteration of the previous demands of the government. He hoped, he wrote the president, that a short and sharp note would persuade Germany to submit on the issue, and thereby save the administration from an embarrassing situation.[20] Apparently Lansing did not expect a lasting settlement of the submarine crisis; his purpose was to tide the nation through a difficult period.

In a preliminary memorandum, the secretary recommended that the American reply should refuse to discuss any *modus vivendi* until Germany recognized the American contentions and offered reparations for the loss of life on the *Lusitania.*[21] Lansing judged that the chief fault of the German note was its failure "... to recognize that property losses may be indemnified by the payment of damages but that the loss of life is beyond indemnification when caused willfully and in violation of law."[22] After thus satisfying the moral dictates of the situation, Lansing's memorandum proceeded to demolish the arguments advanced in the German note of July 8. He rejected as irrelevant the justifications based on Allied violations of international law, and he asserted that the British tactic of arming merchant vessels was not a mitigating factor. Lansing especially condemned the German note for its insulting implication that American neutrality was less than impartial.

Wilson shared Lansing's views on the German note. While awaiting the secretary's advice with the "greatest interest," the president sent Lansing on July 13 his tentative ideas on the nature of the American reply to Germany.[23] Wilson suggested that the reply should insist on a German recognition of the established rules of sea warfare, a demand which he felt should not be difficult to obtain in view of the recent absence of sinkings without warning. Lansing agreed, but pointed out to the president that the German argument that armed merchantmen prevented submarines from surfacing and challenging vessels would sound convincing to the average man; thus he advised that the American reply should refute all the claims raised in the German note.[24] The secretary also expressed concern about the possibility that Germany might continue her refusal to acknowledge the American contentions, and he wondered, fleetingly, if the note should not leave an opening for counterproposals from the German government.

While Wilson pondered these suggestions, Lansing proceeded to draft a sharp note to Germany.[25] Despite his expressed "fears," the secretary was convinced that only a stern position would force Germany to meet the American demands and at the same time satisfy American public opinion. Of the two purposes, he apparently was more concerned with public opinion, which he sought to mobilize by a trenchant restatement of the American position toward submarine warfare. The draft note, sent to Wilson at Cornish, also incorporated Lansing's argument that a retaliatory measure, such as the submarine war zone, was illegal by its very nature and should be discontinued whenever it adversely affected neutrals. The proposed note then examined and rejected the several German defenses and thus, Lansing hoped, destroyed their plausibility. At the end of the note Lansing, having overcome his earlier anxieties, desired to include an extremely curt warning which would notify Germany that any further submarine violations would cause the United States to "... adopt the steps necessary to insure ... respect by all nations."[26] Such a concluding paragraph, Lansing subsequently stated to Wilson, would "... make a very good impression in this country, and of course we cannot ignore the effect of the reply here. ..."[27] Although accepting Lansing's draft and most of his modifications, Wilson rejected the last paragraph as a near ultimatum, unnecessary in view of the general tone of the note.[28] The president evidently felt that public opinion would be satisfied adequately with less threatening gestures.

The note, dispatched to Germany July 21, was a firm restatement of the American attitude toward submarine warfare.[29] Wilson had accepted virtually all of Lansing's suggestions except for the "ultimatum," including the secretary's offhand suggestion that a way be left open for a partial compromise. However, the president proposed a compromise solution to which the secretary was opposed. Wilson inserted in the note an invitation to Germany that, after disavowal of the *Lusitania* sinking, she coöperate with the United States in efforts toward securing "freedom of the seas." Lansing, although realizing that the offer could be construed as an invitation for coöperation against the British blockade, interpreted it to mean merely that Germany should halt the sinking of vessels without warning.[30] He believed that Wilson intended it to mean little more than this, which caused the secretary to criticize freedom of the seas as no advancement beyond the established rules of international law.[31] Nevertheless, Wilson's phrase did offer Germany a way to recede on the submarine issue without loss of prestige. By interpreting freedom of the seas to signify an American proposal for concerted action against the Allied blockade,[32] German public opinion could be prepared for a compromise and the Foreign Office had something concrete to offer Germany's military and naval leaders.

A lull followed the dispatch of the third American note on the *Lusitania*. Two days after the note was sent to Germany, Lansing summoned Bernstorff to the State Department and informed him that the tense situation precluded a further exchange of notes. The secretary warned the ambassador, in emphatic tones, that any future violation would necessarily lead to war. Bernstorff was given to understand that though the American people did not desire hostilities, the government was in a position from which retreat was impossible. The ambassador was greatly disturbed by Lansing's summation of the situation and could see no escape, save possibly through private negotiations for an agreement which would utilize Wilson's idea of the freedom of the seas. Lansing had previously suggested a possible solution through a German admission that although retaliation was justifiable, the agent was responsible whenever neutrals were affected; this would have allowed Germany to make amends for the *Lusitania* without admitting that its actions were illegal or unwarranted.[33] Bernstorff thereupon requested the German Foreign Office to give the United States some assurances on the submarine issue, after which the American government would probably apply pressure against the Allied violations of international law.[34]

While informal negotiations for a settlement of the submarine controversy began, the lull forced the American government to turn its attention to Great Britain and the blockade. Without the diversion of the submarine, public criticism tended to concentrate on the Allies and their increasing interferences with American trade.[35] Token action, at least, was in order.

Great Britain had delayed her reply to the American protest of March 30, 1915. Finally the British government prepared to deliver the reply in June. Upon learning of its unsatisfactory nature, Lansing advised that presentation of the note be further delayed.[36] The secretary feared that otherwise the results might exacerbate public feeling toward the Allies and provide Germany with additional justifications for continuance of intensive submarine warfare.

After the dispatch of the second American note on the *Lusitania*, Lansing recognized that public discontent at the Allied war measures required some kind of action. With the submarine issue temporarily receding, not even the turmoil in Mexico and American intervention in Haiti sufficed to divert attention from the Allied blockade. Although not desirous of taking any action seriously interfering with the Allied prosecution of the war, Lansing was convinced that American trade with the European neutrals was being curbed without adequate cause. The secretary was especially annoyed by what seemed to be the desire of the British government to expand British commerce with the neutrals at American expense. Ambassador Spring-Rice's attention was called to the fact that while American exports to the European neutrals were being curtailed by the Allied naval blockade, British exports to the same areas were increasing.[37] On July 14, 15, and 16, Lansing dispatched three notes to Great Britain, taking exception to the enforcement of the blockade as an unjustifiable violation of international law, and asserting the right of American citizens to trade freely with the European neutrals in noncontraband.[38] Although Ambassador Page became irritated at Lansing's "series of nagging incidents," there really was little cause for alarm within the British Foreign Office.[39] The American government obviously was not prepared to go beyond the stage of mere diplomatic protestations.

Since the British reply to the American protest of March 30 could not be indefinitely held up, the State Department signified its readiness to receive the note, which was then presented July 23.[40] The British note denied the validity of the American objections to the blockade, and after emphasizing German violations of international law and referring to the Lord Bryce report on alleged Teutonic atrocities, asserted that the peculiar conditions of the war made it necessary to interfere with neutral commerce. Otherwise, the British government argued, it would be impossible to exercise the belligerent right to prevent opponents from importing war materials through neighboring neutral ports. The note also contained the usual references to the precedent of the American practice of continuous voyage during the Civil War, and promised not to interfere with bona fide neutral trade. In conclusion, the note expressed the "gratification" of the British government that American trade not only was not suffering but actually was increasing under the impetus of Allied war purchasing, which therefore more than compensated for the loss of the German market. This veiled hint that American obduracy on the blockade issue might lead to withdrawal of war orders, and thus wreck the newly obtained American prosperity, undoubtedly had effect on the American government. President Wilson was, in fact, very favorably impressed with the British note, which he termed "a strong case."[41] Work soon was begun on a counterreply, but the revival of the submarine issue prevented any action for several months.

Cotton was the only real cloud on the horizon of Anglo-American friendship. As the British note had indicated, America generally was too content with the sudden war prosperity to be greatly distraught over the blockade. However, war orders as yet meant little to the cotton producer and shipper, whose trade was being adversely affected by the Allied closure of the German market. Despite the fact that only a trickle of cotton managed to get through the blockade to the Central Powers, Great Britain decided in August, 1915, that cotton would have to be placed on the list of absolute contraband.[42] When rumors of this impending measure began to circulate in the United States, a great howl of protest began to arise from the southern states and the administration was threatened by a revolt by the Southern members of Congress.[43]

Lansing desired to prevent public criticism of the Allies from becoming too intense. His major concern was to preclude the possibility of any coercive action being taken against Great Britain. He therefore felt that it was necessary to try to relieve the fears of the cotton growers. He warned Spring-Rice that placing cotton on the list of absolute contraband would be tantamount to a British admission that the blockade was ineffective, and that America would then have to act on that premise.[44] Lansing added that in such an eventuality, the responsibility for the consequences would rest solely upon the British government. What made the matter all the more embarrassing was that Great Britain had, in October, 1914, given the State Department assurances, which had been widely publicized, that cotton would not be placed on the absolute contraband list. While making dire predictions, which were very disturbing to Spring-Rice at least, Lansing apparently meant that the British government should quietly bar cotton shipments under the blockade, and thereby avoid politically unwelcome publicity.

The British government was unmoved by the secretary's threats and remained adamant on the issue. However, a "compromise" was offered on cotton. Spring-Rice proposed that after cotton was declared absolute contraband, the sufferings of the producers could be relieved by extensive British purchases at ten cents per pound. Bernstorff promptly sought to make diplomatic capital out of the controversy and offered to buy even larger amounts of cotton at a higher price, if the American government would ensure the exportation of the purchases to Germany.[45] Wilson, although willing to entertain the British offer, indignantly rejected the German proposal as a palpable attempt to bribe the United States into smashing the Allied blockade.[46] As a result, no action was taken when Great Britain formally announced, on August 20, the addition of cotton to the contraband list.[47]

Not only did the American government fail to take adequate measures against the British blockade, but it also permitted a further development which bound the nation even closer economically to the Allied cause. The time for repeal of the Bryan policy of prohibiting loans to the belligerents was at hand.

By the summer of 1915, the United States was experiencing an increasing prosperity, based upon Allied war purchases of munitions and supplies. These purchases required vast sums of money and the Allies were beginning to deplete their reserves. Short-term credits, tacitly permitted since October, 1914, no longer sufficed to meet the ever-growing needs. Consequently, Allied officials began to apply pressure in August, 1915, for a reversal of the loan ban, threatening otherwise to ship to America millions of dollars in gold, thereby dislocating the delicate American financial system. To underline the seriousness of the situation, J. P. Morgan and Company, the American financial agents for the Allies, ceased to support British sterling on the market, with the result that prices and stocks soon began to decline.

Thoroughly alarmed by the situation, William Gibbs McAdoo, the secretary of the treasury, immediately began attempts to secure revocation of the ban on loans to the belligerents. In conjunction with Colonel House, who was similarly disturbed by the financial problem, McAdoo wrote Wilson and advocated that the Allies be allowed to float bond issues on the American market.[48] Since the State Department was vitally concerned with all matters relating to neutrality and had originally discouraged the loans, McAdoo felt that it was necessary to secure Lansing's approval of the proposed change. He wrote Lansing on August 23 that it was inconsistent to approve the trade in war materials and yet to deny the means necessary to finance that trade.[49] McAdoo urged the secretary to avoid any action reaffirming Bryan's ban until he could confer with both Lansing and Wilson on the matter. On the following day Lansing received a note from Charles Summer Hamlin, governor of the Federal Reserve Board, which requested a redefinition of the government's policy.[50] Hamlin enclosed a letter from James B. Forgan, president of the First National Bank of Chicago, that referred to a projected large loan to Great Britain and asked for a telegraphic reply stating the administration's attitude thereon. Forgan, conscious of the undesirability of publicity, merely requested that the telegram indicate that the concerned "Parties" would or would not sanction the transaction.[51]

Lansing had never really favored the prohibition on loans. He was convinced that loans to the belligerents were legally compatible with neutrality and, furthermore, considered that the continuance of American prosperity, based upon the Allied war purchases, demanded a liberal credit system. Lansing's concern with America's economic and political interests had been manifested when, in the fall of 1914, he had been instrumental in securing Wilson's approval of short-term credits to the Allies. Therefore, when McAdoo notified him that these credits were no longer sufficient, Lansing promptly responded and wrote Wilson on August 25 that the economic situation demanded some method of funding purchases.[52] Wilson then signified that the interested bankers should be informed orally that the "Parties would take no action for or against such a transaction."[53] In this clandestine manner, the administration completed the reversal of its earlier prohibition.

Although cognizant of the administration's reluctance to reverse publicly the very positive policy it had assumed in 1914, the interested banking groups were not content with Wilson's oral permission. The financiers who were to raise the Allied loans felt that only a formal statement of approval by the government would suffice to break down criticism, and thereby facilitate public subscription to the bond issues. Lansing, therefore, again wrote Wilson and explained in detail the reasons for reversing the ban on loans.[54] American exports, he stated, would exceed imports by $2,500,000,000 by the end of 1915, and yet the Allies could not withdraw gold reserves to meet this imbalance without precipitating a general bankruptcy. Lansing fearfully predicted that if public loans were not floated in America, the Allies would perforce cease their purchases, thus ruining the American economy: "The result [for America] would be restriction of outputs, industrial depression, idle capital, financial demoralization, and general unrest and suffering among the laboring classes."[55] Consequently, the secretary recommended full retraction of the prohibition against loans, especially since public opinion had already crystallized in regard to the belligerents and so would not be swayed by financial interests. Lansing concluded with the rhetorical question: "Can we afford to let a declaration as to our conceptions of 'the true spirit of neutrality' made in the first days of the war stand in the way of our national interests which seem to be seriously threatened?"[56]

Manifestly, the United States could not let itself be crippled by the earlier statement of policy. Although McAdoo's prophecies of future prosperity had influenced the president, Lansing's analysis, stressing not only the economic dangers of the situation but also asserting that considerations of neutrality no longer precluded loans to the belligerents, emphasized a major factor that helped determine Wilson to complete publicly the reversal of the ban policy. The president summoned Lansing and McAdoo to the White House on September 7, and there the decision was made to make public the government's acceptance of the raising of the public loans.[57] Almost immediately thereafter the first of the large Allied loan issues was placed on the market; by early 1917 these loans to the Allies reached the total of almost $2,000,000,000, as contrasted to $27,000,000 extended to Germany.[58]

The administration's tacit sanction of loans to the belligerents not only strengthened the links binding America to the Allied cause, and incidentally removed the sting from the protests made in July and October against the British blockade, but the new policy also stiffened the American stand against Germany.[59] The first loans, raised in the fall of 1915, precipitated a great public debate which sharpened the distinction between Allied and German sympathizers, thus partly negating Lansing's assurance to Wilson that the attitude of citizens would not be affected to any marked degree.[60] Furthermore, opposition to submarine warfare, which threatened to sever the war trade, became more widespread and determined. The matter of loans to the Allies, however, was only a contributing factor to the deterioration of American neutrality. The roots of unneutral involvement lay in the October, 1914, decision to permit the one-sided trade in war materials.

Unfortunately, the benefits derived from the flow of supplies and credits to the Allies were not yet fully apparent to all Americans. As previously mentioned, the brief respite in the submarine crisis tended to concentrate criticism on the Allied blockade, and the British policy toward cotton greatly increased discontent among some Americans. Until wartime prosperity could reach these unblessed shippers and producers, there was a possibility that the State Department might be pushed, albeit reluctantly, into more vigorous reactions than diplomatic protests. The Central Powers, however, unwittingly provided an unanticipated relief—the Austrian protest on the munitions traffic and the famed incident of Dr. Heinrich Albert's brief case were to offer ample public diversion.

The Austro-Hungarian government, ironically in view of the forthcoming loan developments, delivered a protest on June 29 against the American trade in war materials with the Allies.[61] The Austrian note branded the trade as essentially unneutral and urged the United States either to embargo the arms traffic or to use the trade to coerce the Allies into permitting legitimate neutral trade with the Central Powers. Since this protest was practically identical with the German note of December 15, 1914, which had been answered in full, Wilson was inclined to ignore the matter and merely send Austria a note acknowledging receipt.[62]

Lansing disagreed. He recognized a perfect opportunity to lecture the Central Powers on the duties and privileges of a neutral, and thereby to educate the American people on such matters. The continuing agitation in some quarters for an arms embargo would then perhaps be silenced. "Home consumption," as Lansing wrote Wilson, would be the real purpose of the reply to the Austrian protest.[63] Wilson approved the secretary's suggestion, and the work of drafting a full reply was begun. The department's legal adviser, Lester H. Woolsey, summed up the technical aspects of the rebuttal, and Lansing thereupon spent an entire day in broadening the draft note with practical and moral justifications for rejecting consideration of an arms embargo.[64] Lansing designed the note to center around his conviction that peace-loving states traditionally eschewed large armies and armaments, and therefore relied upon neutral importation during times of war to meet defense needs. In the note he stated:

A nation whose principle and policy it is to rely upon international obligations and international justice to preserve its political and territorial integrity might become the prey of an aggressive nation whose policy and practice it is to increase its military strength during times of peace with the design of conquest, unless the nation attacked can, after war has been declared, go to the market of the world and purchase the means to defend itself against the aggressor.[65]

Lansing genuinely believed that international arms embargoes would not only fail to promote world peace but instead would lead to a general armament race. Even worse, an embargo would place small nations with limited industrial facilities at a permanent disadvantage. Lansing ripped asunder the hazy ideas of pacifists and utopians, and emphasized the fact that wars did not result from the mere existence of armaments but rather sprang instead from deeper causes of which arms were only a manifestation. He was fortunate in that his theoretical view of the international arms trade corresponded with his belief that, in the current war, American national interests depended upon an Allied victory. The Allies were on the defensive, and Great Britain, like America, was normally a small land power. If such facts as the existence of the large British Navy and the French military system were ignored, it became quite easy to portray the Allies as resisting an aggressive German militarism based upon long-range rearmament undertaken in years of peace. Thus though Lansing's draft note to Austria did incorporate general concepts possessing considerable validity, the note nevertheless amounted to a severe indictment of the policies and acts of the Central Powers.

Paradoxically, the proposed reply to Austria found Lansing cast in the role of the idealist, contending against Wilson's desire for a purely legal defense of the arms trade. Upon receipt of the draft, Wilson wondered if the note would not have the appearance of a pro-Ally document condemning the Central Powers as militaristic.[66] The president was also then interested in a Pan-American pact centered around control of the manufacture of arms and munitions, and he felt that Lansing's expressions in the note might well conflict with that goal. The secretary answered these questions by asserting that a mere legal defense would rest the entire case for the arms traffic on the single contention that rules could not be changed during wartime, and although he thought such a defense would suffice for Austria, domestic pacifists and humanitarians would remain unconvinced.[67] Lansing also invoked the name of Bryan, now the leader of the pacifists and noninterventionists, whom, he asserted, agreed with Lansing's moral arguments against an embargo. As for the Pan-American pact, the secretary pointed out that it would be unaffected, since there an arms embargo would be combined with territorial and political guarantees against aggression. Finally, Lansing offered to add to the note a statement that the United States was not imputing an aggressive character to the Central Powers, and this, Lansing claimed, would clear the note of any charge of being pro-Ally. Wilson's doubts were removed and he approved the draft note.[68] After the president reworked the phraseology to conform with "Wilsonian flavor," the note was sent to Vienna August 12, 1915.[69]

The reply to Austria fulfilled, in part, Lansing's desire to silence domestic critics of the arms trade. The note was given considerable publicity, and its high moral tone caused Bryan not only to wire his congratulations to the secretary, but also to promise full editorial support in the *Commoner*.[70] Colonel House joined the chorus of approval, writing Lansing that the note had received wide popular approval.[71] Even the Austrian foreign minister, Baron Stephen Burian, was forced to admire the skillful drafting of the note's arguments, although he remained convinced that it was a mere avoidance of the real question of the unneutrality of the arms trade.[72] But even such a moralistic and patently pro-Ally defense paled into insignificance in comparison to the propaganda benefits derived from an ensuing event—the affair of Dr. Heinrich Albert.

Dr. Albert was ostensibly the commercial adviser to the German embassy, but actually his duty was the direction of German propaganda within the United States. American secret service agents had for some time kept Dr. Albert under surveillance. Therefore, when on July 24 Dr. Albert accidentally left his brief case behind upon leaving a New

York City elevated train, an agent promptly seized the brief case and turned it over to Treasury Secretary McAdoo.[73] Upon notification, Lansing hastened to McAdoo's apartment in New York City and the two officials examined the materials within the brief case.[74] They found that the papers, although quite informative about propaganda activities, nevertheless were not of a clearly criminal nature. In view of that fact, and because the brief case had been virtually stolen, Lansing and McAdoo decided that selected documents should be published but without the government's role being revealed. At that point, Colonel House entered the scene. Thus far the two Cabinet officials had ignored House, although the matter centered in his own bailiwick of New York City. House apparently resented his exclusion from so exciting an event, for according to the House diary Wilson ordered the presumptuous Lansing and McAdoo to take no further actions without the Colonel's approval.[75] After this jurisdictional conflict had been settled, it was agreed that selected papers from the captured brief case would be released by Frank I. Cobb of the New York *World*. Cobb began the sensational release August 15, publishing the materials in successive installments.[76]

Propaganda was clearly the purpose of publication. Although the Albert papers failed to indicate espionage, they did show the function of German propaganda and referred to plans for strikes in plants manufacturing arms and munitions for the Allies. Lansing later admitted that the German activities were comparable to those of Allied agents, but he asserted that what made the German propaganda especially distasteful was the systematic attacks, in subsidized newspapers, on the administration.[77] Although Lansing resented these attacks, and particularly those which alleged that he and Wilson were at odds on policy matters, he was deeply concerned with the alleviation of public discontent with the Allies. The outcry from the cotton producers was especially painful, and the secretary came to the conclusion that this discontent was being politically exploited by the critics of the administration, including the German-American bloc. Lansing and McAdoo both hoped that publication of the Albert papers would go far toward silencing such critics.[78]

While the Albert disclosures were being widely publicized as proof of extensive German plots against the welfare of the nation, which resulted in a considerable public hysteria about spies and espionage, the submarine controversy flared up anew. The *Arabic* crisis was at hand.

On August 19, the British White Star liner *Arabic* was torpedoed and sunk with the loss of forty-four lives, including two American citizens.

The informal negotiations for a settlement of the *Lusitania* case were therefore broken off, and the submarine controversy was revived in full intensity.

Lansing's reaction to the *Arabic* sinking centered around his concern with the state of American public opinion. Convinced that the interests of the United States were involved in the war and that the nation probably would have to enter the struggle eventually in order to ensure an Allied victory, he realized that a unified public opinion was necessary before decisive action could be taken. Though his political reasoning was sound, Lansing did allow the martial reactions of the eastern states' press to mislead him for a short period. Consequently he advised Wilson on August 20 that though most Americans did not desire war, they did demand a strong policy toward Germany on the *Arabic* case.[79] The secretary also emphasized the widely held belief that if the government did not now support its previous strong notes with positive action, Germany and the rest of the world would characterize the policy of strict accountability as a mere bluff. He therefore recommended that the seriousness of the situation be indicated by a notice to the press that a special session of the Cabinet was to consider the crisis. Wilson agreed with the general tenor of this advice, but rejected the suggested Cabinet session as unnecessary until the full facts on the *Arabic* were known.[80]

Lansing then followed up his letter with a memorandum, on August 24, analyzing the probable results of hostilities with Germany, which he expected to follow the apparently imminent severance of diplomatic relations.[81] He oriented his analysis toward Wilson's desire to participate in the postwar peace settlement, and he contended that since Germany's friendship had already been irretrievably lost, an American entry into the war would restore friendly relations with the Allies and entitle the United States to a seat at the eventual peace conference. The United States could then exercise its disinterested influence for an equitable settlement, including fair treatment of the vanquished Germany. Lansing, however, realized that not all the American people supported a resort to war, and he closed his analysis with the observation that the commencement of hostilities probably would arouse little popular enthusiasm.[82]

As reports came in from other sections of the nation, particularly from the western states, Lansing concluded that a large part of the American people were relatively indifferent to the *Arabic* sinking. Time was needed to elevate the rest of the country to the pro-Ally and prowar enthusiasms current in the northeastern states. A divided people obviously made immediate hostilities undesirable. However, the government of the United States was in a most embarrassing position, from which retreat was difficult, as a result of the uncompromising policy it had previously assumed toward the German use of intensive submarine warfare. Lansing concluded that the only solution was to warn Germany severely and thereby persuade her to capitulate, at least temporarily, on the submarine issue. He resolved to present Bernstorff with an ultimatum on the *Arabic* case, in full realization that such an unauthorized act might lead to his repudiation and resignation.[83]

Ambassador Bernstorff was well aware of the tenseness of the situation produced by the *Arabic* sinking. He requested the State Department to postpone a decision until the full facts were known, and during the interval he sought a solution through the American note of August 10 on the *Frye* case.[84] The *Frye* note had intimated the possibility of arbitration of the issues between the two nations, if Germany would meanwhile restrain her submarine operations.[85] Bernstorff cabled the Foreign Office and suggested that the essentials of the *Frye* note be applied to the current controversy.[86] Lansing informed the ambassador that the *Arabic* was not subject to prolonged discussion, however, and he urged that Germany end the crisis by disavowing its sinking.[87]

The time seemed propitious to the secretary for presentation of his ultimatum. Since Bernstorff had recently conferred with Wilson, who had demanded an immediate statement on the *Arabic* case, Lansing concluded that the ambassador was ripe for coercion. On August 27, therefore, Lansing summoned Bernstorff to the State Department and told him frankly that unless Germany announced that passenger liners would no longer be attacked without warning, war would follow inevitably.[88] The secretary concluded the interview with the remark that until such a pledge could be given, there was no need for any further conferences on the matter. Bernstorff was quite impressed with the secretary's warning, so much so that he cabled Berlin that the situation was similar to the one which had produced the Spanish-American War, and therefore admitted of no procrastination in settlement.[89]

The warning to Bernstorff undoubtedly facilitated the eventual settlement of the crisis, although Lansing had run little risk in giving the unauthorized ultimatum. A struggle was current in the German government between the chancellory, which desired to conciliate the United States, and the ministry of marine which sought to continue the intensified submarine warfare. The peace party won the struggle, primarily because of the shortage of submarines and the danger of an American war entry adversely affecting Bulgaria, then on the point of casting her lot with the Central Powers.[90] Ambassador Gerard had informed Lansing of this situation August 25, reporting that the Foreign Office was willing to disavow the *Arabic* sinking as contrary to the instructions given submarine commanders.[91] Nevertheless, Lansing's warning did stir Bernstorff to renewed efforts for an acceptable settlement. On September 1, Bernstorff exceeded his instructions and gave Lansing a pledge that "Liners will not be sunk ... without warning and without [making provisions for the] safety of the noncombatants, provided that the liners do not try to escape or offer resistance."[92]

Though Bernstorff's pledge ended the first and most acute phase of the *Arabic* crisis, the value of the pledge was undermined and the controversy continued by the sinking, September 4, of the British liner *Hesperian.*[93] Although no American lives were lost, the event seemed to demonstrate that the German naval leaders ignored the commitments made by their Foreign Office. Additionally, the question of defensively armed merchantmen was raised, with Bernstorff contending that since the *Hesperian* was armed, the pledge was not applicable.[94] Lansing denied that defense and took the position that the only justification for sinking any vessel without provision for the safety of those on board was if a vessel resisted visit and search.[95] Bernstorff then tried to repair the damage, and although no satisfactory explanation was offered for the *Hesperian* incident, he wrote Lansing on September 8 that submarine commanders had been under orders for some time not to sink large liners without warning. These orders had now been extended to cover all liners, and if the *Arabic* was unjustifiably attacked, it was contrary to instructions.[96]

Lansing remained dissatisfied. Not only did he speculate about the true nature of the instructions given submarine officers, but he was greatly displeased by the forthcoming German defense of the *Arabic* sinking. The German note, handed Gerard on September 9, asserted that the *Arabic* had seemed to be attempting to ram the submarine, which had halted the vessel *Dunsley,* and that the submarine officer had therefore submerged and torpedoed the *Arabic.*[97] The note then expressed sympathy for the loss of American lives but refused to acknowledge any obligation for disavowal and indemnities, even if the submarine commander had mistaken the intention of the *Arabic.* By way of compromise, the German government offered to submit the question of liability to The Hague for arbitration, but it excluded the question of the legality of submarine warfare from such consideration.

Lansing considered the note completely unsatisfactory, since the evidence indicated that the submarine officer had full knowledge that no ramming was being attempted. The note seemed to justify the sinking, and it implied that the German Navy was operating under very few restraints. Consequently, the secretary viewed Bernstorff's pledge as practically worthless and recommended to Wilson that the American government either formally demand disavowal of the act or else break diplomatic relations with Germany forthwith.[98]

The seriousness of the *Arabic* difficulty was emphasized by the expulsion of the Austrian ambassador, Dr. Constantin Dumba. The unfortunate Dumba had sinned against the rules of diplomatic propriety by using an American citizen, James F. J. Archibald, to transport dispatches through the Allied lines.[99] Archibald had been captured by the British officials at Falmouth, August 30, and the Austrian embassy's reports were promptly turned over to the American government.[100] Among the papers were a Dumba report outlining plans for strikes by Austro-Hungarian nationals employed in American munitions plants and a letter written by Captain Franz von Papen, the German military *attaché,* which contained unflattering references to the mentality of the American people.

The American government speedily decided to demand the recall of Ambassador Dumba. For a brief moment it appeared that Bernstorff was involved also, and Wilson wrote Lansing that it might be well to seek the recall of both representatives as soon as the *Arabic* case permitted.[101] Bernstorff, however, had wisely refrained from utilizing the services of Archibald and thus was spared.[102] Dumba, upon being informed of Archibald's misfortune, hastily tried to defend his actions to Lansing, citing the paucity of communication means as excuse for using an American citizen as a bearer of dispatches.[103] All was to no avail, particularly since Lansing disliked the Austrian ambassador most heartily. After lecturing Dumba severely on the impropriety of his actions, the secretary informed him that he would soon receive a further communication on the subject.[104] Then, in a swift move, Lansing formally requested the Austrian government to recall Dumba, releasing the news simultaneously to the American press.[105] He justified such an unusual procedure on the grounds that Dumba could not be allowed to save prestige through a mere departure on leave, but had to bear the odium of expulsion in order to give an object lesson to other members of the diplomatic corps.[106]

The Dumba affair stimulated Bernstorff to renewed efforts to solve the *Arabic* dispute. Himself suspect, Bernstorff eagerly tried to redeem the situation, and used the incident to impress upon the German government the determination of the United States to force a final accounting on the submarine issue.[107] The crux of the problem was the State Department's view that the Bernstorff pledge was meaningless unless the German government would disavow the sinking of the *Arabic*. Lansing impressed this aspect on Bernstorff at a conference held September 13, and the secretary requested a full statement on the instructions given submarine commanders. In Lansing's view, a worth-while pledge would have to cover all merchant vessels and not merely passenger liners.[108] Bernstorff promised to do his utmost.

A settlement of the *Arabic* case was finally reached. Bernstorff succeeded in convincing his government that concessions were mandatory, and he secured instructions to meet American demands on the *Arabic* case. Lansing, who had left Washington for a brief respite, met the ambassador at the Hotel Biltmore in New York City for a continuance of the negotiations. There, on October 2, Bernstorff offered a solution wherein Germany would state that the instructions to submarine commanders had been made so exacting as to preclude recurrence of sinkings comparable to that of the *Arabic*. Though liability for the loss of American lives was denied, the proposed note offered to pay an indemnity as an act of friendship.[109] Both Wilson and Lansing objected to the proposed note's justification of the sinking of the *Arabic* and demanded a frank disavowal of the act. They were willing, however, to accept the indemnity as an act of grace if the language were redrafted to obscure that point.[110] Bernstorff accepted these changes and thereupon formally sent the note to the State Department.[111]

With the *Arabic* case closed, the major issue of the legality of unrestricted submarine warfare still remained unsolved. The *Arabic* pledge was vague, failing to clarify both the question of the exemption of merchant vessels from attacks without warning and the differences of viewpoint between the American and German governments on the defensive arming of vessels. In essence, the *Arabic* pledge merely gave assurances of safety to passenger liners. Quite apparently, the German government was not willing to renounce the future use of unrestricted submarine warfare and was making concessions only because of temporary exigencies. Therefore not even the *Lusitania* case could be settled for, although the *Arabic* sinking could be excused as an exceptional occurrence contrary to the instructions given to U-boat commanders, no such plea could be advanced for the *Lusitania*.[112] Thus the

Arabic pledge only established a truce, for both governments had assumed positions on the issue which reduced the possible alternatives to
surrender or an ultimate resort to armed hostilities.[113]

The closure of the *Arabic* case made mandatory the dispatch of the
long-overdue general protest to Great Britain.[114] A sweeping protest
had not been sent since the one on March 30 against the Allied blockade,[115] although in the interval a number of specific cases had been
contested. The lull in the submarine crisis, therefore, once more concentrated public criticism on the Allied exactions levied against the
neutrals, and the State Department was compelled to respond. The
October 21 note to Great Britain was the result, but whereas Germany
had been threatened into compliance with the American demands,
Great Britain merely received another long and fruitless legal protest.

To a considerable degree, the October note was a belated personal
victory for Lansing. He had wanted to protest more thoroughly the
British blockade in March, 1915, and particularly to attack the blockade
as inconsistent with past British practices and with the modified
Declaration of London. Wilson had at that time opposed so legalistic a
protest, which he believed would merely result in futile debate. The
president instead had dispatched a note on March 30 indicating his
faith that Great Britain would use care and discretion in the enforcement of the blockade. Again, during the *Lusitania* crisis, Lansing had
drafted a sharp note to Great Britain, but Wilson had withheld it pending settlement of the submarine controversy. Consequently, no action
was taken until October, 1915, although by that time it was much too
late to accomplish any worth-while results. The blockade was well
established, and the United States had already accepted it in practice
if not in theory.

The mercantilist aspects of the British blockade disturbed Lansing
greatly. Though he had no desire to interfere with the prosecution of
the war, he did object to unnecessary interferences with American commerce. Therefore, little exception was taken to the Allied severance
of neutral trade with Germany, but when Great Britain began to apply
measures that apparently were intended primarily to promote British
commercial interests rather than to prosecute the war, Lansing took
umbrage. In effect, Great Britain was expanding her commerce at
American expense, using the war to defend detention of American exports to European neutrals, on the grounds of enemy destination, while
increasing British exports to the very same areas.[116] Alway responsive
to what he viewed as America's economic and political interests, Lan-

sing found it difficult to tolerate such a gross and materialistic approach
to war. In addition, the State Department was deluged with the protests
of outraged shippers, for since March, 1915,[117] more than three hundred
neutral vessels engaged in the American-European trade had been detained by British authorities. In consequence of these facts, Lansing
was able to persuade Wilson, and even Colonel House, that a sweeping
protest was necessary.[118] The secretary then drafted the note, assisted by
Lester H. Woolsey, and Wilson approved it after making the usual
changes in phraseology.[119] The note was sent to London by special
courier, for Lansing desired a speedy delivery in order to placate dis-
contented Americans and to free the State Department for a resumption of the *Lusitania* negotiations.[120] Even when angered by British actions, the secretary never forgot that Germany was, in his view, the real
opponent.

The long note of October 21 to Great Britain conformed to Lansing's
policy that issues with the Allies should not be pressed too far.[121] In spite
of his resentment of the commercial aspects of the blockade, the note
was truly "submerged in verbosity," although in the legal sense the
protest was comprehensive and convincing. The blockade was contested
as illegal and ineffective, as demonstrated by the Allied inability to
close the Baltic Sea and by the need to place cotton on the list of absolute contraband. The blockade of neutral ports and the practice of
visit and search of neutral vessels in Allied ports were condemned. The
note especially criticized the practice of halting neutral cargoes on the
grounds of enemy destination, and charged that British exports to
European neutrals were increasing in direct proportion to the curtail-
ment of American trade with those countries. In conclusion, the United
States government stated that it could not recognize the validity of the
Allied blockade, and the earnest hope was expressed that Great Britain
would govern its actions by legal principles rather than by expediency.

In spite of Wilson's description of Lansing's note as "an unanswerable paper,"[122] it was vulnerable in several particulars. Not only did the
note fail to assert the right of neutrals to trade with Germany in conditional and noncontraband goods, it also neglected to warn Great
Britain that forcible measures might be taken if American demands
were not met.[123] The note actually amounted to a mere request or plea
for greater consideration. Furthermore, any possible results were
negated by two other developments—loans and House's intervention
plans. During September and October Bryan's ban on loans to the
belligerents was rescinded, and the first of the great Allied bond issues

already was being raised. Clearly, the close economic bonds between America and the Allies precluded consideration of coercive measures against the British blockade—not that Lansing's and Wilson's concept of the nature of the war ever would have utilized such in any case. Finally, Colonel House chose this time to launch his scheme, the outline of which Lansing approved, for American mediation in the European war on the Allied side. House sent Sir Edward Grey, the British foreign secretary, the first letter of the forthcoming exchange on October 17, a few days before the dispatch of the October 21 note.[124]

Thus the October note, described by Page as "a thing of thirty-five heads and three appendices," produced negligible results.[125] Although the British press condemned the protest as unduly severe and discourteous in tone and complained that it even lacked the usual friendly protestations included in the American notes to Germany, the British Foreign Office imperturbably continued on its established course.[126] Sir Edward Grey wrote House that the American demands could not be met without giving up the blockade of Germany, and he trusted that America would not unwittingly ". . . strike the weapon of sea power out of our hands and thereby ensure a Germany victory."[127] He had little cause for alarm; no move was made to act effectively against the British blockade, and Grey was so certain of the reliability of the American government that he delayed a formal reply to the note until April, 1916, when the *Sussex* sinking had once more turned the attention of the United States to Germany.

CHAPTER VI

PUBLIC OPINION AND THE SUBMARINE: FROM THE ANCONA TO THE SUSSEX CRISES

"When the mass of our people are convinced of the real
character of the German Government and are awake to its
sinister designs, the time for action will have arrived."
—Robert Lansing[1]

THE SECOND MAJOR phase of the submarine controversy with Germany followed soon after the *Arabic* pledges were made. This period, which opened with the *Ancona* sinking in November, 1915, and closed with the *Sussex* pledge in May, 1916, was to result in sharpening the submarine issue to the point where a resumption of ruthless U-boat warfare would necessarily lead to hostilities between Germany and the United States.

Lansing's primary concern continued to be centered on the state of American public opinion. His belief remained firm that America's interests demanded an Allied victory and that the United States would probably have to intervene in the war in order to achieve that victory. Intervention, however, was unlikely without a unified public opinion and Lansing therefore continued to shape policies which sharply delineated the submarine issue. At the same time, because of the divided nature of public opinion, he sought to prevent a premature rupture with Germany.

Lansing's attempts to attune policies to the public pulse were not uniformly successful. During the first *Lusitania* crisis and while the *Arabic* case was being settled, he had correctly concluded that the public was not yet ready for decisive action that probably would lead to war, and he had therefore adopted a policy designed to alleviate the situation with Germany. His efforts then had helped to secure the *Arabic* pledges, which had achieved a respite in the controversy. But he evidently misjudged the public reaction in the *Ancona* case, which we will shortly examine, for then he advocated a stern course of action including revival of the *Lusitania* negotiations. This error in judgment might be ascribed to Lansing's tendency to project sentiments current in the northeastern states to the nation at large. He soon realized his mistake and consequently, in view of confidential intimations that intensive U-boat warfare was about to be resumed, he advanced a *modus vivendi* which he hoped would again postpone the inevitable diplomatic break with Germany. This proposed working arrangement, a compromise involving an Allied abandonment of defensive armament in return for a German pledge against resumption of ruthless submarine warfare, was well conceived but ill-timed in its presentation, for it clashed with Colonel House's plans for "mediation-intervention." The proposal also offered Germany a rationalization for a new submarine policy directed against armed merchantmen and, finally, it fed the flames of congressional discontent and rebellion against the foreign policies of the Wilson administration. Nevertheless, though the secretary's proposed *modus vivendi* failed of adoption, it did help to present clearly the submarine issue and the American policy thereto to the American people. The *Sussex* crisis, which followed almost immediately, completed the process of sharpening the issue with Germany.

* * *

In early November, 1915, Lansing revived the *Lusitania* case. Negotiations for a settlement of the *Lusitania* sinking had been held in abeyance for nearly two months, and no urgent reason existed for their renewal. Nevertheless, the secretary began to insist, in an increasingly sharper tone, that the case be closed immediately by a German admission of the illegality of submarine attacks without warning. In effect, Lansing demanded terms which would have renounced the future intensive or unrestricted use of the U-boat, but these terms were too radical in view of the military exigencies of the war for an easy German acceptance. The entire controversy was made to revolve around the question of liability for the American lives lost on the *Lusitania*, with the American government requesting that Germany should complete the *Arabic* pledges with a declaration on submarine warfare that would apply to all vessels and not merely to passenger liners alone.[2]

The reason for the renewal of the *Lusitania* negotiations is somewhat obscure. The formal cause was the desire of Wilson and Lansing to utilize and implement the *Arabic* pledge in a settlement of the earlier case. The severity with which the negotiations were conducted, however, particularly the threats by Lansing that diplomatic relations would probably be severed if Germany did not meet the American demands, indicated deeper purposes. Lansing felt that an entry into the war was almost at hand, and evidently both President Wilson and Colonel House, the latter then maturing his plans for a possible intervention through a proffered mediation, shared the secretary's view that the United States might soon have to enter the conflict. This has led

one historian to conclude that Lansing used the *Lusitania* negotiations
as a device by which diplomatic relations with Germany could be kept
near the breaking point and from which the government could either
advance or retreat in accordance with the manifestations of the popular
will.[3] The evidence tends to support this interpretation. Certainly Lansing was increasingly convinced that intervention was necessary and
that the submarine issue was the only means of achieving that intervention.

In the *Lusitania* negotiations Lansing sought from Ambassador
Bernstorff, with Wilson's approval, an admission of German liability
which would bar a resumption of intensive submarine warfare. Lansing
redefined the American position in an interview with Bernstorff on
November 2, 1915, and he informed the ambassador that, since Germany
had recently conformed to the rules of cruiser warfare, no sufficient
reason existed to prevent a German admission of liability for the American lives lost on the *Lusitania*. The secretary concluded the session with
the statement, thus setting the tone for the remainder of the negotiations, that since the American government had already been "extremely
patient" on the matter, the case would have to be settled "very soon."[4]

The secretary was not completely inflexible, however. In view of the
natural reluctance of the German government to disavow formally the
sinking of the *Lusitania*, Lansing devised a formula which accomplished
the same result but which was couched in more ambiguous terminology.
His formula, approved by Wilson as the best under the circumstances,
required Germany to state that retaliatory measures which affected neutrals adversely were illegal, and that since the later instructions given
submarine commanders recognized that the loss of neutral life through
U-boat attacks without warning was contrary to the rules of warfare,
Germany would now declare the *Lusitania* sinking to be contrary to
international law and would offer a suitable indemnity.[5] The secretary
handed the proposed settlement to Bernstorff on November 17, at the
same time warning the ambassador that the case should be closed immediately; otherwise the state of public discontent might cause the
forthcoming session of Congress to declare war on Germany.[6]

Lansing intended a serious warning.[7] Recent developments, such as
the *Arabic* crisis, the Albert disclosures, and Dumba's expulsion, had
affected the American public.[8] The secretary, however, overestimated
the strength of the popular demand for action, and the Congress which
met in December was sharply and bitterly divided on the question of
the possible American involvement in the war.[9] Indeed, Lansing had so

misinterpreted developments, probably because of his own desires and
the difficulties implicit in the determination of public attitudes, that he
was convinced that war would soon break out, and in December he
notified the War and Navy Departments to that effect.[10]

In the belief that conditions were propitious, Lansing advised President Wilson that an impasse had been reached on the *Lusitania* case.
Bernstorff had just informed the secretary that he doubted if his government would admit liability for the act. Lansing, therefore, wrote
Wilson that Germany apparently was trying to prolong the case indefinitely, and that public opinion demanded decisive action. The secretary then recommended that either diplomatic relations with Germany be broken or that the entire case be laid before Congress for
action.[11] Lansing indicated his preference for the latter course, commenting that the matter would probably lead to war and therefore was
a proper subject for Congress and would best meet the public demand
for action. In addition, with an eye to the forthcoming presidential
election, Lansing noted that the pro-German vote had already been
lost and that care should be taken not to lose the pro-Ally vote as
well. Wilson apparently agreed with the secretary's analysis, and he
outlined a course whereby Bernstorff would be informed that a failure
to meet the American demands on the *Lusitania* case would be regarded
as a repudiation of the *Arabic* pledges.[12] Manifestly, a serious crisis was
in the process of formation, and the president substantially concurred
with Lansing that the time for forcible measures was at hand.

The crisis with Germany was heightened by the *Ancona* case. The
Ancona, an Italian liner, was sunk November 7 by a submarine flying
the Austrian flag.[13] Germany apparently had transferred submarine
operations to the Mediterranean because of the *Arabic* pledges in regard
to the war zone around Great Britain, and was believed to be using the
Austrian flag since Germany was not yet at war with Italy. In spite of
the Austrian flag, Lansing and most other Americans viewed the sinking as a German act, and since the *Ancona* torpedoing followed a rather
brutal shelling of the unarmed vessel in which a number of Americans
lost their lives, popular feeling tended to become more bitter toward
Germany.[14] The American government felt that Austria should have
been bound by the German pledges on the *Arabic* case, but no course
remained except to discuss the submarine question with the Austro-
Hungarian government. The discussion, however, promised to be brief
and rather curt.

Wilson and Lansing were agreed that Austria should be compelled forthwith to repudiate the *Ancona* sinking, in the belief that a stern course toward Austria would prevent German use of the Austrian flag as a cover for ruthless U-boat warfare. Consequently, Lansing drafted a short and severe note which described the *Ancona* sinking as a "wanton slaughter" and demanded that the Austrian government denounce the act as illegal and indefensible, punish the responsible submarine commander, and offer proper indemnities.[15] Although Wilson felt that Lansing's draft was "peremptory," he concluded that it was a necessary presentation, and therefore the note was dispatched to the Austrian government December 6, 1915.[16] To emphasize the seriousness of the situation, Lansing then held two conferences with the Austrian chargé, Baron Zwiedinek, in which he demanded that Austria render immediate compliance to the American demands.[17]

While the *Ancona* case was under consideration, the submarine controversy with the Central Powers was further complicated by the expulsion of Captains Franz von Papen and Karl Boy-Ed, the German military and naval attachés. Since the publication of the Albert papers in August, followed soon thereafter by the Archibald affair, a considerable spy scare had swept over the nation. Lansing, as well as Wilson and other high officials of the administration, was convinced that extensive German propaganda and espionage activities were being conducted in the United States, directed largely at disrupting the munitions and war industries then so busily engaged in meeting the needs of the Allies.[18] The recall of some of the more flagrant offenders would help to put an end to such activities, he believed. Lansing, therefore, sought permission from Wilson on November 29 to take action against Boy-Ed, Von Papen, and the Austrian consul-general, Alexander von Nuber.[19] The secretary also alluded to the possibility of requesting the recall of even higher officials, primarily Ambassador Bernstorff. Wilson readily agreed and authorized Lansing to proceed at once, after allowing Bernstorff an opportunity to withdraw the two German attachés without a formal demand.[20] Wilson later wished to request the recall of Dr. Albert also, but Lansing demurred, on the grounds of the lack of evidence sufficient for criminal action and because Albert was rendering valuable services in aiding American firms to obtain scarce materials such as beet seed, potash, dyes, and medicines from Germany.[21] Consequently, Albert remained as commercial attaché, but Boy-Ed and Von Papen were recalled December 10, 1915.

Ambassador Bernstorff was considerably disturbed, both by the expulsion of Boy-Ed and Von Papen and by the constant pressure and warnings from Lansing in regard to settlement of the *Lusitania* issue. Bernstorff at first had feared that his own recall would be demanded and had anxiously requested reassurances from the secretary.[22] Lansing, reluctantly in view of his distrust and dislike of the ambassador, assured Bernstorff that he was not under suspicion, and he made this aspect clear in the public announcement of the recall of the two attachés. Despite such consideration, mandatory in view of the strained relations between Germany and America, Bernstorff found Lansing's repeated demands for action on the *Lusitania* somewhat irritating. The ambassador wrote Lansing on November 25 that the German government probably would not make further concessions on the *Lusitania,* especially until some concrete results came from the American protest of October 21 to Great Britain, and that he feared continued American pressure would give rise to an effect contrary to that desired by the two governments.[23] When Lansing continued to urge immediate acceptance of his proposed disavowal, Bernstorff replied testily that the delay in reaching a settlement was not his fault, particularly in view of the distractions caused by the recall of the two embassy officials.[24]

The Austrian reply on the *Ancona* was received December 16, and it failed completely to meet the American demands for disavowal and indemnities.[25] The note, which Lansing termed a "special pleading consisting of technicalities and quibbles," requested the United States government to furnish factual data in support of its claims, including the number of American nationals lost in the sinking. Lansing, therefore, drafted a virtual ultimatum to Austria, which after revision by Wilson was dispatched December 19.[26] The American note renewed the earlier request that Austria disavow the act and punish the guilty officials.

The remainder of the *Ancona* negotiations devolved entirely upon Lansing. President Wilson chose this time to marry Mrs. Edith Bolling Galt on December 18, and he departed immediately for a honeymoon at Hot Springs, Virginia.[27] Lansing continued to urge Austrian submission on the issue, and he informed Chargé Zwiedinek that the United States government could not recede from its position.[28] The desperate Austrian government frantically sought some way out of the dilemma, short of a full admission of liability, and pled that insufficient evidence on the case justified arbitration.[29] Wilson, upon being informed of this development, anxiously inquired how the United States, in view of its traditional use of arbitration, could refuse to consider the proposal.[30] The secretary, however, apparently was unperturbed by such doubts.[31]

Lansing's policy of severity toward Austria and Germany, with whom relations were practically at the point of complete disruption, soon received a major jolt. On December 21, Senator William J. Stone, chairman of the Foreign Relations Committee, informed the secretary that the government was much too severe toward the Central Powers and too lenient toward the Allies, and the senator intimated that he could not support the current foreign policies of the administration.[32] Lansing was quite disturbed at Stone's attitude and especially at the senator's refusal to recognize that the loss of life resulting from the submarine attacks was more important than the loss of property resulting from the Allied blockade. Instead of being impressed, Stone merely replied that the British blockade was starving German babies. Stone left the secretary with the definite impression that a large element in Congress would oppose severance of diplomatic relations, on the grounds that it would necessarily lead to war and therefore would amount to an executive usurpation of the congressional power to declare war.[33] In consequence of the Stone interview, Lansing's faith in the martial spirit of Congress began to be shaken, and he warned Wilson that since a break in relations with Austria would probably lead to war, perhaps the entire matter should be submitted to Congress for consideration.[34] Wilson reacted sharply and refused to consider the delegation of a proper responsibility of the executive, the maintenance and severance of diplomatic relations, and he instructed the secretary to continue his present course in the negotiations with Austria.[35]

The Austrian government finally complied with the American demands and notified the State Department that the *Ancona* sinking was disavowed and the responsible submarine officer would be punished.[36] The *Ancona* settlement, however, did not improve German-American relations, which were deteriorating further. On December 31, Bernstorff informed Lansing that the German government could not admit liability for the sinking of the *Lusitania,* and would only offer to arbitrate the amount of an indemnity, solely as an act of friendship.[37] At this stage, news of still another sinking began to arrive. On December 30, the British liner *Persia* had been sunk in the Mediterranean with heavy loss of life, and a new submarine crisis seemed at hand.

The sinking of the *Persia* precipitated a congressional situation quite different from what Lansing had expected. Although no major crisis resulted, since Germany, Austria, and Turkey denied responsibility for the act, the fact that the *Persia* was armed led to a renewed request in Congress that Americans not be allowed to travel on armed belligerent vessels.[38]

The secretary soon realized that he had overestimated the readiness of the American people for war over the submarine issue. The Congress which assembled in late 1915 was sharply divided, with large numbers of Democrats questioning the foreign policies of the administration, and the charge was repeatedly raised that the government had pursued an unneutral course in favor of the Allies.[39] Resolutions were introduced to embargo munitions, prohibit travel on armed ships, investigate the government's policies toward the Allied blockade, and to spur the executive into renewed attempts at mediation of the war. The new session of Congress merely reflected the mounting public confusion and anxiety about the course of the war.[40]

The administration was greatly disturbed by the situation in Congress. Not only did the turmoil in Congress indicate that the masses of the American people were still far from a united demand for war with Germany, a fact which Senator Stone had already made clear, but there was a definite move under way to compel the government to assume a more vigorous policy toward the Allies.[41] Furthermore, Lansing had received intimations that Germany was considering renewal of intensive submarine warfare, which the sinking of the *Persia* seemed to herald. Early in January, 1916, Lansing surveyed the general situation and concluded that the only solution was to attempt to delay the final clash with Germany. In a confidential memorandum, he observed:

> We are not yet ready to meet the submarine issue squarely. Our people are not aroused to a sufficient pitch of indignation at the barbarism of the Germans. It is hard to comprehend this apparent indifference, but the fact that it exists cannot be doubted. . . .
>
> The first effort . . . should be to prevent, if possible, a situation arising which will force this Government into open hostility to the German Government. The time for that has not come. The people are divided in sentiment. I do not believe that Congress would favor drastic action and would be resentful if the President should act without their authorization. It is a humiliating position, but some way will have to be found to postpone definite action until there is a change among a portion of our people.[42]

The expedient adopted by Lansing was an attempt to compromise the armed-ship problem.[43] Lansing hoped that the belligerents would accept a proposed *modus vivendi*, whereby the Allies would abandon the arming of merchant vessels and Germany would agree to conduct U-boat warfare in accordance with the rules of visit and search; in this way a final clash on the submarine issue would be delayed until a more propitious time.[44] It seemed to the secretary that such a proposed compromise would present the Allies with a golden opportunity. Germany had been using the argument that the Allied "defensive" armaments on merchant vessels prevented submarines from surfacing and challenging vessels in the normal way, and although other justifications were also advanced for attacks without warning, the defense based on the vulnerability of U-boats to gunfire was the most plausible and appealing.[45] Lansing believed that the Allies gained little by arming commercial vessels and that they would, therefore, welcome the opportunity to accept the proposal. After all, if Germany refused to accept the working arrangement, or accepted it and later resumed intensive U-boat warfare, her best defense would have been removed and Germany would stand condemned before American and world opinion.[46]

The major fault with Lansing's device was his failure to understand the British attitude toward armed ships. The secretary apparently thought that the submarine's maximum efficiency as a commerce destroyer resulted from submerged attacks without warning on enemy vessels, and he probably realized that even if Germany should accept the *modus vivendi*, the submarine issue would not long remain quiescent, especially since the compromise would not alter the Allied blockade of the Central Powers.[47] Therefore the proposal if adopted would not seriously hamper the Allies. Lansing, however, misunderstood the attitude of the British who proved unwilling to make any arrangements with Germany that would either restrict Allied belligerent rights or ease American disputes with Germany. In fact, British naval leaders were convinced that a surfaced submarine was more efficient than a submerged one, since it could use its deck guns and increased speed to better advantage, whether or not cruiser rules were observed. Consequently, armaments on board a merchant vessel were regarded as a definite advantage in that the submarine was thereby forced to rely exclusively upon submerged torpedo attacks; hence the British government was not willing to forego the use of defensive armaments.[48]

The armed-ship problem had been under consideration by the State Department for several months. During the *Arabic* crisis, Lansing had begun to mature a plan for a special arrangement which he intended to use as a stopgap measure. In addition, he realized that German objections to armaments on merchant vessels had some validity. The American government had, in the circular of September, 1914, recognized the right of defensive armament, which was sanctioned by past international practice. Nevertheless, the State Department had reached an informal understanding with the British government whereby Allied vessels entering American ports removed their guns. In late August, 1915, the British government abrogated the informal agreement and began an extensive program of arming merchant vessels, and armed ships began to arrive once more in American ports.[49] This new program was signaled on August 26, when the British vessel *Waimana* arrived at Newport News armed with a 4.7″ gun mounted aft.[50] Shortly thereafter, Lansing wrote Wilson that defensive armaments on merchant vessels were no longer defensive, and since they had been used offensively against submarines, the government should issue a new circular classifying all armed merchantmen as ships of war.[51] The president was convinced by Lansing's argument, and he agreed to a change in policy as soon as the *Arabic* case was concluded.[52] Wilson and Lansing were also spurred to greater activity by the *Baralong* incident, in which the *Baralong*, a disguised British Q-boat flying the American flag, had sunk a German submarine which was lawfully challenging the British vessel *Nicosian*.[53] The need for revision of the 1914 circular was further emphasized when the German government transmitted to the State Department several captured British documents, which instructed merchant vessels in the best techniques of ramming and resisting challenging submarines.[54]

The aftermath of the *Persia* sinking convinced Lansing that immediate action was required. Not only was the *Persia* armed, a fact which underlined the seriousness of the armed-ship question, but the sinking served to exacerbate congressional fears that the nation was about to be dragged into the war. On January 5, 1916, Senator Thomas Pryor Gore, Democrat of Oklahoma, introduced a resolution to prohibit the issuance of passports to American citizens intending to travel on belligerent vessels.[55] This move was followed by a general attack on the administration's "lax" policy toward the Allied blockade, and demands were made in Congress that steps be taken to defend American commerce against such interferences.[56] Lansing believed that something should be done to relieve the situation and to preclude radical action in Congress, so he wrote Wilson on January 2 that the time had come to revise American policy toward armed merchantmen.[57] Five days later the secretary sent the president a preliminary memorandum on the subject, in which he contended that armament of any type prevented a submarine from safely challenging a merchantman, thus forcing a resort to attack without warning.[58] Wilson approved the memorandum as "reasonable and thoroughly worth trying."[59] The secretary drafted a *modus vivendi* to be proposed to the belligerents, and he sent the draft

on January 17 to Wilson for approval.⁶⁰ This draft rejected the arguments advanced in favor of defensive armaments and requested the
Allies to abandon such armaments in return for a German assurance
that submarines would abide by cruiser rules of warfare. The draft concluded with the warning that the American government was seriously
considering changing its policy and treating armed merchant ships as
ships of war.

Lansing clearly indicated to the president one of his primary reasons
for advancing the proposed solution. He explained that the proposal
should first be presented to the Allied Powers; otherwise Germany
might accept the *modus vivendi* while the Allies either rejected it or
temporized, a result which would "... arouse adverse criticism in the
press of this country and excite public resentment against the Entente
Powers, which appears to be increasing from day to day."⁶¹ Wilson replied immediately and expressed his complete approval.⁶² The proposed
modus vivendi was presented to the Allied representatives in Washington January 18, 1916.⁶³

The January 18 memorandum on armed ships was an ill-timed diplomatic move. In the first place, Lansing was overly optimistic in his
expectation that the Allies would accept the proposed agreement, and
events were to demonstrate that the proposal probably never should
have been made unless the American government had been willing to
force the measure through. Furthermore, the proposal was advanced
at a time when Colonel House was completing an agreement with Sir
Edward Grey, the British foreign secretary, for possible intervention
through a mediation offer, and the colonel viewed Lansing's move as
jeopardizing the success of his enterprise. Lansing's proposal, designed
in part to prevent the renewal of intensive submarine warfare, came in
time to provide the German government with an excellent rationalization for opening U-boat warfare against armed merchant ships. Finally,
Lansing's proposal became known to the public, as he should have
anticipated, and it fed the flames of congressional unrest and rebellion
against the administration.

The Allied Powers reacted instantly and adversely to the January 18
proposal. Convinced that defensively armed merchant vessels possessed a distinct advantage over the submarine, and that the American
proposal was a desperate attempt to avoid involvement in the war, the
Allied governments were not inclined to consider the proposal seri-
ously.⁶⁴ The French ambassador, Jules J. Jusserand, handed Secretary
Lansing a preliminary reply on January 22, in which the French gov-

ernment contended that the proposed arrangements would depend solely on the reliability of a German pledge to restrain U-boat warfare, and an ironic inquiry was made to determine whether the United States was willing to guarantee such a promise.[65] Then, on January 25, Ambassador Page reported the reactions of Sir Edward Grey: "I have only once before seen Sir Edward so grave and disappointed, and that was when he informed me that the British had sent the German government an ultimatum."[66] Grey expressed great anxiety over the matter, Page reported, and the foreign secretary desired to ascertain the address of Colonel House at once, for the State Department's newest proposal placed a different light on his recent conversations with the Colonel. According to Page, British official circles viewed the proposed *modus vivendi* as representing a German victory, and the ambassador closed his report with the ominous observation that it was rumored that the Allies were constructing munitions plants in Canada in order to replace American sources if Germany should succeed in persuading the United States government to "embarrass" the Allies. In view of the Allied dependence upon America for munitions and for all types of goods generally, such a threat should not have been taken too seriously. In any case, the Jusserand memorandum and Page's report clearly indicated that the Allies would reject the proposed working arrangement, and that the rejection would not attempt a logical refutation of Lansing's arguments, which would have been rather difficult, but instead would concentrate on the untrustworthiness of any German pledge.[67]

The preliminary Allied reactions to the *modus vivendi* should have called forth action from the American government, if any action were to be taken at all. Though it would have been far easier to have banned armed ships from American ports at the beginning of the war, before the submarine threat to commerce had developed, it still would have been possible to remedy the situation in early 1916. Although more Allied vessels were armed at that time than ever before, the Allied dependence upon the American market had increased and the Allies would have been compelled by military necessity to accept a new American policy. The United States, however, was in turn largely dependent upon Allied shipping for transportation of its commerce to Europe, especially munitions and war supplies to the Allies, and this economic relationship might have been threatened briefly.[68]

The question of a possible coercion of the Allies was academic in the extreme. Neither Wilson nor Lansing had any actual intention of taking forcible measures on the armed-ship question in the face of Allied opposition. Wilson had viewed the proposal as a genuine effort at a peaceful solution of the submarine problem, and he had hoped that the reasonableness of the proposal would appeal to both belligerent groups.[69] Wilson, however, was pro-Ally in his sympathies, and Lansing certainly had not intended the January 18 *modus vivendi* proposal to unduly embarrass the Entente. In submitting the proposal to the president, Lansing had stated his desire not to disturb the Allies by a premature publication of the move, and the suggested agreement had been sent to the Allies alone, in order to leave the way open for a silent retraction in case they rejected the compromise offer. Evidently the secretary had felt that the move was so reasonable and that its benefits would be so readily apparent to the Allies, for adoption of the proposal by both belligerent groups would sharpen the submarine issue and ensure that a future renewal of U-boat warfare would result in an American entry into the war, that he simply did not expect an Allied refusal. In fact, even after Jusserand's preliminary reply, Lansing was so far from contemplation of forcible measures on the question of armed ships that he threatened Ambassador Bernstorff on January 25 with a severance of diplomatic relations if the *Lusitania* case were not settled immediately.[70]

When Grey's adverse reactions were reported, the secretary naturally was disappointed, and he blamed Page for part of the difficulty. Nevertheless, he still refrained from any decisive action and merely recommended to Wilson that a course of action should be determined, although "I do not think it is necessary for us to act immediately."[71] Lansing made this statement in the full knowledge, given him by the Austrian chargé, Baron Zwiedinek, that the Central Powers were about to declare ruthless submarine warfare against armed merchantmen. Obviously, no real attempt was to be made to bar Allied armed vessels from American ports.

Colonel House received news of Lansing's January 18 proposal with considerable dismay, since the move threatened to disrupt his plans for American mediation-intervention in the war. Although both statesmen agreed on the nature of the war and the probable need for American entry, Lansing realized that this end could not be accomplished until public opinion was ready. House, on the other hand, evidently was more optimistic, and he therefore nurtured a scheme whereby the United States, at a time considered propitious by the Allies, would propose a peace conference to the belligerents on terms not unfavorable to the Entente Powers; if Germany refused the offer, or accepted it and then rejected the terms presented, the United States was to enter the war on the Allied side.[72] Colonel House had secured Wilson's approval, although the president undoubtedly was thinking more of peaceful mediation than of entry into the war.[73] Lansing had also been informed of the plan and had given it a tentative approval, although he made the significant observation that intervention was not only a question of timing but also of the means of accomplishment.[74] As House matured his plans, the secretary's doubts increased, and he wrote Wilson that though the scheme might work, "there are so many problems connected with it—such as boundaries, colonial possessions and indemnities, that I hardly like to express an opinion until it takes more definite form."[75]

Unperturbed by such doubts, Colonel House journeyed to Europe in late 1915 and proceeded to "button up" the scheme with the British foreign secretary, Sir Edward Grey. House had nearly completed the arrangements when Lansing presented his proposed *modus vivendi* to the Allies. The colonel had already expressed concern about the secretary's conduct of the *Lusitania* negotiations, and he had cabled Wilson that he hoped no action would be taken until he had completed the "peace" project with Grey.[76] He viewed Lansing's proposal on armed ships as a gross error, and he feared that the move would cause Grey to doubt Wilson's sincerity in regard to the mediation plans.[77] On February 5, the colonel cautioned Lansing that the problem of armed ships involved "many collateral questions," and he intimated that nothing should be done hastily.[78] Then, when the strident British reaction to the proposed *modus vivendi* became known to him, House cabled the secretary, ". . . I sincerely hope you will leave it in abeyance until I return. I cannot emphasize too strongly the importance of this."[79] By this time Wilson and Lansing realized that the Allies would not voluntarily accept the proposal, and, after the German announcement of February 10 that armed ships would be treated as men-of-war, the president and the secretary were only too glad to heed the colonel's advice to postpone further action.

Colonel House soon returned to Washington, triumphantly bearing the famed House-Grey memorandum.[80] Because of Wilson's modifications of the agreement to intervene, by the insertion of the word "probably," and Allied reluctance to bargain for an American entry that was apparently inevitable, the memorandum was never invoked. House, however, attributed its failure primarily to Lansing's January 18 proposed armed-ship agreement, and although Wilson told the colonel that both he and Lansing were jointly responsible, House blamed Lansing most of all for the ill-timed move.[81] If House's analysis of the cause of the failure of the House-Grey memorandum were completely true, we might well conclude that even though Lansing's proposed *modus vivendi* failed in all other respects, it at least unintentionally prevented what might have been a disasterous attempt to carry out the House mediation-intervention scheme.

The adverse reaction of the Allies and the opposition of Colonel House were enough to defeat the *modus vivendi*. Any remaining chance that positive action might be taken against armed ships was ruined by two other developments—the diplomatic intrigue of Ambassador Bernstorff and the German announcement of February 10 respecting armed ships.

While the January 18 proposed *modus vivendi* was being considered by the Allies, Lansing continued the *Lusitania* negotiations with Ambassador Bernstorff. Settlement of the case was still deadlocked over the question of liability for the American lives lost on the vessel. Lansing maintained an unwavering demand that German admit liability, and thereby declare intensive submarine warfare to be illegal. When Bernstorff offered a proposed settlement by which Germany would pay an indemnity as an act of friendship only, the secretary, with Wilson's approval, rejected the offer as unsatisfactory.[82] Faced with increasing pressure from the secretary, Bernstorff finally offered two alternative solutions. These differed only in phraseology and proffered an indemnity as an act of grace, but in language designed to render the settlement palatable to the people of both nations.[83] Lansing viewed the offer as unacceptable, and he recommended to Wilson that Bernstorff be informed that the United States would have to demand formally an admission of illegality, which, if refused, would probably be followed by the breaking of diplomatic relations.[84] The president agreed with the secretary but advised that the diplomatic rupture be postponed until Colonel House could be consulted.[85] Wilson did authorize Lansing to tell Bernstorff that the negotiations would have to be discontinued. On January 25 Lansing informed Bernstorff that the negotiations would be discontinued and that, if Germany did not soon admit liability for the *Lusitania* sinking, diplomatic relations would be severed.[86] Upon the ambassador's comment that such a step would probably soon be followed by other results, the secretary replied that he and the president had carefully considered the matter and were ready to assume the responsibility for the consequences of a diplomatic break. The thoroughly alarmed ambassador thereupon hastened to draft a new statement of settlement which admitted liability for the American lives lost upon the *Lusitania,* and both Wilson and Lansing pronounced the statement acceptable.[87] Bernstorff then cabled to his government for approval of the step, and there the matter remained temporarily.

At this point in the *Lusitania* negotiations, Lansing learned that Germany was planning to announce a new submarine policy. On January 26 Lansing informally told the Austrian chargé, Baron Zwiedinek, that the American government had submitted to the Allied Powers a proposed *modus vivendi,* which was intended to solve the armed merchantmen-submarine problem.[88] Zwiedinek then informed the secretary that the Central Powers would soon issue a declaration announcing that armed merchant ships would be treated as ships of war and consequently would be subject to submarine attacks without warning. In a most unfortunate hasty reaction, Lansing replied that the sooner the declaration was issued the better. Later, when this had become an unpleasant affair indeed, Lansing tried to defend his maladroit action to Wilson and the Cabinet, on the grounds that Zwiedinek's information had led him instantly to realize that the *Lusitania* case could not be settled until after the new German policy had been announced, for it violated the *Arabic* pledges upon which the *Lusitania* case was to be closed; consequently, it was better to await the new announcement and then force its retraction as part of the *Lusitania* settlement.[89] A much less tortured explanation would be that the secretary, now filled with zeal for his "solution" to the submarine problem, was willing temporarily at least to accept German pressure in persuading the Entente Powers to accept the *modus vivendi.* Zwiedinek evidently understood the secretary's words to imply that the American government desired the Central Powers to help "persuade" the Allies to accept the proposed solution on armed ships, for he cabled the Austrian government that Lansing would "welcome" the announcement.[90]

Lansing attributed the Zwiedinek cable incident to the desire of Bernstorff to bring about his dismissal as secretary. Although Lansing perhaps noticed Zwiedinek's use of the word "welcome," as the cable was sent through the facilities of the State Department, he failed to bring the alleged misinterpretation immediately to the chargé's attention.[91] A few days later, however, he was informed by the secret service, whose agents had tapped the telephone lines of the Austrian and German embassies, that Bernstorff had boasted in a telephone conversation that Lansing had been so indiscreet as to approve in advance the new submarine declaration by the Central Powers, and that the German ambassador intended to use this *faux pas* to force the resignation of the secretary.[92] Lansing, who had long distrusted Bernstorff, apparently now realized his error, and he was readily convinced that a nefarious plot was under way. He concluded that Zwiedinek was an innocent party, forced by Bernstorff into falsely reporting to Vienna as a positive fact that the secretary would welcome the new policy.[93] The secretary's alarm was fully aroused when, on February 9, Zwiedinek showed him a dispatch from the German Foreign Office which stated that the Central Powers would soon publish the declaration "welcomed by Mr. Lansing."[94] Lansing thereupon demanded that Zwiedinek inform his government that the secretary had been misquoted and had not stated that the announcement of the new policy would be welcomed. Although Zwiedinek asserted that he had understood Lansing to have stated that he welcomed the announcement, the chargé had no other choice than to comply with the secretary's demand.[95] Though the Austrian and German governments accepted Lansing's version of the Zwiedinek cable incident, an attempt was made to intimate that the American secretary, through his proposed *modus vivendi* of January 18, was partly responsible for the declaration by the Central Powers on February 10 that armed ships would thereafter be treated as ships of war.[96]

On February 10, 1916, the German government announced that henceforth armed Allied merchantmen would be treated as naval auxiliaries and therefore would be subject to submarine attacks without warning.[97] The German proclamation not only prevented settlement of the *Lusitania* case, then near agreement, but it also dealt the final blow to Lansing's proposed *modus vivendi*.[98] The American proposal of January 18 had requested a mutual agreement among the belligerents, whereby the Allied arming of merchant vessels would be abandoned in return for a German reassurance that submarines would abide by the established rules of sea warfare. Neither Wilson nor Lansing had contemplated any coercion against the Allies who, as the powers using armed merchantmen, would be required to modify their practices in order to activate the proposed working arrangement. Therefore the German announcement of February 10 appeared as a unilateral action designed to exploit the American proposal, and since it manifestly was difficult for a submerged U-boat to distinguish between an armed and an unarmed Allied merchantman, the new German policy amounted to a resumption of ruthless submarine warfare, contrary to the principles for which the American government had contended since February, 1915.

Lansing's proposed *modus vivendi* bore little responsibility for precipitating the German announcement of February 10. The German government had been considering a policy of ruthless submarine warfare for several months, and the decision to limit this attack to armed merchantmen was the result of a compromise between the German Ministry of Marine and the Foreign Office.[99] It was probable that the German naval leaders never wished the proposed armed-ship arrangement to succeed, for they apparently believed it would benefit the Allies through insistence on cruiser rules, but instead had desired both to utilize the proposal as a justification for the February 10 announcement and to ensure its rejection by the Allies at the same time.[100] At any rate, the German government had the United States in the embarrassing position of trying apparently to force the Allied Powers to disarm their merchant vessels, through "coöperation" with the Central Powers in measures to drive armed ships off the high seas. Ambassador Bernstorff did not hesitate to inform Lansing that the German government believed its new policy accorded with the American position as outlined to the Allied Powers in the proposed *modus vivendi*, a proposal which of course had never been formally submitted to Germany.[101] Yet, while thus reopening the submarine issue with the American government, Germany secretly instructed submarine commanders not to attack passenger liners without warning and to use great care in determining whether or not ordinary merchant vessels were armed.[102] Germany therefore doomed the proposed *modus vivendi* and failed to gain much advantage in the process.

By early February, 1916, Lansing's proposed *modus vivendi* had received a series of heavy blows. The Allies had indicated rejection of the compromise, to which Colonel House had added his own strenuous opposition, and Germany had attempted to use the proposal as a justification for a renewal of intensive U-boat warfare. These developments were more than sufficient to end any chance for voluntary acceptance of the proposed working arrangement and to preclude an attempt by the American government at coercion of the Allies through a change in policy toward armed merchantmen. The final blow, and for Lansing an unexpected one, was the tumult produced in Congress when the *modus vivendi* became publicly known.

Rumors of the American proposal on armed ships had been circulating for several weeks when, on January 27, Lansing admitted to the press that a memorandum had been delivered to several of the belligerents. On February 12, the New York *Times* and the Chicago *Herald* ran the full text of the American memorandum of January 18 to the Allies, attributing the source to a "European correspondent."[103] The published text, preceded by a recent press exchange between Lansing and the German chancellor, and following by a few days the German announcement on February 10 of its new submarine policy, created a near sensation in the American press.[104] In general the American newspapers were divided on the merits of the proposed working arrangement, with the more neutral expressing approval of the proposal and such pro-Ally papers as the New York *Times* condemning the plan as unduly favoring Germany.[105]

Lansing had failed to anticipate the effect of the proposed *modus vivendi* on the debates then current in Congress.[106] Since the beginning of the session in December, a number of congressmen had been criticising the foreign policy of the administration, and they had introduced several resolutions directed at curbing travel by American citizens on belligerent vessels and also at restricting the one-sided trade in munitions of war. The publication of the proposal, in conjunction with the newly announced German policy toward armed ships, heightened the popular fear of war and encouraged the opposition within Congress.[107] On the other hand, pro-Ally supporters in Congress, led by Republican Senators Henry Cabot Lodge of Massachusetts and Thomas Sterling of South Dakota, mercilessly flayed the secretary's January 18 proposal as contrary to international law, and they opposed any change in American policy toward armed ships as a surrender to Germany.[108]

A full-scale congressional revolt against the administration was soon under way. Most of the opposition came from within the ranks of the Democratic party, and resolutions were introduced by Senator Gore and by Representative Atkins Jefferson (Jeff) McLemore which would have prohibited American citizens from traveling on belligerent vessels and would have prevented armed ships from using American ports.[109] In effect the administration's policy of insistence on the right of American nationals to travel freely on the high seas was threatened with reversal. President Wilson, never kindly disposed toward what he regarded as coercion, moved immediately to counteract the opposition, and in conferences with congressional leaders, on February 21 and 25, he defended the policy of strict accountability and intimated that a German renewal of ruthless submarine warfare would soon lead to American entry into war.[110] The president, without consulting his secretary of state, who first learned of the matter through the press, wrote Senator Stone on February 12 that though hostilities with Germany were not to be desired, the United States government would continue to demand that Germany fully respect American rights on the high seas. Wilson closed the letter with the statement, "Once accept a single abatement of right, and many other humiliations would certainly follow, and the whole fine fabric of international law might crumble...."[111] Although the president thus ignored the considerable "abatements" already accepted at the hands of the Allies, whose infractions of international law had been quite extensive and numerous, he was able to exert sufficient pressure to defeat the Gore-McLemore resolutions. A measure of party discipline was thereby restored in Congress.

While Congress was in a chaotic state, Lansing began to devise a hasty retreat from the position indicated by the January 18 proposal to the Allied Powers. The secretary now especially regretted the concluding paragraph of the January memorandum, which had stated that the American government was seriously considering treating armed merchantmen as ships of war, and he admitted to Colonel House, according to the latter's Diary, that the move had been a mistake.[112] Lansing, on February 15, issued a press statement which was also sent to the American representatives in Europe, in which he asserted that whereas defensive armaments on merchant ships should be abolished, such an action would have to be agreed to by all the belligerents.[113] If the proposed *modus vivendi* were to be rejected by one of the belligerents, the secretary stated that the United States government would then have to rely upon the previously established rules and therefore would continue to recognize the legality of defensive armaments. Lansing then took a hand in the congressional debates on the McLemore resolution, and he sent Representative Henry D. Flood, chairman of the House Committee on Foreign Affairs, a memorandum on the armed-ship question.[114] The secretary contended in the memorandum that to warn American citizens against travel on armed belligerent ships would be a concession of expediency and thus would amount to a tacit and unneutral approval of submarine attacks without warning against armed merchantmen. Lansing also argued that such a warning or prohibition would be illogical, since armed ships would continue to use American ports, and he concluded with an appeal that nothing be done to embarrass the president's conduct of foreign affairs. Lansing's contention that an act of expediency actually approved the circumstances surrounding unrestricted U-boat warfare was a rather weak argument. Perhaps for that reason, Flood used only that part of the memorandum which dealt with executive control over matters of foreign policy.[115]

The retreat from the January 18 position was soon completed. On March 23 the Allied Powers presented identic notes which reasserted the right of defensive armament for merchantmen, and rejected the proposed *modus vivendi* on the grounds of the unreliability of any German assurances.[116] The State Department thereupon withdrew the proposal.[117] The position taken in September, 1914, toward armed ships was then restated in Lansing's memorandum of March 25, which, after sanctioning the right of defensive armament, stated that a belligerent was not justified in treating an enemy vessel as offensively armed unless it could be proved conclusively.[118] In effect the new American policy statement, which was not then released, placed an absurd and dangerous duty on the commander of a submarine, who would have to surface and presumably be shot at before he could assume that the armed vessel being challenged was in fact offensively armed and therefore subject to treatment as a ship of war.[119] The American government thus once more placed itself squarely athwart the new German policy of ruthless U-boat warfare against armed vessels.

The torpedoing of the *Sussex* on March 24, 1916, must have seemed to Lansing like a breath of spring air which would blow away the confusion and bickerings of the past few months. The administration had defeated congressional attempts to prohibit American travel on belligerent vessels, and it had nullified threats to pass embargo legislation on the arms trade. Consequently, the attack on the *Sussex,* an unarmed French cross-channel passenger vessel, restored the submarine issue with Germany to all its pristine clarity.

Lansing sought drastic action in the *Sussex* crisis. This case seemed well suited as a justification for a break in diplomatic relations, for, though no American lives were lost in the unarmed vessel, a number were seriously injured. At first Germany sought to deny responsibility for the act, but inspection of the *Sussex*'s hull demonstrated that the damage had been inflicted by a torpedo rather than by a mine.[120] Since the *Sussex* attack followed a series of sinkings, including the British vessels *Englishman, Eagle Point, Berwindvale,* and *Manchester Engineer,* it appeared that a new campaign of intensive U-boat warfare was under way. Lansing therefore wrote Wilson that "the time for writing notes" had passed, and he advised that the only measure compatible with American honor would be the severance of diplomatic relations with Germany. The secretary, realizing Wilson's hesitancy, noted that the break in diplomatic relations could be made conditional upon an ultimatum demanding an unequivocal admission of the "illegality of submarine warfare in general."[121] Still vexed by the *modus vivendi* fiasco, Lansing was quite determined that the case should be pushed to its ultimate conclusion, which he admitted to Wilson would probably mean war. His efforts to convince Wilson that drastic action was required were reinforced by Colonel House, who journeyed to Washington, uninvited, to demand the severance of diplomatic relations with Germany.[122] Wilson was very reluctant to take any decisive measures, perhaps because he realized better than either Lansing or House that the country as a whole was not yet prepared for war.[123] The president, in a reply to Lansing's letter of April 27, declared that conclusive proof of the alleged torpedoing of the *Sussex* was needed. He further suggested that conferences were desirable before any definite policy could be adopted.[124]

Lansing soon became discouraged by the president's vacillation and lack of determination.[125] At the Cabinet meetings of March 31 and April 4, a general consensus was expressed that action was necessary, but no definite course was decided upon.[126] Therefore the secretary proceeded to draft a note to Germany which severed diplomatic relations, although he did enclose an alternative paragraph which stated that relations would be broken "... unless the Imperial Government declares unconditionally that it will abandon its purpose and no longer employ its submarines against vessels of commerce."[127] Lansing apparently intended the alternative of an ultimatum, which, since it demanded complete abandonment of submarine warfare was hardly an "alternative," to enable Wilson to take forcible action while clinging to a belief that a "way out" was provided. Although Colonel House praised the draft note as "well written and very much to the point," Wilson continued undecided on the proper course to follow.[128]

The secretary persevered in his efforts to break down the presidential resistance to hostilities with Germany. While Colonel House advocated merely a severe warning to Germany that she abandon her current methods or risk a break in diplomatic relations, Lansing was advancing a course of action which could only result in war.[129] On April 10 the secretary sent Wilson a redraft of the proposed note to Germany, which declared that even if the *Sussex* had been torpedoed by mistake, the act accorded with the general spirit previously manifested by German naval leaders and therefore, "... no apology, no disavowal, no admission of wrongdoing, no punishment of a guilty officer, and no payment of indemnity will satisfy the Government of the United States."[130] Obviously Lansing's draft note meant an almost certain outbreak of war with Germany since the demands he advanced could be met only by a complete surrender of the submarine weapon. Wilson continued to hesitate. While he was revising the secretary's draft note with a more conciliatory tone, the German explanation of the *Sussex* affair was received.

The German note of April 11 was probably decisive in determining Wilson to send an ultimatum to the German government. The note appeared to be an obvious attempt to avoid responsibility since it claimed that "careful investigation" revealed no evidence that a German submarine had attacked the *Sussex*.[131] Wilson, therefore, completed the revision of Lansing's draft note and incorporated therein a conditional ultimatum that threatened to sever diplomatic relations unless Germany ceased her present methods of ruthless U-boat warfare.[132] The secretary was quite disappointed and wrote Wilson that his redraft seemed to say that the American government would postpone action until additional American lives were lost.[133] Lansing argued that sharp action would be more likely to produce the desired German capitulation. On April 15 he wrote the president again and suggested that Wilson's concluding paragraph in the draft be changed to read, "Unless the Imperial Government immediately declares that it abandons its present methods of submarine warfare against passenger and freight-carrying vessels, the Government of the United States can have no choice but to sever diplomatic relations...."[134] With slight alteration by Wilson, Lansing's suggested change was incorporated in the draft, and in this form the note was presented to the German government April 18, 1916.[135] The secretary thus had won a partial victory, since the note served, in effect, as an ultimatum to the German government. Nevertheless, Lansing had failed to achieve a complete break in diplomatic relations, which his original draft would have accomplished.

Before the German government replied to the American note of April 18, several weeks passed of *pourparlers* with Ambassador Bernstorff. Bernstorff sought at first to negotiate with Lansing, but at a conference on April 20 he failed to make much progress, since the secretary virtually demanded a cessation of all submarine warfare and rejected appeals that a German compliance be made more palatable by American action against the Allied blockade.[136] Consequently, Bernstorff succeeded in having the conversations transferred to Colonel House, and Lansing on April 21 drew up instructions on the American case

for the colonel's guidance.[137] Bernstorff continued to speak of the need
for effective American action against the Allies looking toward "freedom of the seas." At the same time, Ambassador Gerard reported that
the German government was considering a compromise reply, which
would attempt to exploit Lansing's January 18 proposed *modus vivendi*
by making pledges only in regard to unarmed vessels. Upon receipt of
this information, Lansing secured Wilson's permission to publish the
March 25 restatement of the American position on armed ships.[138] In
consequence of the firm American attitude and the intimation made by
House and Gerard that settlement of the case would be followed by
renewed attempts to mediate the war, the German government decided
to meet the American demands.[139]

The German reply of May 4 on the *Sussex* case was a long note which
attempted to justify the attack, but at the very end it concluded with
the pledge that merchant vessels would not be sunk without warning
and making provisions for the safety of those on board.[140] The German
government was not yet ready to launch an all-out submarine attack
because of an insufficient number of vessels and a hope that peace
could perhaps be arranged through the good offices of the American
government on terms favorable to the Central Powers.[141] The German
compliance was clearly a conditional one, nevertheless, since the note
stated that if the United States failed in its efforts to secure observance
by Great Britain of the established rules of warfare, and no progress
were made toward the achievement of freedom of the seas, the German
government would have to reserve full freedom of action.

The German note of May 4 was accepted by President Wilson. Lansing considered the reply unsatisfactory and wrote Wilson on May 6
that it had ". . . all the elements of the 'gold brick' swindle with a
decidedly insolent tone."[142] The secretary felt that the last paragraph
of the German note made the acceptance of the American demands
conditional and revocable at any time, and therefore he was convinced
that it should be rejected. He also enclosed in his letter to Wilson a
memorandum by the Joint State-Navy Neutrality Board, which agreed
with the secretary's opinion.[143] Colonel House, however, advised Wilson
to accept the German assurances, arguing that a break now in diplomatic relations could not be justified.[144] The president drafted a reply
accepting the German note, but after Lansing protested that the note
expressed gratification for the German concessions, Wilson accepted a
more curt redraft by the secretary and this note was then dispatched
to the German government.[145] The American note of May 8 accepted the

German pledges in regard to submarine warfare, but stated that the American government trusted that Germany was not making its assurances contingent upon the results of American negotiations with any other belligerent.[146]

Lansing remained dissatisfied with the situation and made an attempt to clarify the issue with Germany. In a press release, approved by Wilson, the secretary stated that American relations with Great Britain were altogether different from those with Germany because of the existence of the Bryan "cooling-off" treaty with the British government and the fact that disputes with Germany involved the question of American lives.[147] Lansing meant thus to inform the German government most positively that there was no reasonable hope that the United States would take any effective steps to modify the British blockade. He was convinced that hostilities with Germany had merely been postponed, and he felt that Wilson had dodged the issue primarily because he hoped to be able to bring about peace negotiations in which Lansing had little faith, and thereby to prevent a final reckoning.[148] Lansing nevertheless was compelled to accept, albeit reluctantly, the current "settlement" of the submarine controversy.[149]

The second phase of the submarine controversy was thus brought to a conclusion by the *Sussex* pledge. The submarine issue had been thoroughly explored, and whereas the *Arabic* assurances had applied primarily to passenger liners, the German promise of May 4, 1916, encompassed a general exemption of all types of belligerent merchant vessels, whether armed or not, from U-boat attacks without warning. The victory scored by America, however, was destined to be most ephemeral. The German government capitulated in the *Sussex* crisis apparently because of a shortage of submarines and a hope that the American government could somehow be used in a peace move. Nine months of relative quiet were to ensue, until the failure of American peace efforts and the exigencies of military necessity led Germany to resume full-scale U-boat warfare. When that point was reached, severed relations and war with the United States became inevitable—the *Sussex* pledge had so clearly defined the issue that no room was left for further diplomatic exchanges.

CHAPTER VII

THE DETERIORATION OF RELATIONS
WITH THE ALLIES

"Nothing in our controversies with Great Britain must be
brought to a head. We must keep the exchanging of notes
because if we do not we will have to take radical measures."
—Robert Lansing[1]

IN THE PERIOD following the *Sussex* pledge, relations with the Allied
Powers became progressively worse. The temporary suspension of the
submarine crisis focused American public criticism on the vexatious
Allied interferences with neutral commerce, and resentment mounted
as new offenses, specifically the censoring of the mails and the blacklisting of American firms, became the subjects of diplomatic exchanges.

Lansing was genuinely disturbed by the situation and tried in every
way possible to prolong the diplomatic controversies with the Entente
Powers. He continued to believe that America was vitally concerned
with the success of the Allied cause, and that American intervention
in the war, for the sake of national interests, was merely a question of
time—renewal of the submarine controversy being, in his view, practically inevitable. In the interval, however, he feared that public
criticism might force President Wilson and the Congress into taking
more energetic action against the Allies, and he dreaded that truly
drastic measures might be applied. Although Lansing's fears were somewhat exaggerated, since the bonds of economic interest and sentiment
made a real clash with the Allies improbable, if not impossible, the
situation was tense and much unpleasantness was in store.

The disputes in 1916 with the Allied Powers, principally Great
Britain, were primarily significant as indices of cumulative American
resentment. The most serious Allied infractions of international law
and violations of neutral rights had occurred in late 1914 and early
1915, when the contraband lists had been greatly enlarged and the
"pseudo blockade" of the Central Powers and adjacent neutrals had
been established. Thus by 1916 the principal features of the Allied
control of neutral commerce were accomplished facts, which no amount
of diplomatic protest was likely to alter. Some unrest and discontent
with the Allied measures had long existed within the United States,
and the absence of the submarine diversion and the fact that 1916 was
a presidential election year forced the State Department to act.

Actually, the Allied censoring of neutral mails and the blacklisting of American firms were not economically important, at least in comparison to the prosperity accruing from the trade in war supplies with the Entente Powers. Moreover, two years of propaganda, building upon the existant predisposition of the majority of the American people toward the Allied cause and the policies pursued by the government toward the German submarine, had sufficed to mold favorably American public opinion, thus making the possibility of truly serious trouble with the Allies unlikely.

* * *

Allied censorship of neutral mails was one of the major controversies in 1916. Before this time little had been done about the mails, but in the desire to isolate Germany effectively and to prevent the importation of contraband goods concealed in packages and letters, the British government began to bring neutral mail ships into port for examination and censorship. The results were that neutral mail was frequently lost or confiscated or delivered after considerable delay. This worked a hardship on American and other neutral business firms. Indeed, suspicion was soon aroused that the British censors delivered trade information and "secrets" to interested British commercial enterprises. In general, past international practice had exempted from examination sealed or first-class mail on neutral vessels, but the Postal Union Convention of 1906 and The Hague Convention XI of 1907, which prohibited such examination, had not been ratified by all the belligerents and consequently were inoperative. On this basis, the Allies were able to counter charges of violations of international law.[2]

Lansing was inclined to sympathize with the British position that censorship was necessitated by Germany's abuse of the neutral mails, which made unreasonable the distinction between sealed and unsealed mail. In addition, he was convinced that America probably would become a belligerent in the current war, and in the desire not to bind future American actions, he conducted the mail controversy with Great Britain ". . . half-heartedly as a matter of form and with no desire to force the issue. . . ."[3] Thus Lansing managed, with willing British cooperation, to extend the dispute from January to October of 1916, at which time the issue was quietly allowed to expire.

The most obnoxious feature of the censorship was the manner in which the Allies obtained jurisdiction over the neutral mail steamers. Nonbelligerent vessels plying between the United States and European neutrals were forcibly taken into Allied ports, where mail and parcel post were leisurely and thoroughly searched; even diplomatic mails were treated thus, occasionally. Public unrest and the legal demands of the situation forced a protest against such practices. Consequently, a note was delivered to the British Foreign Office January 4, 1916, which challenged the legality of the seizures and pointed out that censorship interfered unduly with American commercial transactions.[4] Although Sir Edward Grey, the British foreign secretary, thought that the note was brusque, and Colonel House described it as "peremptory," no concessions were forthcoming.[5] The Allied reply failed to answer Lansing's complaints and instead concentrated on the alleged German abuse of the mails and the absence of definite prewar precedents in regard to the inviolability of sealed mails.[6]

Diplomatic propriety required at least one more exchange of notes on the issue. Before further action was taken, Ambassador Page suggested that the British government be spared the labor of detaining mail ships on the high seas, for he asserted that friendship required that the American government ensure that all mails destined for Europe be routed directly through British ports.[7] In this way, the legal controversy would be reduced, since Great Britain could claim that the mails voluntarily entered British ports and were therefore subject to domestic censorship laws. Such a remedy was too much even for the sympathetic Lansing, and he rejected Page's proposal.[8] The secretary thereupon drafted a stronger note to the British government, which he explained to the president was necessitated by rising public indignation. He further stated that he hoped to follow the note with informal negotiations for a compromise.[9] The note, dispatched May 24, warned that the American government could "no longer tolerate" the abuse of neutral mails, although it admitted the right of the Allies to examine, and confiscate if necessary, merchandise sent by first-class mail and parcel post.[10]

No compromise was obtained. The American note was definitely weak, despite its threatening tone, and the admission that sealed mail could be examined for concealed contraband destroyed most of the American case.[11] The British and French governments were so little concerned in the matter that they delayed a reply for almost five months. When the reply did arrive, October 12, it was found to be no more than a polite rejection of Lansing's demands.[12] The note claimed that the neutral mail ships "voluntarily" entered Allied ports and consequently were subject to the domestic laws there in force. It also asserted that The Hague Convention was inoperative, since six of the belligerents had not ratified it. In conclusion, the note asserted self-righteously that it was assumed that the American government did not classify the Allied practice of searching vessels as comparable to Germany's destroying ships, cargoes, and passengers.

Lansing's reaction to the note well demonstrated one of the reasons why no Allied concessions resulted from the diplomatic exchanges. The secretary wrote the president that he viewed the note as "couched in most friendly terms," and that although it had not altered the controversy, the note had "materially cleared the atmosphere."[13] Presumably, Lansing meant that the issue had been so clearly defined that it now could be settled by compromise or arbitration. A few days later, Lansing informed Wilson that ". . . while we are neutral in the present war, we may be belligerent in the next and may deem it necessary to do certain things which we now regard as extreme restrictions upon the neutrals. It would be most unfortunate to tie ourselves too tightly to a proposition which we would regret in the future."[14] Lansing undoubtedly felt that the United States would probably soon be involved in the current war, and he clearly indicated his reluctance to interfere with the Allied prosecution of the struggle against Germany. Even Wilson indicated his approval of this tacit acquiescence in the Allied practices toward the mails.[15] It was not surprising, therefore, that the formal American protests had failed to win a single abatement of censorship from the Allied governments.

The Allied blockade was well established by 1916, although the diplomatic controversy about its legality continued. On October 21, 1915, the American government had contested the blockade on the grounds that it was inconsistent with international law, and especially so by reason of the blockade of neutral ports and the extension of the doctrine of continuous voyage to conditional contraband goods. Not only had this protest failed to modify the blockade, but the Allies did not answer the note until nearly six months later. As for Lansing, he probably was content to let the issue lie dormant, although he continued to feel that Great Britain was using the blockade to expand her commerce with European neutrals at America's expense. As a legalist, he of course would have preferred that the blockade be regularized in some way and thus brought within the tattered fabric of international law. However, American public criticism in 1916 was such that the blockade issue had to be revived.

Ambassador Page, conscious of the secretary's sense of the legal niceties and of public unrest in America, transmitted a proposed solution to the blockade problem. On January 15, Page informed the State Department that the British ministry had informally asserted that Allied submarines were now able to blockade effectively the Baltic Sea, presumably by using "German tactics," and the question was raised whether the United States would favor a repeal of the March 11, 1915, order in council, which had established the pseudo blockade, with the order to be replaced by a declared legal blockade of Germany.[16] Lansing was impressed with the potentialities of the proposal, which at one stroke would remove most of the American complaints, and he intimated that such an action would be welcomed.[17] In spite of these overtures, the British government failed to proceed along the course indicated by Page, probably because of the unwillingness of the military leaders to abandon the advantages gained by the current blockade of the neutrals adjacent to Germany.

The chief reason for the failure of American executive leaders to exert genuine pressure against the Allied blockade was their concern for the national interests, and especially the security of the nation. Ambassador Page, in a well-reasoned and cogent report on January 22, clearly enunciated America's strategic political interests in an Allied victory.[18] Page stated that the war could not be allowed to end in a stalemate, since such a conclusion would not only lead to a postwar armaments race, but would also affect adversely the balance of power in the Far East. The ambassador reported that high British officials had recently informed him that Japan was seeking large concessions in the Pacific area as the price of her coöperation in the war, and that although the Allied governments had so far withheld approval, they were powerless to do more at the present time. Page wrote that everything depended upon the American attitude:

If the United States should oppose the blockade [of Germany] and the war should end as a draw, Japan will be able to extort her full demands because England will need her Navy indefinitely on this side of the world. If the United States acquiesces in the blockade and the war ends with German defeat, both England and the United States will be in the way of Japan's aggressions. . . . The only hope therefore of a permanent peace lies in such a decisive defeat of Germany as will prevent a new era of armament and a new set of dangerous complications both in Europe and in the Pacific. . . .[19]

For once, Page's views coincided with those of Lansing. The secretary had held for some time this general concept of the significance of the war for America, and he had in July, 1915, specifically recorded the conviction that an Allied defeat or a stalemated war would alter the balance of power and would leave America alone to face a dynamic Japan in the Far East. Lansing, and later Wilson and other American leaders, frequently referred to the war as a conflict between democracy and militaristic autocracy, but always behind or accompanying such idealistic conceptions was an awareness of the power-politics connotation of the current war. Of course, Lansing also meant, by reference to democracy, that an Allied defeat would leave America to face a hostile world and thus would force the United States to engage in peacetime military preparations that would alter profoundly the traditional American way of life. For these reasons, the secretary appreciated the significance of Page's report, and he urged Wilson to examine the report carefully before determining the American policy toward Germany and the *Lusitania* case, which was still under consideration.[20] The president was similarly impressed and he replied that "... the arguments it [Page] urges are evident enough and of considerable weight."[21]

In view of these considerations, it was not strange that nothing concrete was done against the blockade, even when the Allies took further steps to increase its severity. Considerable pressure had long been exerted in Great Britain against the continued acknowledgment of the modified Declaration of London, and many members of Parliament felt that the existence of the declaration was hampering the Navy's blockade of the Central Powers.[22] Although it was difficult to perceive how the emasculated declaration adopted by Great Britain in October, 1914, could conceivably have restrained British prosecution of the war, public criticism forced the Foreign Office to initiate action which finally culminated in the complete denunciation of the declaration. On April 4, Page reported that a new order in council had repealed Article 19 of the modified declaration.[23] This order soon resulted in the abolition of the distinction between conditional and absolute contraband. In effect, all goods became contraband and subject to seizure if they were destined for Germany. Lansing had concluded previously, in January, 1915, that the conditions of modern warfare made the old distinction useless, and therefore he did not object strenuously to the new order.[24] He did, however, consider that the British were guilty of bad manners in issuing a new order before answering the American protest of October 21, 1915, against the old one. The secretary waited until November, 1916, to make the usual formal reservation of rights, however, thereby passing over in relative silence the destruction of one more feature of international law and custom designed to safeguard neutral interests.[25]

Not until April 24, 1916, did the Allies reply to the American protest of October 21, 1915, against the blockade.[26] The note, presented during the height of the *Sussex* crisis with Germany, was a long, virtually insulting rejection of the American demands. The blockade was defended as an extension of established belligerent rights, which had been made necessary by the novel circumstances of the war, in order to prevent Germany from importing war supplies through neighboring neutrals. In answer to Lansing's assertion that the size of modern vessels did not justify departure from the usual modes of visit and search, and in particular the searching of neutral ships in Allied ports, the Allied note appended a statement by Admiral Sir John Jellicoe which ridiculed the view that a vessel of 20,000 tons could be examined as readily as one of 1,000 tons, the average displacement at the time the rules of visit and search were established. The charge that American trade was suffering because of Allied exactions was again denied, and the note pointed out that a recent release by the United States Department of Commerce showed that trade with European neutrals had expanded greatly. Lansing had also stated in the October note that belligerent retaliations were illegal whenever neutrals were adversely affected. The Allied note replied, in a defense which Germany could easily have utilized, "It would seem that the true view must be that each belligerent is entitled to insist on being allowed to meet his enemy on terms of equal liberty of action."[27] In conclusion the note referred to the violation of Belgium's neutrality and other German "crimes," and commented piously that the Allies had nothing to fear from any American championing of the rights of neutrals.

The Allied note closed the blockade correspondence—nothing more could be done by the American government short of coercive action. Lansing and the Joint State-Navy Neutrality Board, after criticizing the Allied note in every particular, concluded that further diplomatic discussion of the blockade would be useless.[28] Wilson was much disturbed by the impasse and wrote Colonel House that Grey should be informed that the United States either had to make an immediate peace move along the lines of the House-Grey memorandum or else firm action would have to be taken against the blockade.[29] Lansing also was upset, especially since he had received definite evidence from his friend Chandler P. Anderson, then attached to the embassy in London, that the British had concluded a secret agreement with Denmark which allowed the reëxportation to Germany of imported British goods, such as cocoa and tea—goods which were blocked as enemy-destined when exported from America.[30] His concern about the economic aspects of

the blockade was increased when the Allies held an economic conference at Paris on June 14–17 and established a preference system intended for postwar trade.[31] The Allies planned to prohibit their nationals from engaging in postwar trade with the former enemy, and
presumably with neutrals blacklisted during the war because of alleged
commerce with Germany. Lansing viewed this development as a serious
threat which, because of its retaliatory elements, would block an equitable and stable peace, and more immediately the scheme would bear
heavily upon the neutrals.[32] He felt that only a conference of the neutrals could block the Allied preference system. Unfortunately, no action
was taken. While this Allied economic threat was under consideration,
Great Britain and France announced on July 7, 1916, that the Declaration of London had finally been abandoned, to which America again
entered a caveat, reserving her rights.[33] Upon this futile note ended
Lansing's long efforts, begun in the fall of 1914, for adoption of the
Declaration of London. Thus also terminated, for all practical purposes,
the diplomatic controversy over the blockade.

By the summer of 1916, the attitude of the American people toward
the Allies had reached a new level of animosity and resentment. Not
only were the controversies with the Entente Powers affected by the
lack of German submarine activity, but the situation was further aggravated by two additional complications: the American presidential
election campaign and the issuance, in July, of the British blacklist.
These developments, when combined with the existent unrest produced
by the Allied blockade and the censorship of the mails, were to produce
an explosive mixture which erupted in the retaliatory legislation passed
by Congress in September, 1916.

Lansing's role in the 1916 election was quite limited. He had never
been active politically, and both he and the president believed that the
State Department should keep out of the campaign so far as possible.
In this way a measure of bipartisanship in matters of foreign policy
would be achieved. Consequently, Lansing refrained from an active
role in the campaign.[34] He could not, however, evince total unconcern
with Wilson's campaign for reëlection against the Republican candidate, Charles Evans Hughes. Although he later admitted that the slogan
that Wilson had "kept us out of war" was a powerful element in the
ultimate victory of the Democratic party, Lansing at the time was
greatly concerned. He believed that the phrase was an unfortunate
choice, for war might come at any time over the submarine issue.[35] He
was convinced, moreover, that the slogan failed to prepare the Ameri-

can people for the probable future sacrifices of waging a war in defense of America's interests and honor. He may also have sensed that the popular desire for continued peace, demonstrated by the reception given the portrayal of Wilson as the preserver of neutrality, strengthened the president's reluctance to enter the war and further determined him to attempt mediation in the great European struggle.

The secretary also had to face Republican political attacks. These partisan barbs, leveled chiefly by Henry Cabot Lodge and Elihu Root, charged that the Democratic administration had failed to settle the *Lusitania* case despite all the talk about strict accountability toward submarine warfare, and that the January 18 proposed *modus vivendi* on armed ships had been a maneuver designed to appease Germany and thereby to achieve a diplomatic "victory" on the submarine issue for domestic political purposes.[36] In addition, the State Department's failure to protest the invasion of Belgium and other alleged German brutalities and flagrant violations of international law was condemned unsparingly. In regard to Belgium, Lansing had long sought a public statement which would point out that the United States government, not being a party to the treaty of guarantee, was not obligated by treaty conventions to protest the violation of Belgian neutrality, and that in any case such protests would be inconsistent with American neutrality.[37] To refute the current Republican attacks, Lansing proposed to Wilson on September 21 that he not only make a speech explaining the failure to protest the invasion of Belgium, but also that he close the *Lusitania* case speedily.[38] The secretary suggested that the case could either be settled on the basis of Bernstorff's offer of January, 1916, or that the record of the long negotiations with Germany be published. In either case, the Republicans would be confounded and the Democratic party would regain any votes lost because of the Lodge-Root attacks. Lansing also proposed, in effect, that the British "lion's tail" be twisted, and more votes garnered by the dispatch of still another "stern," but informal, protest against the blockade and kindred offenses.[39] Wilson was willing to consider the settlement of the *Lusitania* case, if it could be done quietly and without an undue disturbance of existing foreign relations, but when he received the proposed protest to the Allies, he wrote Lansing to take no action without express permission, and he concluded with the admonition, "Let us forget the campaign so far as matters of this sort are concerned."[40] The secretary, thus rebuked for his partisan reaction, then agreed with Wilson that the barbs of the opposition should be quietly endured, although he still felt that the *Lusitania* matter could readily be closed.[41] On this note, Lansing ceased all attempts to refute the Republican attacks.

While the campaign was approaching maximum intensity, the British government adopted the blacklist, a measure that vastly increased American public criticism of the Allies. The measure had been presaged by the British Enemy Trading Act of December 23, 1915, which had prohibited British nationals from conducting commercial relations with enemy subjects or neutral firms having enemy connections. Although this act was purely a matter of domestic legislation, and therefore beyond the scope of international law, Lansing had protested the measure as it bore upon neutral business firms and transactions.[42] The British reply of February 16, which set the tone for the ensuing futile exchanges, rejected the American protest on the grounds that the Enemy Trading Act was merely a domestic law binding solely upon British nationals.[43]

On July 18, Great Britain issued a formal blacklist that applied to eighty-five American firms and individuals.[44] These proscribed persons were denied contact with British commercial groups and were, in addition, precluded from use of any British-owned facilities, including shipping, cables, insurance, and bunker supplies. Although the blacklist did not seriously affect the American economy, its release came at a time when cumulative grievances against Allied measures had aroused considerable popular anger within the United States.[45] The British proscription of American firms, following closely the dispute over censorship of the mails, the "hovering" of British warships off American ports,[46] and the *China* case,[47] seemed to indicate an almost complete disregard by the Allied Powers for American sensibilities. Wilson was greatly disturbed by the blacklist. He wrote House, on July 23, that the "last straw" had been reached, and that he was considering a request to Congress to prohibit loans and restrict exports to the Allies.[48] The entire matter was really unnecessary, since the British were accomplishing far more through the more extensive confidential or secret blacklist than could be achieved through the published proscription.

The summer of 1916 was thus a most anxious period for Lansing. He was so aware of the acuteness of the situation that he left a sick bed, to which he had been confined for several weeks, in order to address the Jefferson County Bar Association at Watertown, New York, June 3, on foreign policy. In this speech, which was widely publicized and very favorably received, Lansing called for patience in public consideration of the nation's relations with the belligerents. He then asserted that though the government would insist on its neutral rights, there was a significant difference in the rights menaced by the opposing belligerents: "Thus the violation of the natural right of life is a much more serious offense against an individual and against his nation than the violation of the legal right of property."[49] The secretary concluded his appeal for public tolerance toward the Allies with a veiled reference to the inhumanity of German submarine warfare, in which he stated that the American government was far more concerned with life than with property, and he bitterly assailed as un-American those materialistic citizens who would place property considerations first. Lansing's address was so patently pro-Ally that even Ambassador Spring-Rice took hope and reported to Sir Edward Grey that Lansing had, with "great courage," attempted to check the rising tide of public indignation.[50] Spring-Rice believed that the secretary's address indicated that no severe action would be taken against the Allies, beyond the usual exchange of diplomatic notes.

It was unfortunate, therefore, that Lansing was absent on vacation when the British blacklist was published. Frank L. Polk, the counselor and acting secretary of state during Lansing's absence, wrote the secretary on July 24 that the blacklist, though not a new development, had touched off an uproar that demanded a strong stand against Great Britain.[51] Wilson and Polk drafted a stern note which protested the blacklist on the grounds of international morality and justice, and pointed out that although the blacklist was admittedly a piece of domestic legislation, it was an affront to the established rights of neutrals.[52] Polk wrote Lansing that the note could have been sharper, but the secretary replied, "It could not be made much stronger and be polite, and of course we must observe our manners."[53] The matter was not to end with a mere protest, however.

Wilson was determined that the Allies should be made to appreciate the depths of American resentment about the blacklist. Polk had suggested that Congress be requested to give the president discretionary powers to restrict loans and exports to the Allies, and this form of threatened reprisal was adopted.[54] Lansing and House were not enthusiastic about this action, and in fact the secretary attempted to reduce congressional anger by informing Representative Claude Kitchin on August 17 that there was no substantial evidence of the existence of an extensive British confidential blacklist.[55] Lansing made this statement despite the knowledge, supplied by Consul General Robert P. Skinner, that a secret list of several thousand names undoubtedly existed. Nevertheless, when Wilson had determined on the adoption of countermeasures, the secretary had to endorse publicly the proposed retaliation.[56] In reality, he had little to fear. The legislation adopted, embodied in the Shipping Board Act of September 7 and the Revenue Act of September 8, merely authorized the president to refuse clearance and port facilities to vessels declining to transport American goods because of the blacklist.[57] The legislation thus fell far short of an embargo and though perhaps it could have been used successfully, it never was invoked. The secretary of commerce, William C. Redfield, sent Lansing a study of Anglo-American trade, which concluded that application of the retaliatory measures would threaten the basis of American prosperity, since the closure of American ports to British vessels would disrupt the trade in war materials and would probably be followed by British countermeasures.[58] America was too deeply enmeshed with the Allies to jeopardize her economic welfare by forcible retaliation. The blacklist, and even the blockade, were minor factors compared to the prosperity flowing from the trade in war material and supplies with the Allies.[59]

Great Britain did make a few concessions in regard to the blacklist. The British government was naturally concerned about the retaliatory legislation, mild though it was, and it was especially fearful of any possibility that the United States might convoy merchant vessels through the Allied blockade. Thus though the formal Allied reply of October 11 on the blacklist failed to make a single concession, Grey privately admitted that publication of the list had been a blunder, and he intimated that the number of listed American firms would be reduced.[60] Lansing accepted the offer to scale down the list, an action which eventually was accomplished, but he refused to follow Ambassador Page's suggestion that Polk be sent to London for conferences on the matter.[61] Thus ended the controversy, and it is noteworthy that a few months later, when America had entered the war, the United States also resorted to use of the blacklist—a use far more extensive than that which it had protested in the summer of 1916.[62]

The election of 1916 resulted in a narrow Democratic victory, and Wilson was enabled once more to concentrate on matters of foreign policy. For a time the prospects of success had appeared so dim that Wilson had, at the suggestion of House, devised a plan for the smooth transition of power to his expected successor, Charles Evans Hughes.[63] According to the plan, Lansing would resign after the election and Wilson would appoint Hughes to the office of secretary of state; thereupon, Wilson and the vice-president would also resign, and Hughes would succeed to the office of president four months in advance of the legal date. House informed Lansing of the plan, and after initial surprise at such unorthodoxy, the secretary approved the idea as sound and patriotic statesmanship in view of the delicate foreign situation.[64] On election night, November 7, Lansing and other Democratic leaders gathered at the Hotel Biltmore in New York City for a "victory" dinner, but as the depressing returns came in, the celebration began to resemble a "morgue-like entertainment."[65] Victory was recorded, however, as the returns came in from the Western states; Wilson embarked upon another four-year term. For Lansing, the election meant a continuation in the office of secretary of state, and from this position he soon was to realize the fulfillment of his policies—American intervention in the war.

As the year 1916 drew to a close, reports to the State Department indicated that Germany was preparing to resume unrestricted submarine warfare. After nine months of quiescence, during which time America had signally failed to reduce in the slightest the rigors of the Allied blockade, military necessity was to cause Germany to resort to the weapon which gave the greatest promise of speedily ending the war. The controversies with the Allies, which hardly could have led to hostilities in any case, soon faded into the background. Wilson prepared his final efforts at peaceful mediation, and the failure of his attempts was to leave the American government, in view of its past policy declarations, with no alternative except intervention in the war.

Chapter VIII

AMERICA ENTERS THE WAR

"I hope that those blundering Germans will blunder soon
because there is no doubt but that the Allies in the west are
having a hard time and Russia is not succeeding in spite of
her man power. The Allies must *not* be beaten."

—Robert Lansing[1]

THE FINAL PHASE of American neutrality centered around the efforts of President Wilson to mediate in the war. The failure of those attempts, together with the German launching of unrestricted submarine warfare, removed the last hope that America could remain out of the great European conflict.

The American efforts for peace were made in desperation and were doomed from their initial conception. America had lent herself rather fully to the Allied cause, and had placed the nation in opposition to the efficacious use of the submarine, thus tacitly accepting the numerous Allied violations of international law while demanding of Germany full compliance with the rules of war. The German government, responding to military exigencies, prepared in late 1916 to resume unrestricted U-boat warfare, partly on the assumption that America as a belligerent could hardly be any more useful to the Allies than she was as a neutral. America's last possibility of remaining at peace, and the only consideration of value to Germany, was that Wilson might be able to persuade the Allied Powers to enter peace negotiations. Unfortunately for him, the Allies were not willing to make peace while the military situation gave Germany the advantage, and so efforts for a peaceful settlement failed.

* * *

The election of 1916 apparently reinforced President Wilson's pacifism.[2] Wilson had long desired to mediate the conflict and thereby to render an invaluable service to mankind. The Allied unwillingness to make peace while Germany was militarily successful and the fact that he was strongly sympathetic with the Entente cause had prevented Wilson from making a strong public bid for mediation. Thus, though sending Colonel House on private peace missions, Wilson had avoided participation in several proposed neutral conferences dedicated to ending the war.[3] Moreover, the House-Grey memorandum of early 1916 seemed to indicate that at one time the president was thinking in terms

[145]

of a mediation effort that might well result in armed intervention in the war, unless peace could be made on terms favorable to the Allies. Soon, however, Wilson reverted to a more neutral mood, encouraged by the failure of the Allies to invoke the House-Grey agreement and by the popularity of the 1916 Democratic slogan that Wilson had kept the nation out of war. In fact, the president believed that he had largely won the election on the basis of this slogan and that the majority of the American people expected him to preserve American neutrality. Thus when indications began to arrive that Germany was about to re-sume intensive U-boat warfare, Wilson saw that he could no longer delay a major peace "offensive." Wilson's mediation attempts in the winter of 1916–1917 were desperate efforts to end the war before America was involved by the submarine issue.[4]

Lansing was opposed to any American attempts at mediation of the war. Although he did not relish the prospect of actual war and blood-shed, he found it difficult to envisage a satisfactory alternative to an American intervention in the conflict. Upon receiving intimation of Wilson's mediation plans, Lansing recorded his objections in private memoranda, emphasizing his fear that the Allied Powers, whom he believed to be unwilling to make peace, would be embarrassed by the president's proposals. He wrote:

I am most unhappy over the situation, because on no account must we range ourselves even indirectly on the side of Germany . . . .

The amazing thing to me is that the President does not see this. In fact he does not seem to grasp the full significance of this war or the principles at issue. I have talked it over with him, but the violation of American rights by both sides seem to interest him more than the vital interests as I see them. That German imperialistic ambitions threaten free institutions everywhere apparently has not sunk very deeply into his mind. For six months I have talked about the struggle between Autocracy and Democracy, but I do not see that I have made any great impression. . . .

I only hope that the President will adopt the true policy which is "Join the Allies as soon as possible and crush the German Autocrats." If he takes drastic measures against Great Britain, he will never be forgiven; if he attempts to mediate now, he will commit a grave error, because I am sure nothing will come of it, and I hope nothing will.

As to my own position. I will never sign an ultimatum to Great Britain. I will act in favor of mediation though with great reluctance, but I would not do it if I thought it would amount to anything.[5]

This memorandum, written during the height of American resentment at the British sea war measures, indicated how far Lansing's thinking about the war had progressed. Lansing was speaking increasingly in terms of an ideological conflict with Germany. The temper of the times and the democratic tradition in America, to which Lansing subscribed emphatically, made it convenient to speak of a quite realistic concern about security, international politics, and economic factors in terms of democracy. In addition, Lansing meant by the phrase "democratic conflict with autocracy" that a German victory would force upon America the assumption of a heavy armaments burden for reasons of defense, and such a development might basically alter America's democratic institutions.

Lansing's memoranda revealed the serious difficulties existing between the president and his secretary of state. Lansing even went so far in his opposition to mediation as to impute to Wilson selfish motives. He felt, as he recorded later, that although the president had originally sought to mediate the war because of altruistic impulses, he now was primarily interested in his own role. He was obsessed with the idea of participating personally in the peace conference and, by achieving a stable peace, to make the American president the premier citizen of the world.[6] Although Lansing's criticisms of Wilson's motives were harsh and possibly unjust, his belief that mediation could not succeed, because of Allied unwillingness to treat on Germany's terms, was borne out by events. Lansing also believed, and perhaps correctly, that merely to settle the war on an inconclusive note would achieve at most only a temporary truce. The president was constitutionally charged with the conduct of foreign relations, and Lansing, holding such radically different views, probably should have resigned his office. That he did not was because he believed that by remaining in office he could continue to exert persuasion on the president and thus eventually to guide him along the "right" path.

Several months later, when Wilson's mediation plans had assumed more definite form, Lansing again recorded his objections. In the belief that it was ". . . imperative that we draw nearer to rather than away from the Allies," and that a peace proposal at the present time would embarrass and anger the Allied Powers, he opposed any peace moves whatsoever.[7] More importantly, Lansing's memorandum clearly foreshadowed his later break with Wilson at the Paris Peace Conference. Wilson at the time was tentatively formulating plans for a postwar international organization, the future League of Nations, and he considered a mutual territorial guarantee as vital to the projected collective security system. Lansing believed that Wilson's planned organization was faulty, not only because he objected to supranational authorities and guarantees involving force, but also because he felt that membership in any type of international organization should be restricted to democratic nations.[8] Lansing shared the belief, long current in America, that the masses of common people everywhere essentially desired peace, and that a democratic state, controlled by popular will, tended by its very nature to be peaceful and nonaggressive. Since a league could function only if its members were reliable, nondemocratic states should be excluded, and the resulting league of democracies would be so stable as not to require guarantees based on force. Although the secretary's conclusion that Wilson's projected league would probably fail was prophetic, his reasoning as to the innate pacifism of democratic states was more questionable. The real significance of his views, however, lay in their opposition to what was to become Article X of the League Covenant, the heart of the covenant.

The president's determination to offer mediation to the belligerents was increased by indications that Germany was considering resumption of intensified submarine warfare. On September 14, 1916, Ambassador Gerard reported that the German foreign secretary, Gottlieb von Jagow, had complained of the American munitions supplies which were then enabling the Allies to continue the Somme offensive, and that Von Jagow had commented bitterly that forty-one Allied munitions vessels had recently been allowed to pass safely through the English channel merely because some American might be aboard.[9] The German government was at the crossroads; the current military situation was in their favor and they would have preferred a peace at this point. Since a decisive land victory, however, was improbable, and continuation of the war meant a slow economic strangulation by the Allied blockade, Germany felt constrained either to move for a favorable peace or to renew the U-boat campaign, which was the one remaining hope for a swift military decision. The chancellory, anxious to avoid renewal of the submarine warfare and the inevitable American intervention, began to act on the peace front. Gerard cabled, September 25, that Germany was anxious for peace, and this overture was repeated October 9, at the direct order of Kaiser Wilhelm.[10]

With the distractions of the election over, Wilson began to put his plans into motion. Colonel House[11] and Lansing were both opposed to mediation and were convinced that the Allied Powers would reject any offer. Undeterred, Wilson submitted a draft proposal for the equivalent of mediation to House and Lansing which demanded that the belligerents define the goals for which they were contending. On this point

House and Lansing did succeed in persuading the president to modify the note, which was changed to a request instead of a demand, for a statement of war aims.[12] Unable to praise the redrafted note, the secretary wrote House that at least it was less objectionable than the original draft.[13]

Lansing did not abandon all efforts to block the proposed "mediation" note. On December 8, he wrote the president that the recent submarine attacks on the *Marina, Arabia,* and other vessels demonstrated that the *Sussex* pledge had been violated, and he therefore recommended that diplomatic relations with Germany should be severed.[14] Again, on December 10, the secretary wrote that the U-boat situation required immediate action, and he pointed out that America's interests and democratic principles necessitated support of the Allies. In regard to the mediation move, Lansing indicated the dilemma which it posed: "But suppose that the unacceptable answer comes from the belligerents whom we could least afford to see defeated on account of our national interest and on account of the future principles of liberty and democracy in the world—then what?"[15] The president, who shared Lansing's view in part but who was obstinately determined on his course, apparently made no attempt to answer the secretary's question.

Even the arrival of the German peace bid did not deter the president. In an ill-timed move, which made Wilson's mediation efforts appear to be part of the German plan, the German government requested the United States to transmit to the Allies a proposal that peace negotiations be commenced.[16] Lansing immediately utilized the German move to argue with Wilson that the mediation overture be indefinitely postponed, since the Allies would certainly not consider it after the rather boastful German overture. Lansing's position was supported by secretaries Houston and McAdoo, at the Cabinet session of December 15, but Wilson refused to abandon his plans.[17] The German note was forwarded to the Entente Powers December 16, and its delivery was coupled with the intimation that the American government was about to make an unrelated peace move of its own.[18] Lansing returned Wilson's mediation draft note December 17, with the comment that the note was much superior to the previous draft.[19] Wilson dispatched the note in that form on December 18.[20] The Allied reaction fulfilled the secretary's expectations, and exception was taken especially to Wilson's apparent classification of the two belligerents' war aims as being on the same moral level. Ambassador Page reported that the British officials were greatly hurt and angered, and that it was said that the king had "wept."[21]

In an attempt to reassure the perturbed Entente Powers, Lansing dealt Wilson's mediation move a crushing blow. In a press statement made on the morning of December 21, the secretary commented to the assembled reporters and correspondents that the dispatch of the mediation note emphasized that the foreign situation was highly critical, and that "... we are drawing near the verge of war ourselves, and therefore, we are entitled to know exactly what each belligerent seeks, in order that we may regulate our conduct in the future."[22] Although he later rationalized the press statement as merely designed to make clear to the Allies and to the American people that the American note had no connection with the earlier German peace overture, there seems little doubt but that his true purposes were larger.[23] A more adequate explanation would be that Lansing sought to inform the Allies, then disturbed by Wilson's note, that they could rest assured that the United States would probably soon enter the war on their side. In addition, he felt that his statement would aid the solidification of American public opinion and thus acquaint the people with the fact that hostilities were near at hand. Lansing intimated these purposes in a letter to his friend, Edward N. Smith of Watertown, New York. Lansing wrote: "For the present, however, I must bear the blame of having made an unpardonable blunder, and I do so with perfect equanimity, knowing that my action accomplished what it was intended to accomplish."[24] It was even possible that the secretary sought, deliberately, to undo completely the mediation note of December 18. At any rate, the American press reacted to Lansing's statement with headlines that war was near with Germany, and Allied officials were greatly comforted by the event.[25]

Not so President Wilson. Grievously disappointed and "dreadfully worried" that Lansing's press interview would ruin the prospects of success for his note, the president displayed not a little anger.[26] The hapless secretary was summoned to the White House, where Wilson peremptorily demanded that the press statement be retracted. Lansing refused, arguing that he had merely stated a palpable truth of which Wilson himself was quite conscious, but he did agree, reluctantly, to issue a second statement to the effect that there was no intention of changing the nation's policy of neutrality.[27] It has been contended that Lansing's press action ruined Wilson's mediation proposal.[28] However, the note had little chance for success in any case because of the opposition of the Allied powers to peace negotiations while Germany held the military advantage. Nevertheless, Lansing's statement certainly did not aid Wilson's mediation offer, and it probably did stiffen Allied resistance to the proposal. It also had one other effect—Wilson had recently given signs of depending more on Lansing than on House for general advice, and the press "blunder" ended that trend.[29]

Wilson's mediation attempt failed. In an effort to secure a frank statement of war aims, Lansing had notified the belligerent powers that all replies would be treated confidentially, and he asserted that the only role desired by President Wilson was to serve as a clearinghouse for exchanges between the contending powers.[30] Not only were the Allies then opposed to peace, but both they and the Central Powers were unwilling to allow Wilson a large hand in any negotiations that might result. The German government merely wanted Wilson to open the process, after which they preferred direct exchanges with the Allies. Consequently, Ambassador Bernstorff was instructed to this effect, and Foreign Secretary Arthur Zimmermann, the successor of Von Jagow, commented that American indiscretion and meddling made it impossible to conduct negotiations through the United States.[31] The formal German reply to Wilson's note failed to state any war aims and, instead, expressed a desire for a belligerent conference to be held on neutral grounds.[32] A concession was made to Wilson, however, in that the German note stated a willingness to coöperate after the war in the establishment of an international peace organization. The Entente Powers likewise failed to respond favorably to Wilson's note. Some general war aims were indicated, but they were completely unacceptable to Germany.[33]

President Wilson, nevertheless, persevered in his efforts for peace. The failure of the December 18 proposal determined Wilson to make one more attempt, using an address to the Senate as the vehicle for persuading the belligerent governments and peoples that the time for an end to the slaughter had come. The president prepared the first draft of the speech and showed it to Colonel House January 11, 1917.[34] Lansing, who was holding a Cabinet dinner that evening, had not yet been restored to the president's good graces and thus was kept uninformed for the time being.[35] After securing the colonel's approval of the address, Wilson took Lansing into his confidence and had the secretary examine the draft—a step made necessary by Wilson's desire to transmit the printed address to American embassies abroad. Lansing spent an hour with Wilson on January 12, during which he tried to persuade the president to delete from the message the phrase "peace without victory," which the secretary believed would arouse bitter criticism in the Allied nations, especially since Sir Arthur James Balfour, the new

British foreign secretary, had just given a speech emphasizing the need for peace through a decisive victory.[36] In addition, Lansing privately objected to the manner in which the address was to be given, since it obviously was an attempt to override the belligerent governments and appeal directly to their people. The secretary, steeped in diplomatic propriety, could not condone such a method.[37] He was unable to alter the president's plans. The speech was delivered to the Senate January 22, 1917, and consisted of a renewed plea for peace negotiations and a settlement based on justice.[38] Once more no immediate results, other than indications of Allied displeasure, were forthcoming.[39]

The failure of Wilson's efforts at mediation, and the Allied rejection of the German peace overture of December 12, sealed the fate of American neutrality.

In early January, the German government decided to renew the intensive U-boat warfare. Germany was faced by a virtually stalemated land war on the one hand and an ever-tightening Allied blockade on the other, and therefore feared a protracted war which would end in her own defeat and collapse. The only hope for a decisive victory appeard to be the submarine, whose unrestricted use would, it was hoped, reduce Great Britain to surrender by cutting off her imports, especially of foodstuffs and war materials. In the past Germany had restricted the use of the submarine because of the American threat to sever diplomatic relations. As Lansing had pointed out in a memorandum in February, 1915, Germany really had little to lose from American entry into the war and much to gain through a restored freedom of action in underseas warfare.

By early 1917, American neutrality had lost virtually all value to Germany. Through its policies sanctioning and promoting the munitions and contraband trade, loans and credits to the belligerents, and by its tacit coöperation and acceptance of the Allied blockade and control of neutral commerce, the United States had become closely bound to the Allied cause. Not only had America become economically a part of the Entente war effort and had failed to preserve noncontraband trade with the Central Powers, but she also had placed herself in opposition to the submarine warfare. Thus no ties of mutual interest, economic or political, existed to moderate either the American position toward Germany and the U-boat or Germany's use of that weapon. When Wilson's peace efforts failed, therefore, the German government decided that the price of continued American neutrality—restriction of the submarine— was not worth the cost of German victory, and possibly even of survival itself. It seemed that America could hardly aid the Allies any more than she had already, and it was believed that unrestricted U-boat warfare would win the war before American military forces could arrive in Europe. Consequently, at the military conferences held at Pless January 9, Germany's leaders decided to launch unrestricted submarine warfare.[40]

The State Department soon received reports concerning the German intentions. On January 8, before the final decision was actually made, the American ambassador to Turkey, Abram I. Elkus, relayed information that high German officials, recently returned from Berlin, intimated that a new U-boat campaign was about to be launched, and on January 11, Ambassador Gerard confirmed this report.[41] Shortly thereafter, the German government began to lay the basis for the change in policy, and Ambassador Bernstorff presented Lansing on January 10 with a memorandum on armed merchant vessels.[42] The German memorandum cited extensive evidence, in the form of captured British orders, that demonstrated that Allied merchantmen were using their defensive armaments for offensive purposes, and this evidence was asserted to furnish the conclusive proof demanded by the American memorandum of March 25, 1916. The memorandum then asserted that, in conformity with the position advanced by Lansing in his January 18 proposed *modus vivendi,* all armed merchantmen should be classified as public ships of war. Lansing, distressed by this attempt to exploit his earlier fiasco in regard to the armed-ship problem, wrote Wilson that he believed the German memorandum to be merely an attempt to justify the resumption of intensive submarine warfare.[43] The armed-ship question thus reopened the problem of U-boat warfare.

Lansing believed that the time for decisive action had arrived. For several weeks, he had viewed the increasing pace of U-boat warfare as ample proof that the *Sussex* pledge was being violated. On December 21, he wrote the president that a definite course of action should be determined, and that there was no further excuse for delaying the severance of diplomatic relations, threatened by the American government in the *Sussex* crisis, for Germany ". . . has assumed that we intend to submit to the sinking of American vessels with Americans on board without carrying out our threat."[44] Lansing had felt for some time that only a shortage of submarines was restraining the German government, and although he had not expected the new campaign to be launched under mid-winter conditions, he was forced to conclude that Germany was about ready to act.[45] On January 28, he recorded his belief that America's entry into the war was practically at hand:

...I have felt that the American people were not wholly convinced of the real menace of Germany, and that, therefore, we ought to keep at peace if possible until the nation as a unit demanded war. If our people only realized the insatiable greed of those German autocrats at Berlin and their sinister purpose to dominate the world, we would be at war today. I am certain that they do not appreciate the danger and I am not sure that the President does, although he may be hiding his true feelings and purposes....

Sooner or later the die will be cast and we will be at war with Germany. It is certain to come. We must nevertheless wait patiently until the Germans do something which will arouse general indignation and make all Americans alive to the peril of German success in this war. When that time comes, as it will come because of German folly, I am convinced that the President will act and act with vigor.

I hope that those blundering Germans will blunder soon because there is no doubt but that the Allies in the west are having a hard time and Russia is not succeeding in spite of her man power. The Allies must *not* be beaten. It would mean the triumph of Autocracy over Democracy; the shattering of all our moral standards; and a real, though it may seem remote, peril to our independence and institutions....

I hate the horrors of war but hate worse the horrors of German mastery. War cannot come too soon to suit me since I know that it must come at last.[46]

Lansing's memorandum, which was followed within three days by the German announcement of unrestricted submarine warfare, displayed his consciousness of three important factors in the transition of America from neutrality to war: the need to unify American public opinion, the vacillating indecisiveness of President Wilson, and the significance of the European war to the national interests of the United States. The secretary had long realized that no really decisive action could be taken until the American people fully appreciated the threat posed by Germany for America's security and institutions, and he had perceived that this "enlightenment" would best be promoted by the German conduct of intensive submarine warfare. In reality, little could be done effectively until the German submarines sank more vessels bearing American citizens and thus provided a simplified moral and emotional stimulus. In addition, Lansing realized that Wilson, despite his pro-Ally sympathies, was torn between his moralist concepts of national honor and duty, and his pacifist inclinations, with the result that the president required also the submarine issue in order to agree to take the nation into the war. Finally, Lansing's memorandum indicated his understanding of the fact that America's immediate and long-term interests, economic and political, were dependent upon an Allied victory, a victory which he believed that the Allied Powers, unaided by America, were unlikely to achieve. He was also cognizant early in 1917 of the fact that the condition of the Entente Powers was deteriorating; the time had arrived for American intervention.

In view of his belief that America should soon enter the conflict, Lansing reacted negatively to German overtures concerning armed merchantmen. The German memorandum of January 10 was an offer, a final one, to "compromise" the submarine issue by limiting ruthless warfare to armed ships. Of course, since practically all Allied vessels were armed, this would have amounted to full use of the submarine. Even if America had, at such a late date, compelled the Entente to abandon defensive armament, it was probable that the German naval leaders would have found some other rationalization for the resumption of intensive U-boat warfare. In any case, Lansing was unwilling to alter basically the American approval of defensive armaments on belligerent vessels. After transmitting the German memorandum to Wilson, and requesting his views thereon, the secretary forwarded a report from Ambassador Page, dated January 5, which stated that if America should change its policy toward armed ships, British vessels would boycott American ports.[47] Although Lansing must have realized that the British threat was an idle one, precluded by Allied dependence upon America for war materials, he made no reference in his recommendations to the obvious fact that the United States possessed a great economic weapon capable of coercing the Entente Powers. Instead, Lansing resubmitted the armed-ship question, January 17, to the Joint State-Navy Neutrality Board, and the board agreed with him that the American policy recognizing defensive armaments should not be reversed.[48]

President Wilson, however, was torn by doubts about the situation. He wrote Lansing on January 24 that he wondered if the recent British practices of attacking challenging submarines did not require a change in the American policy toward armed merchantmen.[49] Again, on January 31, the president expressed the belief that the Allies were using defensive armaments for offensive purposes, and he termed the question of whether their guns were used only for defensive ends as more important than the question of their number, caliber, and location.[50] Wilson thus pointed out the essence of the problem upon which, if the American government had acted earlier, it might have been possible to settle the armed-ship problem sensibly, since as Lansing had emphasized in his January, 1916, proposed *modus vivendi,* any type of armament readily became offensive against the fragile submarine. Lansing had now completely abandoned his earlier position, which he had attempted only as a delaying process, and he proceeded to draft a memorandum on armed ships which was markedly in favor of the Allied

Powers.[51] This memorandum, dated January 30 and transmitted to the president on the following evening, concluded that intent or purpose determined the character of armament, and that a merchant vessel *claiming* defensive purposes could carry up to four 6″ guns, mounted in any location and manned by special gun crews not on active or detached military service, without assuming the characteristics and designation of a public ship of war.[52] In an accompanying letter to Wilson, on January 31, Lansing urged that the memorandum be speedily approved and issued, to prevent Germany from assuming that the American government by its silence had acquiesced in the German policy against armed ships.[53] Although Lansing's memorandum was not acted upon, owing to developments soon to follow, Wilson informed the secretary on the night of January 31 that he doubted the soundness of Lansing's arguments.[54]

On January 31, Germany announced that unrestricted submarine warfare would be launched. Lansing was engaged in writing still another letter to the president, in which he advocated that the government meet the apparently imminent U-boat warfare against armed vessels with a "firm and uncompromising position," when Ambassador Bernstorff arrived to present the announcement.[55] Bernstorff handed the secretary a formal communication which stated that after February 1 all vessels, neutral or belligerent, entering the war zones around Great Britain, France, and Italy would be sunk without warning.[56] The German government did offer to allow one American passenger liner, clearly marked and illuminated at night, to make a voyage each week to the British port of Falmouth. At the same time, Bernstorff sent to Colonel House Germany's statement of war aims, which included rectification of the German boundaries with France and Russia, the restoration of colonies, and mutual economic compensation and indemnities.[57] Immediately after Bernstorff left his office, Lansing sent the papers to the White House and directed the War and Navy departments to prevent the disabling of the German vessels stranded in American ports; this notification came too late, for Bernstorff had previously instructed the skeleton crews aboard the vessels to wreck the machinery.[58]

President Wilson was extremely reluctant to face the issue presented by the German declaration. For the past two and one-half years, he had approved policies which had in effect bound the nation economically to the Allies, and he had accepted Lansing's advocacy of the doctrine of strict accountability toward the use of the submarine, but now that

Germany had decided, at last, to proceed with the most effective use of the U-boat regardless of the American attitude, Wilson found it difficult to accept the logical fruits of his policy. Lansing hastily arrived for a conference at the White House on the night of January 31, and for almost two hours he urged that diplomatic relations with Germany be ended.[59] He argued that American honor was clearly involved, and that in his mind the only real question was whether it would not be best to declare war immediately. Wilson was undecided, and after references to numerous Allied violations of American rights and the need to preserve neutrality in order to serve the world upon the conclusion of peace, he expressed a fear that war with Germany might endanger the supremacy of "white civilization" in the world.[60]

House and Lansing joined forces to help resolve Wilson's indecision. The colonel, upon receipt of the German news, had hurried to Washington, where he joined Wilson and Lansing in conference on February 1. House and Lansing jointly urged that diplomatic relations be discontinued, without waiting for a German overt act.[61] The secretary hammered on the theme that ". . . peace and civilization depended on the establishment of democratic institutions throughout the world, and that this would be impossible if Prussian militarism after the war controlled Germany."[62] Wilson, who was soon to become the great advocate and spokesman of the "crusade for democracy," appeared unimpressed at the time and, instead, expressed fear that such a policy might destroy the German nation. On the following day, Lansing wrote Wilson that Bernstorff should be handed his passports, and that war should be declared on Germany as "an enemy of mankind."[63] The secretary pointed out that merely to sever relations and warn American vessels to remain in port would accomplish the very object sought by Germany, that of disrupting the flow of goods to the Allies, whereas a declaration of war would show that America was determined to eliminate the German ruling military clique and would give the United States a prominent place at the peace conference, which was one of Wilson's fondest desires. In this way, the secretary contended, a just peace could be ensured and America would add "tremendous moral weight to the cause of human liberty and the suppression of Absolutism."[64] Lansing's idealistic expression, in part a genuine conviction that the American way of life was endangered and in part undoubtedly framed to appeal to the moralistic side of Wilson's nature, demonstrated that, at this point, the "realistically minded" secretary was occupying the position later to be assumed by the president.

The debate continued at the Cabinet session of February 2. Here Wilson expressed "astounding surprise" at the German declaration of unrestricted submarine warfare, although Lansing had not been thus surprised, and in view of the secretary's repeated warnings, the president should not have been.[65] Lansing again stressed the idea that only the universal triumph of democratic principles would ensure permanent peace, and that the best way to promote this situation, and to protect America's national interests, would be for the United States to join the Allies.[66] Wilson replied that he was not convinced of this argument's validity, although he had previously told Lansing that he did share the belief that democracy was the only sure basis of peace. Wilson's reluctance to act was supported by Cabinet members William B. Wilson, secretary of labor, and Albert S. Burleson, the postmaster-general. The other members agreed with Lansing's views, especially William Gibbs McAdoo, secretary of the treasury, and the secretary of agriculture, David F. Houston.[67] Lansing suspected that the indecisive Wilson was merely countering his arguments in order to canvass thoroughly the situation, and his surmise was probably correct. Wilson was too deeply rooted in the American democratic tradition to question seriously the assertion that democracy was per se peaceful and non-aggressive, and would, therefore, best promote world peace.

The president finally capitulated. Under constant pressure from Lansing and House, and faced by the painful alternatives of either decisive action or a humiliating retreat from the position assumed during the *Sussex* crisis, Wilson agreed to sever diplomatic relations with Germany. At an early conference February 3, Wilson informed the secretary of his decision.[68] Greatly relieved that the tension was over, and overjoyed that the wisest course had been adopted, Lansing hastened to the State Department and began to draft the necessary diplomatic communications. That afternoon, at two o'clock, Wilson informed Congress of the momentous step, and at the same time Ambassador Bernstorff was handed his passports.[69] Although a declaration of war was still several months away, American neutrality was at an end.

The period from February 3 to April 6 was a twilight zone between peace and war, a period of psychological preparation of the American people for the struggle ahead. In a way it also was a transitional phase for President Wilson. With a disturbed feeling that continued American neutrality might be the only assurance of a stable postwar world, and torn between his concepts of plighted honor and his concern for humanity on the one hand, and on the other his deep abhorrence of war and bloodshed, the president appeared to be psychologically incapable of making a clear decision. Only with great reluctance had he brought himself to the point of severing diplomatic relations with Germany, a course forced upon him by the past policy decisions of the government. He could not bring himself actually to face the prospect of war. Consequently, overt German acts had to be awaited which would make the decision for him.

Lansing was ready for war. In fact, this state of preparation was hardly a new development, for he had been in a martial mood since early 1915. After appraising the war and determining its significance to America, Lansing had decided that the needs of America required an Allied victory and that the country should actively promote that goal. Thus when Wilson finally severed relations with Germany, in considerable part because of Lansing's steady barrage of arguments and memoranda, the secretary desired the logical concomittant of a formal entry into the conflict. He viewed delay with an ill-concealed impatience. His eagerness for action, however, was tempered by his appreciation of the need to prepare both the American people and the president for intervention. He wrote, on February 27:

> The psychology of the situation is the real problem which has to be solved. I wish this was not so and that no question existed as to the attitude of all the American people in the present crisis. Unfortunately this is not the case. Whatever our inclination may be we cannot act without carefully feeling out the ground in advance.[70]

Lansing, therefore, tried to be patient as he advocated policies for action to Wilson. For the American people a most useful instrument was soon found in the Zimmermann telegram. However, it was first necessary to endure the president's last desperate attempts at peace.

Wilson manifested his desire to avoid hostilities by his plan to create a common neutral front and thus compel the belligerents to seek peace or, at least, to bring about a cessation of unrestricted U-boat warfare. In a second "peace" effort, the president sought to detach Austria from the war. Lansing believed that in spite of the gravity of the situation Wilson still thought he could persuade Germany to retract the January 31 submarine announcement.[71] Consequently, the president had Lansing, on February 3, dispatch an invitation to the remaining neutral nations to follow the American precedent and sever diplomatic relations with Germany. Lansing opposed this action vigorously and argued that it could not succeed. He felt that it should not be attempted, since

failure would needlessly humiliate the American government.[72] The
sole aspect of the appeal which interested the secretary was that in this
way Latin America could, because of the power of the United States, be
unified behind American leadership. He soon took steps to force Panama
and Cuba, virtual protectorates of the United States, first to break
diplomatic relations and later to declare war on Germany.[73] In addition,
he made an address before the governing board of the Pan American
Union, on February 7, in which he bitterly castigated Germany as a
brutal and ruthless power against whom America had been forced to
take action; this speech was circulated throughout the Latin American
capitals.[74] Except for Latin America, the neutrals did not respond to
Wilson's invitation for joint action, and thus ended one possible avoidance of hostilities.[75]

In the hope that peace might somehow be preserved, Wilson prepared
a memorandum entitled "Bases of Peace," which he evidently intended
to submit either to a congress of neutrals or directly to the belligerents.[76]
This memorandum, transmitted to Lansing for analysis on February 7,
was an outline for the later covenant of the League of Nations.[77]
Wilson's bases of peace contained four major articles or points, which
called for mutual guarantees of political independence, pledges of territorial integrity, mutual assurances against economic warfare or acts
interfering with equal trade opportunities, and provisions for naval
and land limitations of armaments. Lansing believed that Wilson's continued efforts to mediate the European war were preposterous, since
the Allies were far too elated over the American severance of diplomatic relations to entertain peace overtures.[78] On returning the memorandum to the president, the secretary commented that any guarantee
of territorial integrity should take into consideration those countries
with heavy and expanding populations, and he noted that it was doubtful if boundaries could be rigidly drawn without thus laying the basis
for future conflict.[79] In this comment, Lansing not only referred to what
was to be known as the problem of *lebensraum,* but he also indicated
his conviction, in regard to the later slogan of the "self-determination of
peoples," that boundaries in Europe could not easily be drawn on the
basis of ethnic lines and groups. As for armament limitations, the
secretary asked the president several pertinent questions of the type
which troubled the postwar disarmament conferences. He inquired how
the proper amount of armaments would be determined and upon what
basis, and how the limitations would be enforced and by whom. Lansing
concluded his analysis of Wilson's bases of peace with the remark,

"These questions are to me very perplexing and very real, and I cannot feel that they should remain unanswered until after the proposal of such an article as this."[80]

Wilson preferred vague and inspiring ideas, but he found it most difficult to analyze closely such concepts and translate them into practical achievement. Despite the secretary's comments, then and later, Wilson was to enter the Paris Peace Conference nearly two years later still without having clearly reasoned out his concepts and plans. After returning the memorandum to the president, Lansing also indicated his objections, as a convinced "nationalist," to any projected supranational executive authority.[81] This, too, was to be a source of future conflict between the president and his secretary of state. However, the general failure of the neutrals to respond favorably to the invitation for joint action prevented at that time a further development of the president's embryonic league plans.[82]

Wilson's second plan to avert hostilities was through the attempted detachment of Austria from the war. If accomplished, he believed this would discourage and render Germany more reasonable.[83] Lansing supported this move, since he believed it had some chance for success and would greatly weaken Germany.[84] Consequently, the Austrian announcement of unrestricted submarine warfare was not acted upon nor released for publication, and it was intimated to the Austrian government that America was willing to act as an intermediary and would try to secure peace for the Dual Monarchy on the basis of Allied reassurances against dismemberment.[85] On February 8, Lansing sought Allied assurances on this point, only to receive the disappointing reply that the Entente Powers were committed to the desires for territorial rearrangements, at Austria's expense, by Italy, Roumania, and Serbia, and in addition that Austria was valuable in the war as a drain on German resources.[86] Although Ambassador Page cabled February 21 that the Allies had changed their policy and were now anxious to detach Austria from the war, and were willing to give territorial reassurances, the Austrian government replied that it could not enter peace negotiations without German participation.[87] Since the Allies were not willing to negotiate with Germany and make peace on Germany's terms, the move to detach Austria from the war failed. Lansing still persisted in his efforts, even arranging a secret meeting between the Austrian ambassador-designate, Count Tarnow Tarnowski, successor of Dumba, and a representative of the Russian government, General Sosnowski.[88] Sosnowski tried to impress on Tarnowski that the Allies were certain to win the war, and that Austria's only salvation lay through formation of a "United States of Central Europe," which would meet the national aspirations of the subject peoples within the Dual Monarchy. These efforts failed, and when America formally entered the war, Austria severed diplomatic relations.[89]

Lansing continued to advocate an immediate entry into the war. In a letter of February 13, he sought to nullify Wilson's resistance to Allied pressure and to encourage his ambitions for an important role at the peace conference. He wrote that the Allies were no longer enthusiastic for American participation in the conflict because they feared Wilson would prove too generous to the enemy when peace was made.[90] Lansing then joined Joseph Tumulty, Wilson's private secretary, in a move to arm American merchant vessels.[91] On February 21, the secretary presented a memorandum advocating that merchant vessels be equipped with guns and gun crews, a position which he restated on March 6 to include naval personnel in the gun crews.[92] Lansing defended this measure, which was almost certain to lead to an armed clash with German submarines, as necessary because Germany had ignored international law and thus forced the United States to resort to the elemental and primitive law of self-defense. Wilson was persuaded, and on February 26 he went before Congress and requested authorization for the projected arming.[93] Unfortunately for the administration a small group of pacifists, led by Senator Robert M. La Follette, defeated the bill by a filibuster as the session drew to a close.[94]

At this juncture, the German Foreign Office and the British intelligence service came to the administration's aid. Ambassador Page transmitted February 24 an intercepted cable from the German foreign secretary, Arthur Zimmermann, to the German embassy in Mexico. The cable proposed that in advent of war with America, Mexico should join Germany in the struggle, in return for which she would receive large sections of the southwestern United States.[95] The German note also alluded to the possibility of an alliance with Japan. Although these proposals were not evil or despicable, in view of the current state of German-American relations, except that the message had been transmitted over the facilities of the American State Department, Lansing immediately perceived the cable's utility in molding American public opinion. He arranged, with President Wilson's permission, to have the cable released through E. M. Hood of the Associated Press.[96] The effect on the American people was electrifying, and the affair did much to convince the public that Germany was a menace to America.[97] Lansing was further surprised and pleased when Zimmermann admitted the authenticity of the intercepted cablegram.[98] Not the least part of his satisfaction with the incident came from what he believed would be the favorable results in Mexico, where he had long suspected that extensive German propaganda and anti-American activities were taking place.[99]

With the failure of the armed-ship bill in Congress, the government sought to accomplish the arming of merchant vessels by other means. Lansing advised Wilson on March 6 that the 1819 Neutrality Statute did not preclude this arming, and he recommended that the Navy supply the guns and gun crews.[100] On March 8 the secretary wrote the president that the present state of near-war was unsatisfactory and, in effect, met Germany's desires by avoiding hostilities and yet keeping American ships out of the war zone.[101] Lansing asserted that it was up to the United States to provide or provoke the *casus belli,* and he recommended again that merchant vessels be armed, and thus American public opinion would be guided and molded by effective executive leadership. Wilson accepted the secretary's advice, and on March 12 it was announced that all American vessels entering the war zones would be armed.[102]

By mid-March, Lansing believed that the overt German act awaited by Wilson had occurred. On March 19 he recorded his views that the recent sinkings of the American vessels *Illinois, City of Memphis,* and *Vigilencia,* together with the Zimmermann telegram, had settled the issue and that at long last the American people were ready for war.[103] A few weeks earlier he had received a cable from Ambassador Page, warning that the Allies were on the verge of financial collapse; although the secretary had already favored war and had realized that the Allied cause was definitely not prospering, Page's communication probably increased his desire for an immediate entry into the conflict.[104] Lansing hurried to the White House and relayed the news of the recent German sinkings, but much to his surprise and disappointment, he found that Wilson was still reluctant to act.[105] When Lansing urged that the Russian Revolution of March, 1917 (which made it possible to classify all the Allies as democracies) and the stirrings of unrest within Germany made the present time ideal psychologically for a declaration of war, the president expressed the fear that the pacifists in and out of Congress would stir up great resistance.[106] Lansing then wrote House and requested his aid in forcing a decision by the vacillating president, a request which met prompt compliance.[107] On the same day, March 19, the secretary sent the president a long letter which repeated his earlier oral arguments for a declaration of war.[108] Lansing asserted that ". . .the Allies represent the principle of Democracy, and the Central Powers, the principle of Autocracy, and . . . it is for the welfare of mankind and for the establishment of peace in the world that Democracy should succeed."[109] Lansing then pointed out that an immediate decision for war would strengthen liberal forces in Russia and in Germany, give the Allies moral support to match their recent military "successes," satisfy the American people, and finally would increase America's influence and enable her to play a decisive role at the eventual peace conference. Lansing realized the most efficacious method of influencing the president, and his references to the future peace conference and America's role therein undoubtedly appealed greatly to Wilson.

The Cabinet meeting of March 20 was a momentous one. At this session, Wilson posed two questions to the group, whether he should call a special session of Congress and what should be said then to the Congress.[110] All the members agreed that no course remained but war. Lansing again urged that the present moment was propitious for action and that the Russian Revolution offered a wonderful opportunity to wage a war in the name of universal democracy; this should receive the emphasis, rather than the issue of the loss of American ships and lives alone. According to his notes, Lansing stated to the Cabinet:

> The time for delay and inaction has passed. Only a definite, vigorous and un-compromising policy will satisfy or ought to satisfy the American people. . . . We are at war now. Why not say so without faltering?[111]

Wilson, however, remarked that he did not see how he could address Congress with a speech centering on the theme of a war for democracy, with references to the Russian Revolution. Lansing countered that this could be done, at least through an indirect attack on the acts of the autocratic German government.[112] Upon conclusion of the session, Wilson ordered Lansing and the postmaster general, Albert S. Burleson, to make the necessary arrangements for a special session of Congress, now scheduled for April 2. In no other way did the president indicate that he had decided for war.

Lansing did not know definitely until the last day what Wilson had decided to request in his speech to Congress.[113] The president was keeping the address a close secret, fearing that otherwise great pressure would be exerted by various Cabinet officials for changes therein. Nevertheless, Wilson incorporated in his war address of April 2 nearly all the ideas which Lansing had repeatedly urged on him for several months.[114] Not only did the president portray the conflict as a war for democracy and perpetual peace, but he also stressed the recent Russian Revolution as a vital factor demonstrating the dynamic impact of democratic principles. Lansing was greatly pleased, particularly when Colonel House wrote him: "One of the best parts of the President's Address was his statement in regard to democracy being essential to permanent peace and I know you are gratified beyond measure to have your ideas brought to the fore so prominently at this time."[115] The secretary in a letter to House on April 4 rejoiced that ". . . it has worked out most splendidly."[116]

The existence of a state of war was formally recognized by Congress in joint resolution on April 6, 1917.[117]

Lansing could well be satisfied. His policies, dedicated to the national interests of America as he conceived them, had finally been fulfilled through the entry into war. His constant pressure and idealistic appeals had, in large degree, helped to persuade the reluctant Wilson to lead the nation into the great European struggle. In spite of his past annoyance at the president's indecision and penchant for delay, Lansing now realized more then ever before that an attempt to have secured a declaration of war in 1915 or 1916 would have met with failure. He wrote his friend, Edward N. Smith, on April 7: "The only course practicable was to wait, to suffer further indignities, and to make every effort to bring about peace, so that the lukewarm would grow hot and the cold lukewarm. It was to wait the time when there could be no question but that a substantial majority favored war."[118] In his final Diary entry for the neutrality period, Lansing recorded:

> The decision is made. It is war. It was the only possible decision consistent with honor and reason. Even if Germany had not so flagrantly violated our rights we were bound to go to the aid of the Allies. I have trembled lest the supreme necessity . . . would not be manifest to Congress. Some of our Senators and Representatives seem to be blind to the danger to civilization even now. They only see the infringement of our rights, and compared with the great issue they seem so little. Why can they not see that we must never allow the German Emperor to become master of Europe since he could then dominate the world and this country would be the next victim of his rapacity. Some day they will see it however.
>
> Now to make ready our millions and send them overseas to bring victory to the cause of Liberty. It will be a long struggle but in the end we will win.[119]

Chapter IX

CONCLUSIONS

INTERPRETATIONS of the factors and events underlying the American entry into the war on April 6, 1917, have ranged from single causality to more complex explanations. One of the earliest interpretations of the causes of involvement was the "submarine theory," which contended that an America trying to preserve neutrality was forced into the conflict by the German violation of neutral rights and lives. Subsequently, the "revisionist" school of the 1930's attacked the submarine-neutrality theory, supplanting it with explanations stressing the biased character of American neutrality, the extent of economic and financial entanglement with the Allies, and the culminating actual involvement in the struggle, partly to save the embattled Entente and partly because an enraged Germany finally struck back at her covert antagonist. Finally, in recent years, some writers began to view intervention as a means of protecting the national interest by ensuring an Allied victory and maintaining the Atlantic community.

While space precludes anything more than a cursory presentation and evaluation of these interpretations, some tentative conclusions can be essayed. The revisionists at least have been responsible for a critical reëvaluation of the neutrality-submarine thesis. Their work demonstrated that the United States had been neutral only in a formal or technical sense, that in actuality the American interpretation of international law and practice rather consistently favored the Allied Powers, that the nation's economy was soon closely bound to these Allied states, and that the officials and most of the citizens of "neutral America" were far from neutral in thought and action. On the other hand, the early revisionist suggestion that the country entered the war to save its own economic stake in the Allied cause has been rejected as unfounded. Certainly the majority of Americans were not conscious of national interests as significant in the war; the actual intervention, as far as the public was concerned, came because of violated rights and "inhumane" German acts.

The question of whether the one-sided character of American neutrality caused Germany to retaliate by unrestricted U-boat warfare is still subject to debate. The German decision for unrestricted action was based largely on military exigencies and the desire for a full victory over Great Britain, to be obtained by halting all British imports and exports. Therefore, a recent scholar has concluded, there probably was little the United States government could have done to avert unrestricted submarine warfare, which had little relationship to the American munitions trade except as the existence of that trade provided the German government with a moral justification or rationalization.[1] It must be noted, however, that the German chancellory and Foreign Office restrained for a time the naval and military leaders on the basis of doubts of the submarine's efficacy, fears as to significance of an American entry, and hopes for a negotiated peace—and such efforts to stay the hand of the military were continued by the Foreign Office up to the final decision in 1917. In this connection, it is interesting to recall Lansing's private note of May, 1916, recorded just after the *Sussex* crisis, in which he expressed the belief that Germany had capitulated on the submarine issue because of fears of the postwar trade ostracism and commerical war, planned by the Allies.[2] The evidence, therefore, tends to support the view that a slightly different American policy could have changed or at least have postponed the decision for full-scale underseas warfare—and a delay of only two months would have witnessed the outbreak of the Russian Revolution and the subsequent shift in German and Allied military expectations.

Although the concept of endangered national security and favorable balance of world power was not widely held by American citizens, it was the viewpoint of high administration officials and advisers. At first glance President Wilson, wrapped in his own moralistic values and ideas, seems to have been immune to such views; in fact a recent study maintains that at no time during the final critical period of American neutrality—February to April, 1917—did Wilson express recognition of the necessity for intervention on either security-national interest or idealistic-ideological grounds.[3] It should be observed, however, that his war message did stress ideological concepts and goals, which Lansing and others urged upon him during the last months of neutrality and which quite probably were in Wilson's mind as he pondered the issue of war versus continued armed neutrality. Furthermore, the president in the past had given several indications that he was cognizant of and appreciated arguments that vital American security and ideological interests demanded an Allied victory, even at the cost of American intervention. His policy changes have led one recent analyst to conclude that Wilson clearly understood the significance of balance-of-power concepts for American policy, hence his shifts from courses emphasizing neutral rights to mediation and collective security approaches.[4]

Finally, the examination of Lansing's career reveals that Wilson had been influenced heavily by the policy recommendations and briefs of an official who as counselor and secretary sought to base policy toward Europe and Latin America on concepts of national security interests and on ideological factors. That the intervention was publicly justified on the grounds of violated national rights indicates no more than that even the most enlightened officials in a democracy are dependent on public opinion and must deal with it on its own terms and level.

The submarine factor, therefore, should be viewed primarily as the immediate cause of hostilities; behind it lay the fact that the United States and Germany held sharply conflicting views of their respective national interests. For the United States, these interests were encompassed within the framework of a benevolent neutrality, oriented toward the Allied Powers and reflecting a mixture of popular sentiment, economic connections, outraged moral sensibilities, and some concept of a national security and ideological interest; for Germany, survival and victory over her opponents, regardless of the means necessary. The neutrality policies of the United States government interacted with German policies to take America into the armed struggle.

Robert Lansing bore a large share of the responsibility for American intervention in the war.

Lansing's policies were founded on his concept of America's national interests. Although by birth and education he was a member of the eastern upper classes, and therefore was strongly Anglophile in his sentiments and attitudes, his analysis of the significance for America of the European war was derived from his training and practical approach to international affairs. He realized that America was part of the world system of nation states and that her relative position therein and her long-term welfare depended upon the stability of the *status quo*. During the early months of the war he had contented himself with pursuing policies which both aided American economic interests and either benefited or left unharmed the Entente cause; gradually he came to view Germany as a positive threat necessitating intervention. By mid-1915 Lansing was recording in his private diary the conviction that an Allied defeat or even an indecisive conclusion of the war would profoundly alter the world's political balance in a way inimical to America, and would deprive the nation of the support of British power in the Far East and the Atlantic. Although most Americans, basking in the past century of peace and nonentanglement with Europe, were confident that the Atlantic and Pacific moats adequately secured the nation, Lansing recognized that America was not isolated and that, in fact, her past peaceful and prosperous development had largely resulted from the preëminent position occupied by Great Britain in the nineteenth century. With prophetic vision, Lansing foresaw, in the advent of a British defeat, the possibility of a German-Japanese-Russian alliance which would menace America's security, her homeland as well as her overseas territories, and her economic interests; this fearful prediction achieved a large measure of reality in the years 1939–1941. In addition, Lansing made no attempt to delude himself, and while Wilson and other leaders talked of America's strict neutrality, he realized that the nation was far from genuinely impartial. In a memorandum of February 15, 1915, Lansing took account of America's support of the Allies, and he predicted that Germany would soon force hostilities in order to gain a larger freedom of action. Gradually Lansing came to advocate an early American participation in the conflict as the only certain means of safeguarding the nation's interests by ensuring an Allied victory.

Lansing's considerations of national security and welfare clearly involved ideological factors. As a product of the American democratic tradition, he felt that democracy and its institutions were unalterably in conflict with autocracies, and that though the latter were aggressive and often amoral, democracy by its very nature was more pacific and dedicated to the progress of mankind. Specifically, he feared that a German victory would compel America to abandon its traditional way of life and to assume heavy peacetime armaments. If this occurred, he thought that individual liberties would be curtailed and the very foundations of American democratic institutions undermined. Finally, Lansing was interested in the immediate economic needs of America, as was well demonstrated by his position and arguments in behalf of the munitions trade and the approval of credits and loans to the Allies. Nevertheless, throughout the period of American neutrality, he was more concerned with the broader interests of the nation, the security and future welfare of the people, which he tended increasingly to speak of in terms of ideology and the democratic crusade.

In terms of specific policies, Lansing's primary concern was to use his influence to ensure that all possible measures for an Allied victory were taken. This meant that nothing should be done to interfere with the Allied prosecution of the war and that diplomatic protests should be long and inconclusive, designed to satisfy public opinion and to maintain legal reservations of right for postwar settlement on the one hand, and, on the other, to prevent any of the controversies from degenerating into positive action of a coercive or retaliatory nature. Within this context, Lansing sought to foster American commerce through working agreements with the Entente; he was always ready to oppose vigorously British measures which unnecessarily, from the standpoint of winning the war, interfered with neutral trade. Again, Lansing sought to enable the Allies to use the American market for war purchases, and to resist all attempts to close or restrict this trade. On the reverse side, he attempted to keep the submarine controversy with Germany to the forefront, while at the same time he tried to delay the final crisis until the American people were prepared for a more active role in the conflict.

The concepts and policies of Lansing were successfully translated into concrete actions and results. He influenced President Wilson through suggestion and quiet but persuasive argument. Wilson was relatively uninformed about international law, and Lansing, both as counselor and secretary of state, supplied many of the requisite interpretations and recommendations which enabled the president to transform his devotion to national honor and duty into actual policies. Wilson received the credit for the results because his was the final responsibility for executive decisions and because of his penchant for recasting Lansing-drafted documents into Wilsonian phraseology— for example, the Neutrality Proclamation and the notes to Germany on the February, 1915, war zone proclamation, and *Lusitania, Arabic,* and *Sussex* notes were based largely on Lansing memoranda. It was Lansing who formulated and drafted the armed-ship and the contraband-trade circulars, who helped to reverse the Bryan ban on loans, and who, in large part, shaped the American course of acquiescence to the Allied blockade and of private arrangements therewith. Equally important, Lansing had a major responsibility for American policy toward submarine warfare, even to the point of coining the phrase "strict accountability," and he clearly asserted the unqualified right of American citizens to travel in safety on belligerent vessels. In addition to his role in formulating the basic neutrality policies of the nation, Lansing constantly urged the president to break diplomatic relations with Germany and to enter the war on the Allied side—this, of course, on moral and ideological grounds. Understanding the psychology of Wilson, Lansing presented courses of action in such a way as to appeal to two of the president's predilections: Wilson's preference for written communications, which he could "mull over" without outside disturbance or pressure, and his devotion to idealistic and moralistic concepts of honor, duty, and righteousness. Lansing, whose views in many ways antedated those of the president, constantly urged the identity of American and Allied democratic interests, and his plethora of arguments for intervention in the conflict were instrumental in Wilson's final decision for war.

In an evaluation of Lansing's role and achievements, we must conclude that America was fortunate to possess at the helm of the State Department a statesman of large caliber, who was capable of surveying the scene and of acting on a reasoned course designed to promote the nation's interests. Despite the near-Machiavellian character of some of his policies, Lansing was striving for noble and worthy goals. Within the limited confines of office, he sought nothing less than to preserve and advance the nation's security, welfare, and future tranquillity. The immediate results of the war met all of Lansing's expectations: Germany was defeated, a structure of power favorable to America was established, and dynamic democracy appeared to be universally triumphant. That postwar leaders in Europe and America were to waste the fruits of victory and to allow, if not abet, the rise of a new ideological and military menace, was in no way the fault of Lansing or his objectives. Perfection and omniscience are not required of statesmen, but rather it is demanded that they possess a large measure of realistic vision and the ability to act upon it. Lansing met these requirements.

NOTES

[1] For a brief outline of Lansing's earlier life, see the following: Julius W. Pratt, "Robert Lansing," *The Dictionary of American Biography* (31 vols., ed. by Dumas Malone, 1933), X, 609–611, and his "Robert Lansing," in Samuel Flagg Bemis, ed., *The American Secretaries of State and Their Diplomacy* (10 vols., New York: Alfred A. Knopf, 1927–29), X, 47–175; Editorial comment, *American Journal of International Law*, VIII (1914), 336–338; Lansing to Senator James A. O'Gorman, March 8, 1913, Lansing Papers, 1911–1928, Manuscripts Division, Library of Congress.

[2] Charles E. Hill, "John Watson Foster," *The Dictionary of American Biography*, VI, 551–552. Foster served as President Benjamin Harrison's secretary of state in 1893.

[3] While at Paris, Lansing met Viscount Ishii, the secretary to the Japanese legation, with whom he was later to negotiate the Lansing-Ishii Agreement. Kikujiro Ishii, *Diplomatic Commentaries* (Johns Hopkins University Press, 1936—translated by W. R. Langdom), 122; John W. Foster, *Diplomatic Memoirs* (2 vols., Boston and New York: Houghton Mifflin Co., 1909), II, 38.

[4] Upon the completion of this work, Lansing wrote an article on the various aspects of the Arbitration: "The North Atlantic Fisheries Arbitration," *American Journal of International Law*, V (1911), 1–31.

[5] Secretary Knox to Lansing, January 15, 1913, Lansing Papers. This arbitral tribunal first met on May 13, 1913, in Washington, and then held its next session in June at Ottawa, Canada. The final session was held in March–May, not to meet again until October, 1923, because of the war. In the early sessions Chandler P. Anderson was arbitrator for the United States and Sir Charles Fitzpatrick for Great Britain. Henri Fromageont of France, president of the tribunal, opened the May 13 session with a speech praising Lansing and his British counterpart, Cecil Hurit, for their ability and distinguished records. United States State Department, *American and British Claims Arbitration, under the Special Agreement Concluded between the United States and Great Britain, August 18, 1910; Report of Fred K. Nielsen* (Washington: G.P.O., 1926), 18. Also, Lansing to J. Reuben Clark, June 20, 1913, and Lansing to W. W. Willoughby, May 27, 1913, Lansing Papers.

[6] *Amer. Jour. of Internat. Law*, VIII (1914), 336–338.

[7] Robert Lansing and Gary M. Jones, *Government, Its Origin, Growth and Form in the United States* (New York and Chicago: Silver, Burdett & Co., 1902), 251 pp.

[8] For a brief account, see Oscar S. Straus, *Under Four Administrations: from Cleveland to Taft* (Boston and New York: Houghton Mifflin Co., 1922), 333–336.

[9] Robert Lansing, "Notes on Sovereignty in a State," *American Journal of International Law*, I (1907), 105–128, 297–320. His "Notes on World Sovereignty" was not published then because of its speculative nature. After the war, when the League of Nations created interest in discussions of world government, the article appeared in the journal's 1921 issue, XV, 13–27. At the same time the Carnegie Endowment for International Peace collected the articles into one monograph, entitled *Notes on Sovereignty from the Standpoint of the State and the World* (Washington: Carnegie Endowment for International Peace, No. 38, 1921), 94 pp.

[10] Lansing to John N. Carlisle, December 20, and Carlisle to Lansing, December 23, 1912, Lansing Papers. Lansing stated in his letter, "I would not like to be a candidate and be turned down."

[11] James Brown Scott to F. R. Coudert, January 21, 1913, Lansing Papers.

[12] Purcell to O'Gorman, February 7, 1913, Lansing Papers.

[13] F. R. Coudert to J. B. Scott, and Lansing to O'Gorman, March 8, 1913, Lansing Papers.

[14] Lansing noted that Wilson did not know how to conduct a diplomatic reception,

having recently attended one that was no more than a vast mob. Lansing to A. Mitchell Innes, January 14, 1914, Lansing Papers.

[15] Harley Notter, *The Origins of the Foreign Policy of Woodrow Wilson* (Baltimore: Johns Hopkins University Press, 1937), 250; Jennings C. Wise, *Woodrow Wilson, Disciple of Revolution* (New York: Paisley Press, 1938), 156.

[16] Memorandum by Lansing to the State Department, March 11, 1914, Lansing Papers.

[17] Philip C. Jessup, *Elihu Root* (2 vols., New York: Dodd, Mead & Co., 1938). II, 320; Josephus Daniels, *The Wilson Era; Years of Peace, 1910–1917* (Chapel Hill: University of North Carolina Press, 1944), 437. Daniels, generally a sharp critic of Lansing, agreed that Root's defense of Lansing was correct: "Root undoubtedly spoke truly, for, however one might differ with Lansing, all who were associated with him regarded him as upright and honorable."

[18] Lansing had previously served as a State Department legal counsel under Elihu Root, and he was recommended by Root in 1914 for the position of counselor. This has led Charles Callan Tansill to conclude that because Root aided Wilson in the repeal of the Panama Tolls Act, a working alliance had been formed whereby Root was permitted to fill several important posts within the State Department. On this premise, Tansill infers that Root was Lansing's mentor, and that Lansing through Root served as the tool of Wall Street and the dollar diplomacy of the past.—Tansill, *America Goes to War* (Boston: Little, Brown & Co., 1938), 166–168. However, my examination of the Papers of Elihu Root in the Manuscripts Division, Library of Congress, indicates that Lansing and Root were not really on intimate terms. Undoubtedly, Root's aid did help Lansing to secure the appointment as counselor, but the support of many others was also involved. Both as counselor and later as secretary of state, Lansing did receive advice and suggestions from many sources, none of which indicated any form of tutelage or subservience. In fact, Lansing's actions within the Department did not always please Root; during the controversies with the Allies over neutral rights, Root was fearful that Lansing's notes might cause serious trouble and concluded that Lansing lacked imagination and reliability of judgment.—Philip C. Jessup, *Elihu Root*, II, 319–320, 330.

[19] *Congressional Record*, 63d Congress, 2d Sess., 5178; J. B. Scott to Lansing, April 1, 1915, Lansing Papers. Cone Johnson of Texas was confirmed as solicitor of the department on the same day.

[20] The position of undersecretary of state was not established until 1919, when Frank L. Polk, then counselor, was designated undersecretary. Graham A. Stuart, *American Diplomatic and Consular Practice* (New York and London: Appleton-Century Co., 1936), 68–69, 82.

[21] For a brief and critical account of Bryan's political appointments, see Robert Edward Annin, *Woodrow Wilson, a Character Study* (New York: Dodd, Mead & Co., 1924), 163–165.

[22] Joseph C. Grew, *Turbulent Era, A Diplomatic Record of Forty Years, 1904–1945* (2 vols., Boston: Houghton Mifflin Co., 1952), I, 120–121. Grew evidently then classified Lansing as a Republican and wrote that this appointment and that of William Phillips as third assistant secretary explained Bryan being allowed to place his friend, Cone Johnson, as solicitor.

[23] *The Nation*, March 25, 1915, 331.

[24] *American Journal of International Law*, VIII (1914), 336–338; *The Outlook*, April 4, 1914, 740–741. The *Outlook* editorial, though friendly to Lansing's appointment, viewed pessimistically that of Cone Johnson, the "political friend" of Bryan.

[25] For an intimate portrayal, see David F. Lane, "Robert Lansing as His Friends Know Him," *Colliers*, November 13, 1915, 22–24. Lansing's favorite club was the Fortnightly Club of Watertown, established for literary purposes, but which every

summer held a two-week outing at Galloo Island at the eastern end of Lake Ontario. Among this circle Lansing was known for his passion for fishing and prodigious drinking of cold coffee.

[26] William Gibbs McAdoo, in his *Crowded Years, the Reminiscences of William Gibbs McAdoo* (Boston and New York: Houghton Mifflin Co., 1931), 339, describes Lansing as a "quiet, undemonstrative, even phlegmatic sort of man," with little interest in politics and decidedly conservative.

[27] Lansing to Rev. David Lander, May 3, 1915, Lansing Papers. Lansing in April, 1921, wrote Rev. J. E. Freeman of the Washington Church of the Epiphany that he felt Christianity was becoming too utilitarian and materialistic, that believers were in danger of losing sight of spiritual values and of faith, as opposed to mere morality demonstrated in good works.

[28] Lansing to Edward N. Smith of Watertown, December 20, 1917, Lansing Papers. Lansing understood the need for greater governmental controls in a period of war crisis.

[29] Lane, "Robert Lansing," *Colliers*, November 13, 1915, 23; Cordell Hull, in his *Memoirs* (2 vols., New York: Macmillan Co., 1948), I, 82, described Lansing (in February, 1916) as lacking the broad international view on economics and tariffs.

[30] Lansing to Senator James A. O'Gorman, March 8, 1913, Lansing Papers.

[31] Lansing to Jacob Ten Eyck, August 16 and 19, 1912, Lansing Papers.

[32] Vittorio Emanuele Orlando, "Wilson and Lansing," *Saturday Evening Post*, March 23, 1929, 6–7. Lansing's habit of constantly sketching caricatures of people was probably a psychological release compensating for his otherwise highly inhibited personality. See W. C. Redfield, *With Congress and Cabinet* (Garden City, N.Y.; Doubleday, Page & Co., 1924), 80, for an account of Lansing's constant sketching at Cabinet meetings.

[33] Lansing to W. W. Willoughby, February 12, 1913; Willoughby to Lansing, January 3, 1914, Lansing Papers.

[34] "Force and Material and Moral Impulses," May 23, 1922, Confidential Memoranda, Lansing Papers. These Memoranda Books have been incorrectly termed "Diaries."

[35] Robert Lansing, *War Memoirs of Robert Lansing, Secretary of State* (New York: Bobbs-Merrill Co., 1935), Foreword, 7–9.

[36] Judge G. W. Reeves to Lansing, April 21, and Lansing to the Postmaster General, April 30, 1914, Lansing Papers.

[37] Lansing-Treasury correspondence of June 4, 9, and 12, 1914, Lansing Papers.

[38] Lansing to Boaz Long, April 29, 1914, Lansing Papers.

[39] Jessup, *Elihu Root*, II, 265–266.

[40] Lansing to Bryan, June 12, and Wilson to Bryan, June 13, 1914, State Department File 817.812/168, Foreign Affairs Section, National Archives. For a brief discussion of the Nicaraguan situation, see Graham H. Stuart, *Latin America and the United States* (New York and London: Appleton-Century Co., 1943, 4th ed.), 347–348.

[41] Charles W. Hackett, *The Mexican Revolution and the United States, 1910–1926*, World Peace Foundation, No. IX (1926), 339–341; Henry Bamford Parkes, *The Mexican Nation* (Boston: Houghton Mifflin Co., 1950, rev. ed.), 285–322.

[42] For a more detailed account, see Stuart, *Latin America and the United States*, 151–153; Hackett, *Mexican Revolution*, 342–343.

[43] Foreign investments in Mexico as of 1911 have been estimated as $1,058,000,000 for the United States, $321,000,000 for Great Britain, and $143,000,000 for France. For an account of these investments and of Anglo-American oil rivalry, see Scott Nearing and Joseph Freeman, *Dollar Diplomacy, A Study in American Imperialism* (New York: Huebsch and The Viking Press, 1925), 84–90.

[44] Notter, *Wilson*, 223–224, 228.

[45] James M. Callahan, *American Foreign Policy in Mexican Relations* (New York: Macmillan Co., 1932), 544.

[46] D/S File 812.00/11510½, Archives. Lansing noted that Thomas Jefferson (*Writings*, ed., H. A. Washington, VII, 628) held that since such actions often resulted in war, Congress alone had the right to sanction their use.

[47] The Shimonoseki case concerned the sudden closing of the Inland Sea by the Lord of Choshu in 1863, at the order of the Japanese shōgun, effected by firing on an American ship attempting to pass through the straits of Shimonoseki. An American warship promptly bombarded the town and in the following year a joint expedition, composed of British, French, Dutch, and American vessels, forced the local rulers to reopen the area. The Greytown, Nicaragua, incident arose from British and American rivalry concerning the Mosquito Coast. After the American minister was hurt in a local riot, the United States government authorized the use of force in the protection of American property and lives. The result was the destruction of the town by an American warship on July 13, 1854. See Harold M. Vinacke, *A History of the Far East in Modern Times* (New York: F. S. Crofts & Co., 1941, 4th ed.), 95–96; Mary Wilhelmine Williams, *Anglo-American Isthmian Diplomacy, 1815–1915* (Washington: American Historical Association, 1916), 171–180.

[48] Notter, *Wilson*, 289–290.

[49] Lansing to Bryan, April 17, 1914, D/S File 812.00/11432½; Memorandum on the Powers of the President to Use Armed Force, April 19, 1914, D/S File 711.12/30½, Archives.

[50] Ray Stannard Baker and W. E. Dodd, eds., *The Public Papers of Woodrow Wilson* (6 vols., New York: Harper Bros., 1925–1926) III, 99–102.

[51] D/S File 711.12/29½, Archives.

[52] D/S File 711.12/31½, Archives.

[53] Stuart, *Latin America and the United States*, 155–156.

[54] Lansing to Bryan, May 1, 1914, D/S File 812.00/11800½, Archives.

[55] For a brief discussion of American cattle and oil interests in Mexico and their agitation for military intervention, see Parkes, *Mexican Nation*, 344–345.

[56] Memorandum on the Mexican Situation, May 4, 1914, D/S File 812.00/11984½, Archives.

[57] Memorandum of May 9, 1914, D/S File 812.00/11986½, Archives.

[58] Memorandum of June 3, 1914; Wilson to Bryan, June 4, 1914; D/S File 812.00/24265, Archives.

[59] Bryan to Wilson, June 10, 1914, The Papers of Woodrow Wilson, Manuscripts Division, Library of Congress.

CHAPTER II: THE ESTABLISHMENT OF AMERICAN NEUTRALITY

[1] See my article, "Robert Lansing and the Formulation of American Neutrality Policies, 1914–1915," *Mississippi Valley Historical Review*, XLIII (June, 1956), 59–81.

[2] Alice M. Morrissey, *The American Defense of Neutral Rights, 1914–1917* (Harvard University Press, 1939), 49.

[3] H. C. Peterson, *Propaganda for War, The Campaign Against American Neutrality, 1914–1917* (Norman: University of Oklahoma Press, 1939), 5–6.

[4] H. Schuyler Foster, Jr., "How America Became Belligerent: A Quantitative Study of War News, 1914–17," *American Journal of Sociology*, XL (January, 1935), 468; Millis, *Road to War*, 62–63.

[5] Peterson, *Propaganda for War*, 33–35. Also see James Duane Squires, *British Propaganda at Home and in the United States from 1914 to 1917* (Harvard University Press, 1935), 42–68.

⁶ Tansill, *America Goes to War*, 3–15; Dexter Perkins, *America and Two Wars* (Boston: Little, Brown & Co., 1944), 20–30.

⁷ Lewis Einstein, "The United States and Anglo-German Rivalry," *National Review*, January, 1913, 736–750. In 1910, the influential naval publicist, A. T. Mahan, wrote that "the condition and strength of Great Britain is a matter of national interest to every other community." Upon the outbreak of the great war, Mahan stated to a reporter his belief that American interests would be seriously affected by a German victory. The Navy General Board apparently reflected Mahan's views, for in 1906 the board had stated that German naval plans threatened the Monroe Doctrine, so that close Anglo-American relations were advisable.—A. T. Mahan, *The Interest of America in International Conditions* (Boston: Little, Brown & Co., 1910, 1915), 75–76; and Forest Davis, *The Atlantic System, the Story of Anglo-American Control of the Seas* (London: George Allen & Unwin Ltd., 1943), 187, 205. For a survey of naval thinking, see Alfred Vagts, "Hopes and Fears of an American-German War, 1870–1915," *Political Science Quarterly* (1939 and 1940), Vol. 54, 514–535, and Vol. 55, 53–76.

⁸ See his "Consideration and Outline of Policies," July 11, 1915, Confidential Memoranda, Lansing Papers.

⁹ Walter Lippmann advanced the thesis of national interests motivating the American war entry in his *United States Foreign Policy: Shield of the Republic* (Boston: Little, Brown & Co., 1943), 33–34. In the Preface (dated January 1, 1917) to his *The Stakes of Diplomacy* (New York: Henry Holt & Co., 1915), xiii–xviii, Lippmann described the United States as the "tacit partner" of the Entente Allies, because of the national interests. Other leading citizens who shared views comparable to those of Mahan and Einstein were the historians George Louis Beer, George Burton Adams, Albert Bushnell Hart, and Roland G. Usher; and among administration figures, in addition to Lansing, Walter Hines Page, Colonel Edward M. House, and James W. Gerard. Some less prominent citizens were also cognizant of the German threat to the balance of power as it related to the Western Hemisphere.—Letters to the Editor, October 16 and 18, and November 10, 1914, and editorials of October 14 and 19, 1914, New York *Times*. For a fuller discussion, see Robert Endicott Osgood, *Ideals and Self-Interest in America's Foreign Policy, the Great Transformation of the Twentieth Century* (University of Chicago Press, 1953), 114–134, 154–170. Arthur S. Link, *Woodrow Wilson and the Progressive Era, 1910–1917* (New York: Harper & Bros., 1954), 279–280, recognizes that Lansing and House shared Lippmann's views of the national interest, but he contends that Wilson, who made all final decisions, was not greatly influenced by these views of his advisers. This apparently underestimates the fact that though Lansing's concept of the national interest was not fully shared by Wilson, the latter adopted many of Lansing's policy recommendations which were in effect based on such views of the nation's vital interests.

¹⁰ Lansing to the Rev. M. H. Gates, October 10, 1914, Lansing Papers. Lansing returned to the department from his vacation on the day before Austria declared war on Serbia.

¹¹ John W. Foster to Lansing, September 16, 1914, Lansing Papers. Foster was ardently pro-Ally, writing Lansing on September 3, 1915, that he hoped Wilson would not further embarrass the Allies with another mediation offer, as "... the power of Germany must first be broken." Foster, as an experienced diplomat and former secretary of state, exerted considerable influence over Lansing's thought.

¹² For a brief account of the war dislocations, see John Bach McMaster, *The United States in the World War* (2 vols., New York and London: Appleton & Co., 1918), I, 16; Walter Millis, *Road to War: America, 1914–1917* (Boston: Houghton Mifflin Co., 1935), 33–41.

[13] James Brown Scott to Lansing, August 10, Lansing to Bryan, August 11, and Lansing to Chandler P. Anderson, September 3, 1914, Lansing Papers.

[14] Lansing to Wilson, November 5, 1914, Lansing Papers; Wilson to Josephus Daniels, secretary of the Navy, November 6, 1914, Papers of Josephus Daniels, Manuscripts Division, Library of Congress.

[15] Ray Stannard Baker, *Woodrow Wilson, Life and Letters* (8 vols., Garden City, New York: Doubleday & Doran, 1935–39), V, 3. For the text of the proclamation, see Baker and Dodd, *Public Papers of Woodrow Wilson*, III, 151–156.

[16] Lansing Memorandum on A Public Appeal to the American People, August 9, 1914, D/S File 763.72111/32½, Archives.

[17] James Brown Scott, ed., *President Wilson's Foreign Policy, Messages, Addresses, Papers* (New York and London: Oxford University Press, 1918), 66–68.

[18] For a brief critical discussion of international maritime law, see J. M. Kenworthy and George Young, *Freedom of the Seas* (London: Hutchinson & Co., 1928), 26–28.

[19] Kenworthy and Young, *Freedom of the Seas*, 58–61.

[20] For the text, see Carlton Savage, ed., *Policy of the United States toward Maritime Commerce in War* (2 vols., Washington: G.P.O., 1936), II, 163–179. Articles 22, 24, and 28 established the contraband categories and the free list. The free list included such items as cotton, rubber, ores, and other materials destined to be important to modern war economies. Foodstuffs were classified as conditional contraband. Articles 1 and 2 related to blockades, and 30–32 to the application of continuous voyage.

[21] Kenworthy and Young, *Freedom of the Seas*, 61–64; M. W. W. P. Consett and O. H. Daniel, *The Triumph of Unarmed Forces, 1914–1918* (London: Williams & Norgate, 1923), 6–14; Louis Guichard, *The Naval Blockade*, translated by C. R. Turner (New York: Appleton & Co., 1930), 13–14. Additional reasons for the British rejection were fear of the Prize Court unduly favoring neutrals, the provision of Articles 55–56 in regard to converting merchant vessels into naval auxiliaries, and the inflexibility of the contraband lists.

[22] International law as of 1914, without the declaration, has been summarized as the following: a blockade to be legal must be enforced; "free ships, free goods," applying even to enemy goods on board a neutral, if not bound for a blockaded port; absolute contraband consisted of goods used exclusively for war, and could be captured en route through a neutral; and conditional contraband not subject to continuous voyage. See Philip C. Jessup, ed., in the preface to Edgar Turlington's *The World War Period*, Vol. III of *Neutrality, Its History, Economics and Law* (New York: Columbia University Press, 1936), 4 Vols.

[23] Edwin M. Borchard and W. P. Lage, *Neutrality for the United States* (New Haven: Yale University Press, 1940, 2d ed.), 59–60, assert that there was no good reason to seek adoption of the declaration in 1914, as existing rules were adequate; in addition, the declaration in several ways departed from precedent with new innovations.

[24] Notter, *Foreign Policy of Woodrow Wilson*, 347–349; Seymour, *American Diplomacy During the World War*, 55. Baker, *Wilson, Life and Letters*, V, 185, views Wilson as seeking to relieve the southern and western farmers through adoption of the declaration, as well as striving to maintain an economic balance between the belligerents.

[25] United States Department of State, *Papers Relating to the Foreign Relations of the United States, 1914, Supplement* (Washington: G.P.O., 1928), 216. Cited henceforth as *For. Rel., 1914 Supp.*

[26] *For. Rel., 1914 Supp.*, 215–216.

[27] Page to Bryan, August 22, 1914, *For. Rel., 1914 Supp.*, 218–220.

[28] Tansill, *America Goes to War*, 140–141.

[29] Lansing to Page, September 26, 1914, *For. Rel., 1914 Supp.*, 225–232. Some confusion has existed as to the origins of this note, many frequently attributing it exclusively to Cone Johnson. Research in the State Department Archives indicates that though the final draft note was the product of Lansing and Johnson, it was based on the earlier analysis of Dr. James Brown Scott, dated September 9. Scott, whose memorandum was quoted extensively in the final note, was more critical of the British actions.—D/S File 763.72112/135½, Archives. See also Tansill, *America Goes to War*, 141; Burton J. Hendrick, *The Life and Letters of Walter Hines Page* (3 vols., Garden City, New York: Doubleday, Page & Co., 1926), I, 378–379.

[30] United States State Department, *Papers Relating to the Foreign Relations of the United States; The Lansing Papers, 1914–1920* (2 vols., Washington: G.P.O., 1940), I, 247–248.

[31] House records in his Diary entry of September 30 the story of Wilson reading aloud several pages from his history on the causes of the War of 1812, drawing a parallel between his own position and that of James Madison. See Charles Seymour, ed., *The Intimate Papers of Colonel House* (4 vols., Boston and New York: Houghton Mifflin Co., 1926–28), I, 303–304; Notter, *Foreign Policy of Woodrow Wilson*, 347–348.

[32] Seymour, *Intimate Papers*, I, 306–307.

[33] Stephen Gwynn, ed., *The Letters and Friendships of Sir Cecil Spring-Rice* (2 vols., Boston: Houghton Mifflin Co., 1929), II, 233–234. Spring-Rice interpreted the entire controversy as arising from the desire of the State Department lawyers to put up a historical fight and thus have themselves quoted in the law books. In a letter to Sir Edward Grey on October 20, he described Lansing as a lawyer accustomed only to handling small claims, with the "lawyer's instinct to make good his case." (p. 238).

[34] Seymour, *Intimate Papers*, I, 307–308. The September 26 dispatch was never used except for information and informal conversations. See Bryan to Page, October 1, 1914, in Savage, *Maritime Commerce*, II, 208–209.

[35] Lansing to Wilson, September 28, 1914, *For. Rel., Lansing Papers*, I, 248–249.

[36] Lansing to Page, September 28, 1914, *For. Rel. 1914 Supp.*, 232–233.

[37] Morrissey, *American Defense of Neutral Rights*, 33–34, terms the entire negotiations a major defeat resulting from inept diplomacy.

[38] Robert Lansing, "The Difficulties of Neutrality," *Saturday Evening Post*, April 18, 1931, 6–7.

[39] Memorandum by Lansing, September 29, 1914, *For. Rel., 1914 Supp.*, 233–235.

[40] Britain soon began an extensive system of effective control over neutral commerce through the embargoes and nonexportation agreements which she forced on the smaller European neutrals.

[41] *For. Rel., Lansing Papers*, I, 249–250.

[42] Page to Bryan, September 29, 1914, *For. Rel., 1914 Supp.*, 233.

[43] Tansill, *America Goes to War*, 148.

[44] Spring-Rice to Lansing, October 1, and Lansing to Spring-Rice, October 2, 1914, Wilson Papers.

[45] Tansill, *America Goes to War*, 152–154.

[46] Spring-Rice to Wilson, October 5, 1914, Wilson Papers.

[47] *For. Rel., 1914 Supp.*, 244–246.

[48] *For. Rel., Lansing Papers*, I, 252–255; Tansill, *America Goes to War*, 154.

[49] Lansing to Page, October 16, 1914, *For. Rel., 1914 Supp.*, 250–252. Grey and Spring-Rice justified the new order in council as absolutely necessary to keep Germany from freely importing through the contiguous neutrals. They appealed to American practices during the Civil War, conveniently overlooking the fact that the

United States had not applied continuous voyage to conditional contraband entering Mexico. Recourse was also made to the soon all too familiar argument that American trade was increasing to the neutrals, thus compensating for loss of the German market. Grey asserted that Britain had to choose between serious controversy with the United States, or else abandon all attempt to curb German importations; hence he urged American acceptance of the proposed order. Wilson was impressed with the sincerity and earnestness of the British explanations. See Spring-Rice to Wilson, October 15, 1914, *For. Rel., Lansing Papers*, I, 250–252.

[50] Tansill, *America Goes to War*, 157–159; James Wilford Garner, "Violations of Maritime Law by the Allied Powers during the World War," *American Journal of International Law*, XXV (1931), 26–49; Hendrick, *W. H. Page*, I, 369–370; and Borchard and Lage, *Neutrality for the United States*, 60–61.

[51] *For. Rel., 1914 Supp.*, 249–250. For a detailed analysis of the American negotiations for the declaration, see Richard W. Van Alstyne, "The Policy of the United States regarding the Declaration of London at the Outbreak of the Great War," *Journal of Modern History*, VII (1935), 434–447.

[52] Josephus Daniels, *Wilson Era: Years of Peace*, 573, claims that Page at least told Wilson his views, but House and Lansing concealed theirs under a mask of neutrality. The record fails to substantiate this thesis, Lansing repeatedly expressing his views to Wilson, especially after the submarine controversy arose.

[53] Lansing, "Difficulties of Neutrality," *Saturday Evening Post*, April 18, 1931, 102–104. Lansing blamed much public criticism of the department on Page's actions, which could not be publicly revealed.

[54] Page to Bryan, October 15, 1914, *For. Rel., 1914 Supp.*, 248–249.

[55] Wilson to Page, October 16, 1914, *For. Rel., 1914 Supp.*, 252–253. House later warned Page of Bryan's and Lansing's dissatisfaction with his conduct, and of the need in the future to avoid unneutral expressions in dispatches to the State Department. See House to Page, December 4, 1914, in Seymour, *Intimate Papers*, I, 312.

[56] Van Alstyne, "Declaration of London," *Journal of Modern History*, VII, 445, terms this an amazing statement in view of Page's forthcoming irregular suggestions to Grey on the *Dacia*. Grey praised Page's advice as ". . . of the greatest value in warning us when to be careful or encouraging us when we could safely be firm." Viscount Grey of Fallodon, *Twenty-Five Years, 1892–1916* (New York: Frederick A. Stokes Co., 1937), 2 vols. in 1, 110.

[57] Page to Wilson, October 21, 1914, in Hendrick, *W. H. Page*, III, 181–187.

[58] Page to House, October 22, 1914, *ibid.*, 380–384. Page accused Lansing of treating Britain like a criminal, by seeking to bind her future actions.

[59] Page to Bryan and Grey to Spring-Rice, October 19, 1914, *For. Rel., 1914 Supp.*, 253–254.

[60] Page to Bryan, October 20, 1914, *ibid.*, 255–256.

[61] *Ibid.*, 257–258.

[62] Grey to Spring-Rice, October 24, 1914, *For. Rel., Lansing Papers*, I, 257; Baker, *Wilson, Life and Letters*, V, 219.

[63] This is the view of Morrissey, *American Defense of Neutral Rights*, 33–34, and Baker, *Wilson, Life and Letters*, V, 217.

[64] See Charles C. Hyde, *International Law Chiefly as Interpreted and Applied by the United States* (2 vols., Boston: Little, Brown & Co., 1922), II, 402–405; James Wilford Garner, *International Law and the World War* (2 vols., London and New York: Longmans, Green & Co., 1920), I, 399–401.

[65] Tansill, *America Goes to War*, 246–247.

[66] The *Adriatic* and *Merion* arrived in September, carrying four and six guns respectively. The British ambassador, to prevent the delay of determining their status, promised that the vessels would depart without their guns. Despite these

assurances, the *Merion* sailed with her guns still mounted. Bryan was inclined to deliver a sharp comment, but Lansing had the note withheld after Spring-Rice protested that it reflected on the honor of the British government. See Bryan to Spring-Rice, September 9, 1914, Lansing Papers.

[67] Lansing to Bryan, September 13, 1914, D/S File 763.72111/158, Archives. This memorandum was based in part on the findings of the State-Navy Neutrality Board.

[68] Wilson to Lansing, September 17, 1914, D/S File, 763.72111/174½, Archives; *For. Rel., 1914 Supp.*, 611–612, 618–620.

[69] Gerard to Bryan, October 15, and Lansing to Gerard, November 7, 1914, *For. Rel., 1914 Supp.*, 613–614. Lansing added to the note the comment that no armed merchantman had visited the United States since September 10, 1914.

[70] Morrissey, *American Defense of Neutral Rights*, 12–14. See also Tansill, *America Goes to War*, 249–250, and Borchard and Lage, *Neutrality for the United States*, 83–90.

[71] Lansing to Wilson, September 12, 1915, *For. Rel., Lansing Papers*, I, 330–331.

[72] Elton Atwater, *American Regulation of Arms Exports* (Washington: Carnegie Endowment for International Peace, Division of International Law, Monograph No. 4, 1941), 2–7.

[73] Atwater, *American Regulation of Arms Exports*, 8; Hyde, *International Law*, II, 572–579; Garner, *International Law*, II, 376–378.

[74] The munitions trade increased from an estimated $49,000,000 in 1913 to approximately $1,000,000,000 in 1916. For a penetrating analysis of the trade, see J. V. Fuller, "The Genesis of the Munitions Traffic," *Journal of Modern History*, VI (1934), 280–293.

[75] Lansing Memorandum on Revision of the Neutrality Laws, December 22, 1914, D/S File 763.72111/1430, Archives.

[76] Lansing to Wilson, October 10, 1914, *For. Rel., Lansing Papers*, I, 113.

[77] Wilson to Bryan, October 13, 1914, *ibid.*, I, 113. Wilson believed that embargoes as a coercive weapon not only were ineffective but led to actual hostilities, as demonstrated in the Jefferson and Madison administrations.—Notter, *Foreign Policy of Woodrow Wilson*, 347–349.

[78] *For. Rel., 1914 Supp.*, 573–574.

[79] See previous citation, Lansing's letter to Wilson, October 10, 1914.

[80] According to a poll taken in early 1915, the majority of opinion, especially in the industrial East, opposed an arms embargo.—*Literary Digest*, June 26, 1915, 225–226.

[81] Morrissey, *American Defense of Neutral Rights*, 17–19; and Atwater, *American Regulation of Arms Exports*, 24–25, 30–31.

[82] Sir Edward Grey, as Wilson, was conscious of the "lessons" of the War of 1812 and particularly feared American recourse to an embargo, which he was convinced would fatally injure the Allied cause. See George Macaulay Trevelyan, *Grey of Fallodon* (London and New York: Longmans, Green & Co., 1937), 306–309.

[83] Grattan, *Why We Fought*, 31.

[84] On the legality of loans by private citizens in a neutral state, see Hyde, *International Law*, II, 744–747, and Garner, *International Law*, II, 408–410.

[85] William Jennings and M. B. Bryan, *Memoirs of William Jennings Bryan* (Philadelphia: John C. Winston Co., 1925), 375–376.

[86] Bryan to Wilson, August 10, 1914, *For. Rel., Lansing Papers*, I, 131–132.

[87] Baker, *Wilson, Life and Letters*, V, 175–176.

[88] Bryan to J. P. Morgan and Co., August 15, 1914, *For. Rel., 1914 Supp.*, 580. Link, *Wilson and the Progressive Era*, 151, asserts that the ban was actually intended to protect the security market, with Bryan wrongly injecting the neutrality issue.

[80] For a detailed discussion of war purchasing, see Richard W. Van Alstyne, "Private American Loans to the Allies, 1914–1916," *Pacific Historical Review*, II (1933), 180–193.

[90] Tansill, *America Goes to War*, 74–78.

[91] Baker, *Wilson, Life and Letters*, V, 185–187.

[92] Lansing to Wilson, October 19, 1914, *For. Rel., Lansing Papers*, I, 134. The American government was most anxious to secure a new commercial agreement that would replace the 1832 agreement, denounced in 1911. The reply to the overture, however, clearly indicated that the requested loan would be improper.

[93] Memorandum by the Russian ambassador, October 20, 1914, *For. Rel., Lansing Papers*, I, 135.

[94] Lansing to Wilson, October 20, 1914, *For. Rel., Lansing Papers*, I, 135.

[95] McRoberts to Lansing, October 23, 1914, *For. Rel., Lansing Papers*, I, 136–137; United States Senate, *Hearings Before the Special Senate Committee on the Investigation of the Munitions Industry*, 74th Cong., 2d sess., 7664–7665. McRoberts emphasized his bank's zealousness in stimulating the "unprecedented and unusual" buying by the Allies.

[96] Lansing to Wilson, October 23, 1914, *For. Rel., Lansing Papers*, I, 137–140.

[97] Lansing Memorandum of a conversation with President Wilson, October 23, 1914, *For. Rel., Lansing Papers*, I, 140.

[98] *For. Rel., 1914 Supp.*, 820.

[99] Lansing has been savagely condemned for his role in the credits arrangement. Tansill, *America Goes to War*, 74–78, marvels at an acting secretary of state personally conveying messages to the agents of the bankers and concludes that this proved he was a tool of Wall Street. See also A. M. Arnett, *Claude Kitchin and the Wilson War Policies* (Boston: Little, Brown & Co., 1937), 138–139. Charles A. Beard, who in a previous work, *The Devil Theory of War* (New York: Vanguard Press, 1936), 42–43, had accused Lansing of making the decision behind Bryan's back, retracted the charge in a subsequent article entitled "New Light on Bryan and the Wilson War Policies," *The New Republic*, June 17, 1936, 177–178. Beard there contends that Bryan knew of and approved the policy on credits, but desirous of maintaining his public reputation as author of the loan policy, deliberately kept his own role shrouded in secrecy and silence.

[100] See Clifton James Child, *The German-American in Politics, 1914–1917* (Madison: University of Wisconsin Press, 1939), 42–63, and Carl Wittke, *German-Americans and the World War* (Ohio Historical Collections, V, 1936), 55–66.

[101] Wilson to Lansing, December 1, 1914 (enclosing Münsterberg's letter of November 10), *For. Rel., Lansing Papers*, I, 161–165.

[102] Lansing to Wilson, December 9, 1914, *For. Rel., Lansing Papers*, I, 166–179.

[103] Memorandum on the Münsterberg Letter, sent to Wilson on December 9, 1914, *For. Rel., Lansing Papers*, I, 167–179. Lansing based his paper in part on the analysis furnished by the State-Navy Neutrality Board, D/S File 763.72111/1074½, Archives.

[104] See Frank L. Owsley, "America and Freedom of the Seas, 1861–1865," in Avery Craven, ed., *Essays in Honor of William E. Dodd* (University of Chicago Press, 1935), 194–256.

[105] Borchard and Lage, *Neutrality for the United States*, 69–71. The *Peterhof* was a British vessel seized in 1863 while on a voyage from London to Matamoros, Mexico. The cargo, mostly military equipment, was allegedly intended for the Confederacy. The Supreme Court ruled, in 1866, that the capture was illegal, as a neutral was entitled to trade with another neutral in conditional and noncontraband. This decision, however, only came after the war and in no way interfered with the Union's war efforts.

106 Baker, *Wilson, Life and Letters*, V, 188.
107 Wilson to Lansing, December 10, 1914, enclosing the telegram from Paul Fuller, Benjamin F. Tracy, and Frederick R. Coudert, *For. Rel., Lansing Papers*, I, 179–180.
108 Lansing to Wilson, December 10, 1914, *ibid.*, I, 180–181.
109 Wilson to Lansing, December 14, 1914, *ibid.*, I, 182.
110 *Ibid.*, I, 166, 184.
111 Bernstorff to Bryan, December 15, 1914, *For. Rel., 1914 Supp.*, 646–647. The reply to Bernstorff, on December 24, noted his admission of the legality of the arms traffic but rejected his argument for the supplying of belligerent warships from American ports. *Ibid.*, 647–649.
112 *For. Rel., Lansing Papers*, I, 115–116, 183.
113 Lansing to Bryan, January 1, 1915, *ibid.*, I, 185–188. Lansing also listed other methods of publicity which could be used.
114 For the text of the Bryan-Stone letter, see *For. Rel., 1914 Supp.*, vii–xiv.
115 Lansing wanted to leave out the reassertion of Bryan's loan ban and insert an explanation of the differences between "credits" and loans, but Bryan refused. See Lansing to Wilson, September 26, 1915, *For. Rel., Lansing Papers*, I, 144–147.

CHAPTER III: THE DIE IS CAST FOR WAR

1 "Consideration and Outline of Policies," July 11, 1915, Confidential Memoranda, Lansing Papers.
2 The term "neutrality" in international law and practice describes the position of a power which in effect promises to treat the belligerents equally and impartially in return for respect of its rights and its desire to remain at peace. In this sense, formal or technical neutrality can be distinguished from a more genuine neutrality of spirit. Many of the American policies were technically neutral and applied equally, in theory, to both belligerent sides. In practice, however, the American interpretations of international law consistently favored the Allies; and, more importantly, the belligerents were not treated equally for while acquiescing in Allied acts, the United States demanded of Germany the fullest observance of international law. Neutrality also requires a *sensitive observance* of abstention and impartiality, which the development of the unilateral war trade hardly supported.
3 For a discussion of naval tactics during the war, see Kenworthy and Young, *Freedom of the Seas*, 68 ff.
4 Turlington, *Neutrality, World War Period*, 4–5, 67.
5 As quoted by James Brown Scott, "Robert Lansing, Counselor for the Department of State," *The American Review of Reviews*, April, 1915, 424–427.
6 "Cruel and Inhuman Acts of War," May 25, 1915, Confidential Memoranda, Lansing Papers. Also see "Future Considerations on Neutrality," May 19, 1915, D/S File 763.72111/1430, Archives. In this series of memoranda, made in anticipation of a postwar Hague conference, Lansing expressed the opinion that a neutral zone or safety belt, within which belligerent actions were prohibited, might be advantageous and possible of achievement; here he clearly foreshadowed the Western-Hemispheric safety belt adopted during the World War II neutrality period. He also felt that joint neutral activity might be considered as a preventive of belligerent excesses in sea warfare. Lansing noted that the submarine should be considered from all angles and that revisions might be required in international law to encompass this new weapon. Entries of December 22 and 30, 1914, January 13, February 12 and 13, 1915, *ibid.*
7 Entry of May 3, 1915, Confidential Memoranda, Lansing Papers.
8 Lansing to Bryan, August 28, 1914, *For. Rel., Lansing Papers*, I, 29–32.
9 Lansing to Bryan, January 23, 1915, *For. Rel., Lansing Papers*, I, 192–194.
10 Lansing to Sir Charles Fitzpatrick, January 9, 1915, Lansing Papers, Lansing

stated that the American note of December 26, 1914, did not "... in any way affect the friendly relations..." existing between the United States and Great Britain. He indicated that the real purpose of the note was to relieve growing industrial resentment in America and thus prevent an increase in bitterness by many Americans toward British maritime acts. He reminded Fitzpatrick that now was the time to be patient and "... trust our friends."

[11] In 1928, Lansing described the harshness of the notes as intended for home consumption only.—Lansing to Julius W. Pratt, June 24, 1928, Lansing Papers.

[12] Robert Lansing, *War Memoirs of Robert Lansing* (Indianapolis: Bobbs-Merrill, 1935), 128–129. This book was not published until 1935, seven years after Lansing's death. The editors state in the preface that the volume was published substantially as left by Lansing. Several historians have questioned the representative character of the *Memoirs*, averring that the book does not collate too well with the State Department's published *Lansing Papers*, which allegedly shows Lansing as more genuinely neutral. Richard W. Leopold, "The Problem of American Intervention, 1917: an Historical Retrospect," *World Politics*, II (April, 1950), 405–425, records these comments on the *War Memoirs* and notes (fn., 414) that no one has yet collated Lansing's *Memoirs* with the article he wrote for the *Saturday Evening Post*, published April 18, 1931, entitled "Difficulties of Neutrality." Upon careful comparison of the article with the *Memoirs* (as well as a study of two other articles appearing in the *Post* June 20 and July 19, 1931, which treat the purchase of the Virgin Islands and Wilson's peace efforts in late 1916), the author fails to find any significant differences. In comparing the *War Memoirs* with the published *Lansing Papers*, it should be kept in mind that the latter, besides being incomplete, relate only to official correspondence. Lansing's Confidential Memoranda show no significant differences in relation to the *War Memoirs*, and in conjunction with the House Papers and Diaries portray Lansing as pro-British and as repeatedly urging war with Germany. Correspondence with Wilson naturally emphasized the submarine as necessitating war, but Lansing's private records indicate his broader political motives. The *War Memoirs*, although not including all his private notes, are representative of Lansing's thoughts during the neutrality period.

[13] Lansing cabled Page on October 28 that the United States was reserving the right to protest any particular article placed on the contraband list. *For. Rel., 1914 Supp.*, 260.

[14] Lansing to Page, October 24, 1914, *ibid.*, 288–289.

[15] See Grey, *Twenty-Five Years*, 110, 115–116. Armin Rappaport, *The British Press and Wilsonian Neutrality* (Stanford University Press, 1951), 5, points out that the English press maintained a careful scrutiny of the government's conduct of the war and raised a storm of criticism and condemnation whenever attempts were made to conciliate the United States by a relaxation of the blockade.

[16] Page to Bryan, October 26, 1914, *For. Rel., 1914 Supp.*, 289.

[17] Lansing to Gerard, October 28, and Gerard to Lansing, November 11, 1914, *For. Rel., 1914 Supp.*, 290–291.

[18] Lansing to Spring-Rice, October 29, 1914, in Savage, *Maritime Commerce*, II, 223–224.

[19] Lansing to Page, October 31, 1914, in Savage, *Maritime Commerce*, II, 224–225; Page to Bryan, November 9, 1914, *For. Rel., 1914 Supp.*, 342–343.

[20] Lansing to Spring-Rice, November 7, 1914, *For. Rel., 1914 Supp.*, 339–340.

[21] Bryan to Spring-Rice, December 24, 1914, in Savage, *Maritime Commerce*, II, 239–240.

[22] "Future Considerations on Neutrality," January 9, 1915, D/S File 763.72111/1430, Archives.

[23] Lansing was sufficiently annoyed by what he regarded as unnecessary British

extensions of the contraband lists to consider one form of "retaliation." Discovering that the British Navy was using the manifests of vessels leaving American ports, published by the Treasury Department, to aid the intercepting and searching of these ships on the high seas, Lansing persuaded Secretary McAdoo to halt the publication. The British government expressed great alarm and accused the United States government of seeking to conceal contraband cargoes destined for Germany. In answer to Page, who requested permission to assure the Foreign Office that the American government was not trying to aid its citizens in the war trade with Britain's enemies, Lansing defended the right of Americans to trade with all the belligerents and refused to consider protests bearing on matters of domestic concern. However, after the working agreements on trade were concluded with Britain, the State Department reversed its stand and again permitted the publication of the manifests. See *For. Rel., 1914 Supp.*, 332–333; Tansill, *America Goes to War*, 181–182.

²⁴ C. Hartley Grattan, *Why We Fought* (New York: Vanguard Press, 1929), 166–167.

²⁵ Page-Bryan correspondence of December 6 and 9, 1914, *For. Rel., 1914 Supp.*, 356–358, 361.

²⁶ For a more detailed discussion, see Ethel C. Phillips, "American Participation in Belligerent Controls, 1914–1917," *American Journal of International Law*, XXVII (1933), 675–693.

²⁷ The involvement of the State Department is clearly revealed by an examination of the correspondence of Lansing's successor as counselor, Frank L. Polk. Polk wrote Lansing September 22, 1915, that he was reminding the British government of the need to handle such trade matters unofficially. On December 13, 1915, Polk sent Colonel House an informal memorandum, for guidance in conversation with the Allies on trade issues, which described the working agreements made with private firms. The Papers of Frank L. Polk, in the House Collection, Yale University Library.

²⁸ Lansing to Sir Charles Fitzpatrick, January 9, 1915, Lansing Papers; Baker, *Wilson, Life and Letters*, V, 233. Morrissey, *American Defense of Neutral Rights*, 43–45, points out that the shippers and exporters were comparatively quiet, as in 1812, and that the most vociferous critics of British sea measures came from groups outside commercial circles. The *Wall Street Journal*, in the December 31 issue, ridiculed assertions that American trade was suffering from British interferences with copper shipments.

²⁹ *For. Rel., Lansing Papers*, I, 257–258.

³⁰ Baker, *Wilson, Life and Letters*, V, 231–232.

³¹ Bryan to Page, December 26, 1914, *For. Rel., 1914 Supp.*, 372–375. In defense of British actions, Garner, "Violations of Maritime Law by the Allies," *Amer. Jour. of Internat. Law*, XXV (1931), 26–49, asserts that consignment of goods "to order," the usual American practice, became a subterfuge concealing the German destination of the detained cargoes. In connection with the detained cargoes, held by Britain on the ground of enemy destination, Richard W. Van Alstyne, *American Diplomacy in Action* (Stanford University Press, 1947), fn., 761–762, prints a letter from David Hunter Miller in February, 1943, wherein Miller states that although the department's notes were sound legally they had little relation to reality. This was because the assumption that the seized American cargoes were American owned was false; actually, the cargoes were purchased by German agents, a fact which only became known later during the 1927 negotiations with Great Britain over the war claims. Miller concluded that the Allies were therefore entitled to seize these cargoes as German owned.

³² The note was so inconclusive that even Page was pleased, terming it an "ad-

mirable" paper. Page to Bryan, December 28, 1914, *For. Rel., Lansing Papers,* I, 259–261.

[33] Great Britain, *Correspondence between His Majesty's Government and the United States respecting the Rights of Belligerents, Command Papers* (London: His Majesty's Stationery Office, 1915), Cd. 7816, 3–6; United States Department of State, *Papers Relating to the Foreign Relations of the United States, 1915, Supplement* (Washington: G.P.O., 1928), 299–302.

[34] Lansing to Wilson, January 11, 1915, *For. Rel., Lansing Papers,* I, 261–265.

[35] Wilson to Bryan, January 14, 1915, *For. Rel., Lansing Papers,* I, 266.

[36] Great Britain, *British and Foreign State Papers, 1914–1920* (London: His Majesty's Stationery Office, 1918–1923), 777–792; *For. Rel., 1915 Supp.,* 324–334.

[37] See Tansill, *America Goes to War,* 566–570.

[38] A. J. Peters to Lansing, October 14, 1914, Lansing Papers.

[39] Lansing to Wilson, October 19, 1914, *For. Rel., Lansing Papers,* I, 104–105. The State-Navy Neutrality Board disagreed with Lansing, holding that such transfers were contrary to established practice.

[40] Wilson to Lansing, November 23, 1914, *For. Rel., Lansing Papers,* I, 107.

[41] Lansing to Wilson, November 23, 1914, *For. Rel., Lansing Papers,* I, 107–109. In a letter to Secretary McAdoo February 25, 1916, Lansing expressed the opinion that if the federal government clearly stated its intention to allow these vessels to be treated as any other neutral vessel by the belligerents, Allied opposition would soon be overcome.—Lansing Papers.

[42] Wilson's Second Annual Address to Congress, December 8, 1914, in Scott, *Wilson's Foreign Policy,* 71–83.

[43] The *Dacia* affair closed the question of transfer of ownership. Certain American citizens purchased the vessel from the Hamburg-American line for one-third its value and dispatched the ship with a cargo of cotton to Germany. British public opinion was greatly aroused by the well-publicized affair, comparing it, inaccurately, to the *Trent* case in the Civil War. As a result of Ambassador Page's suggestion, the British government allowed the French Navy to make the seizure, thus avoiding a further strain on Anglo-American relations. For the correspondence, see *For. Rel., 1915 Supp.,* 674–677, 682–683; *For. Rel., Lansing Papers,* I, 110. Page's role is presented by Hendrick, *W. H. Page,* I, 394–395.

[44] Guichard, *The Naval Blockade,* 25–26.

[45] Spring-Rice to Bryan, November 3, 1914, in Savage, *Maritime Commerce,* II, 226–227.

[46] Gerard to Bryan, February 4, 1915, *For. Rel., 1915 Supp.,* 94.

[47] Lansing to Wilson, February 5, 1915, Wilson Papers; Baker, *Wilson, Life and Letters,* V, 247.

[48] Lansing's draft note to Germany, sent to Wilson on February 6, 1915, Wilson Papers.

[49] The exact origin of the phrase "strict accountability" is obscure. Both Baker, *Wilson, Life and Letters,* V, 247, and Notter, *Foreign Policy of Woodrow Wilson,* 388, agree that Lansing first used the term in a written form but feel that perhaps Wilson had suggested it to the counselor in their previous consultations over the German war zone. There is no particular reason why Wilson should be credited with the phrase, which was not very literary in form, but rather had more of the appearance of a common legal expression.

[50] Lansing to Wilson, February 7, 1915, Wilson Papers. Gerard's copy of the German memorandum arrived on February 10.

[51] Bernstorff to Bryan, February 7, 1915 (received February 8), in Savage, *Maritime Commerce,* II, 264–267.

[52] Baker, *Wilson, Life and Letters,* V, 247–252.

⁵³ Bryan to Gerard, and Bryan to Page, February 10, 1915, *For. Rel., 1915 Supp.*, 98–100, 100–101.

⁵⁴ Grey Memorandum to Page, February 19, 1915, *Command Papers*, Cd. 7816, 20–21.

⁵⁵ Gerard to Bryan, February 17, 1915, *For. Rel., 1915 Supp.*, 112–115.

⁵⁶ Lansing's comments on the newspaper text of the German note of February 16, 1915, *For. Rel., Lansing Papers*, I, 354–361.

⁵⁷ Bryan to Wilson, February 18, 1915, *For. Rel., Lansing Papers*, I, 361–363; Baker, *Wilson, Life and Letters*, V, 256.

⁵⁸ Lansing to Bryan, February 18, 1915, D/S File 763.72111/1691½, Archives.

⁵⁹ Baker, *Wilson, Life and Letters*, V, 256–258.

⁶⁰ Bryan to Page and Gerard, February 20, 1915, *For. Rel., 1915 Supp.*, 119–120. Part of the compromise called for neutral supervision of the distribution of imported foodstuffs in Germany, necessitated by the Allied charge that Germany had nationalized food for military purposes. In January, some American exporters, backed by German money, had purchased the vessel *Wilhelmina* and loaded it with foodstuffs destined for the port of Hamburg. Britain met this test case by seizing the cargo on the ground that the German Federal Council decree of February 1 nationalized food and made no distinction between civilian and military supplies. This ended any real hope for an American trade to Germany in foodstuffs, which, as conditional contraband, was legal under international law. See J. C. Crighton, "The *Wilhelmina*: an Adventure in the Assertion and Exercise of American Trading Rights during the World War," *American Journal of International Law*, XXXIV (1940), 74–88.

⁶¹ Charles Seymour, *American Diplomacy during the World War* (Baltimore: Johns Hopkins University Press, 1934), 59–60.

⁶² Gerard to Bryan, March 1 and 4, 1915, *For. Rel., 1915 Supp.*, 129–130, 132.

⁶³ Page to Bryan, March 13, 1915, *For. Rel., 1915 Supp.*, 140–143.

⁶⁴ Lansing Memorandum on Relations with Germany, February 15, 1915, *For. Rel., Lansing Papers*, I, 367–368.

⁶⁵ Spring-Rice to Bryan, March 1, 1915, *For. Rel., 1915 Supp.*, 127–128.

⁶⁶ For a detailed discussion of continuous voyage and the Allied pseudo blockade, see Herbert W. Briggs, *The Doctrine of Continuous Voyage* (Baltimore: Johns Hopkins University Press, 1926), 122–144.

⁶⁷ Lansing to Bryan, March 2, 1915, *For. Rel., Lansing Papers*, I, 270–271.

⁶⁸ Bryan to Wilson, March 3, and Wilson to Bryan, March 4, 1915, *For. Rel., Lansing Papers*, I, 271–273.

⁶⁹ Bryan to Page, March 5, 1915, *For. Rel., 1915 Supp.*, 132–133.

⁷⁰ Lansing probably knew that Great Britain had pursued a course during the Napoleonic Wars, 1803–1812, designed to exploit belligerent rights for the purpose of capturing the continental market for British commerce.

⁷¹ Lansing Memorandum on the order in council, March 20, 1915, *For. Rel., Lansing Papers*, I, 280–281.

⁷² Wilson to Bryan, March 22, 1915, *For. Rel., Lansing Papers*, I, 281.

⁷³ *For. Rel., Lansing Papers*, I, 278–279.

⁷⁴ Page to Bryan, March 21, 1915, *For. Rel., 1915 Supp.*, 146–147.

⁷⁵ Page to Bryan, March 21, 1915, *For. Rel., 1915 Supp.*, 146–147.

⁷⁶ Lansing to Bryan, March 22, 1915, *For. Rel., Lansing Papers*, I, 281–285.

⁷⁷ Lansing to Bryan, March 23, 1915, *For. Rel., Lansing Papers*, I, 286–287.

⁷⁸ Wilson to Bryan, March 24, 1915, *For. Rel., Lansing Papers*, I, 288–289.

⁷⁹ Lansing Memorandum on the Proposed Note to Great Britain, March 24, 1915, *For. Rel., Lansing Papers*, I, 290–291.

⁸⁰ Bryan to Wilson, March 29, 1915, *For. Rel., Lansing Papers*, I, 295–296. For

the text of the note, see Bryan to Page, March 30, 1915, *For. Rel., 1915 Supp.*, 152–156.

[81] Lansing in a March 25, 1915, interview by Samuel K. Ratcliffe, a London journalist, refuted the charge that America was interested primarily in profits and asserted that the United States had been most "friendly and considerate" toward the Allied Powers. *For. Rel., Lansing Papers*, I, 291–293.

[82] Tansill, *America Goes to War*, 250–251.

[83] The *Frye* case was not as serious as the *Falaba*. This case concerned the sinking of an American vessel, the *William P. Frye*, by the converted German cruiser *Prinz Eitel Friedrich*. Lansing wrote Joseph Tumulty, Wilson's secretary, on March 12, 1915, that he had been reserving the 1828 Commercial Treaty with Prussia for just such an event.—Wilson Papers.

[84] Lansing's views accorded with past general practices under international law. However, the question of the submarine, with its limited space and vulnerability to attack, had not been provided for. See John Bassett Moore, *A Digest of International Law* (8 vols., Washington: G.P.O., 1906), VII, 485–487, 518; Garner, *International Law*, I, 355, 364–367; Hyde, *International Law*, II, 482–485.

[85] For a contrary view, see Borchard and Lage, *Neutrality for the United States*, 182–183; and John Bassett Moore, "America's Neutrality Policy," New York *Times*, May 16, 1937, Magazine Section, p. 1. Only three Americans lost their lives through German attacks on American vessels up to February, 1917.

[86] Lansing to Bryan, April 2, 1915, *For. Rel., Lansing Papers*, I, 365–366.

[87] Bryan to Wilson, April 2, 1915, Bryan Letter Books, Manuscripts Division, Library of Congress. Chandler P. Anderson, one of the department's legal advisers, supported Bryan's views, contending that Thrasher's death was merely incidental to the destruction of the *Falaba;* hence the proper course for the State Department was to present claims for compensation.—Link, *Wilson and the Progressive Era*, 162–163. Anderson noted in his diary on April 5 that Lansing felt that public opinion would not be satisfied with weak measures in a case involving American life, hence there could be no debate of the legality of killing nonbelligerents.—See Edward H. Buehrig, *Woodrow Wilson and the Balance of Power* (Bloomington: Indiana University Press, 1955), 24–26.

[88] Wilson to Bryan, April 5, 1915, *For. Rel., Lansing Papers*, I, 369.

[89] For an interesting analysis stressing Wilson's psychological make-up, see Richard Hofstadter, *The American Political Tradition and the Men Who Made It* (New York: Alfred A. Knopf, 1949), Chapter X, 234–278.

[90] See Wilson's letter to Bryan of April 3, 1915, accepting Lansing's contention about the duty of the government to defend its citizens' right to travel on belligerent vessels, *For. Rel., Lansing Papers*, I, 368.

[91] Lansing's Draft Instructions to Gerard, *For. Rel., Lansing Papers*, I, 370–371.

[92] Lansing to Bryan, April 5, 1915, *For. Rel., Lansing Papers*, I, 369–370.

[93] Bryan to Wilson, April 6, 1915, *For. Rel., Lansing Papers*, I, 372.

[94] Wilson to Bryan, April 6, 1915, *For. Rel., Lansing Papers*, I, 372–373.

[95] Bryan to Wilson, April 7, 1915, *For. Rel., Lansing Papers*, I, 374–376.

[96] Baker, *Wilson, Life and Letters*, V, 266–267.

[97] Lansing to Wilson, April 10, 1915, *For. Rel., Lansing Papers*, I, 377.

[98] Wilson to Bryan, April 22 and 28, 1915, *For. Rel., Lansing Papers*, I, 377–378, 380. In the April 28 letter Wilson did indicate that he still had some doubts as to the proper course to adopt.

[99] Bernstorff to Bryan, April 4, 1915, *For. Rel., 1915 Supp.*, 157–158.

[100] Lansing to Bryan, April 11, 1915, *For. Rel., Lansing Papers*, I, 117–118.

[101] Rustem Bey had made a statement September 8, 1914, to the Washington *Star*, flailing the general attitude of Americans toward Turkey and drawing a parallel

between the Armenian massacres and the American lynchings of Negroes in the South and the "watercures" of rebellious natives in the Philippines. Lansing recommended his expulsion, but because of the delicate situation of Christians within Turkey, Wilson turned this advice down. Happily, however, Rustem Bey concluded that his usefulness as ambassador was destroyed and so departed at his own volition. See *For. Rel., Lansing Papers*, I, 68–72, 74.

[102] William Phillips to Lansing, April 17, 1915, *For. Rel., Lansing Papers*, I, 119.

[103] Bryan to Bernstorff, April 21, 1915, *For. Rel., 1915 Supp.*, 160–162.

[104] Lansing to Bryan, May 1, 1915, *For. Rel., Lansing Papers*, I, 381–382.

[105] Lansing to Bryan, May 3, 1915, *For. Rel., Lansing Papers*, I, 383–384.

[106] Lansing to Bryan, May 5, 1915, *For. Rel., Lansing Papers*, I, 384–385. For a few days Lansing was virtually willing to ignore the *Falaba* for the clearer issue of the American vessels.

[107] See the previously cited memorandum of February 15, 1915, *For. Rel., Lansing Papers*, I, 367–368.

[108] "Consideration and Outline of Policies," July 11, 1915, Confidential Memoranda, Lansing Papers. This memorandum was published in Lansing's *War Memoirs*, 19–21, with the exception of the section speculating on a possible future German-Russian-Japanese military coalition.

[109] See Squires, *British Propaganda*, 74–75.

[110] The *Lusitania* did not arouse a unanimous demand for war.—Seymour, *American Diplomacy During the World War*, 94–95.

[111] Although he had earlier been pessimistic about the military value of an American war intervention, Lansing had now apparently revised his estimates.

[112] Lansing, *War Memoirs*, 28.

[113] For a critical presentation of Lansing's role during the *Lusitania* crisis, see Tansill, *America Goes to War*, 290–321; Borchard and Lage, *Neutrality for the United States*, 136–137.

[114] Bryan felt that nations behaved similarly to individuals, and that the way to stop hostilities between either was simply to separate them and allow time for the cooling of passions. For a discussion of Bryan's beliefs and ideas, see Merle E. Curti, *Bryan and World Peace* (Smith College Studies in History, XVI, Nos. 3 and 4, 1931), 113–116.

[115] Lansing to Bryan, May 9, and Wilson to Bryan, May 11, 1915, *For. Rel., Lansing Papers*, I, 387–388, 392.

[116] Bryan to Wilson, May 9, 1915, *For. Rel., Lansing Papers*, I, 386. Solicitor Cone Johnson wrote Lansing on May 15, "Babies and bullets ought not to go on the same ship."—Lansing Papers.

[117] A. J. Peters to Lansing, May 8, 1915, *For. Rel., Lansing Papers*, I, 385–386. (For a later report, see 428–436.)

[118] Considerable doubt has long existed on this question. Thomas A. Bailey, "The Sinking of the *Lusitania*," *American Historical Review*, XLI (1935), 54–73, has concluded, after a thorough study of the documents, that the vessel was probably unarmed and deserved to be classified as a belligerent merchantman on a regular trans-Atlantic passenger trip.

[119] Lansing Memorandum on the *Lusitania*, May 10, 1915, *For. Rel., Lansing Papers*, I, 389–390. On May 17, Lansing sent Wilson an elaboration of the above memorandum on alternatives, 407–408.

[120] Lansing to Bryan, May 10, 1915, *For. Rel., Lansing Papers*, I, 391–392.

[121] Bryan to Wilson (undated, probably May 12, 1915), *For. Rel., Lansing Papers*, I, 392–394.

[122] Lansing to Bryan, May 12, 1915, enclosing the draft note to Germany, *For. Rel., Lansing Papers*, I, 394–398.

[123] Bryan to Gerard, May 13, 1915, *For. Rel., 1915 Supp.*, 393–396.

[124] Bryan to Wilson, May 12, 1915, *For. Rel., Lansing Papers*, I, 400–401.

[125] Wilson to Bryan, May 13, 1915, *For. Rel., Lansing Papers*, I, 402.

[126] For an account of this episode, see Baker, *Wilson, Life and Letters*, V, 340–341; Tansill, *America Goes to War*, 300–304; James Kerney, *The Political Education of Woodrow Wilson* (New York and London: The Century Co., 1926), 376; Paxton Hibben and C. Hartley Grattan, *The Peerless Leader, William Jennings Bryan* (New York: Farrar and Rinehart, 1929), 344–345; M. R. Werner, *Bryan* (New York: Harcourt, Brace & Co., 1929), 246; and David Lawrence, *The True Story of Woodrow Wilson* (New York: George H. Doran Co., 1924), 145–146. Lansing may have intimated an intention to resign if the tip or statement desired by Bryan was issued, feeling that otherwise his position would be undermined within the department. Entries of May 12–13, 1915, Lansing Desk Diary.

[127] Wilson to Bryan, May 13, 1915, *For. Rel., Lansing Papers*, I, 403.

[128] Bryan to Wilson and Wilson to Bryan, May 13, 1915, *For. Rel., Lansing Papers* I, 403–404.

[129] Lansing to Bryan, May 14, 1915, *For. Rel., Lansing Papers*, I, 404–405. Lansing claimed that the Executive had no authority to forbid travel on belligerent vessels, but admitted that an official warning would be almost as effective as a prohibition.

[130] Wilson to Bryan, May 14, 1915, *For. Rel., Lansing Papers*, I, 406–407.

[131] Lansing to Bryan, May 15, 1915, *For. Rel., Lansing Papers*, I, 296–299.

[132] Seymour, *Intimate Papers*, I, 443.

[133] Wilson to Bryan, May 20, 1915, *For. Rel., Lansing Papers*, I, 411.

[134] Memorandum of a conversation between Spring-Rice and Lansing, May 27, 1915, D/S File 763.72112/12931, Archives.

[135] See *For. Rel., Lansing Papers*, I, 408–410, 413–416.

[136] Lansing, *War Memoirs*, 30–31. Lansing partly blamed the Dumba incident for the unsatisfactory nature of the forthcoming German reply on the *Lusitania*. This was hardly justified, as Bryan was widely known both as a pacifist and as an almost negligible factor in the State Department.

[137] Curti, *Bryan and World Peace*, 205–207, agrees with Lansing that Dumba was too astute to fabricate an entirely false story, and stresses Bryan's deep agitation as causing him to be over-confiding to a foreign diplomat. Curti, however, maintains that the episode had little effect on the German *Lusitania* note, since the repudiation of the Dumba affair was known several days in advance and both Dumba and Bernstorff were reporting on the danger of a break in relations.

[138] Gerard to Bryan, May 29, 1915 (received May 31), in Savage, *Maritime Commerce*, II, 327–330.

[139] Lansing to Bryan, June 1, 1915, *For. Rel., Lansing Papers*, I, 417.

[140] Lansing to Bryan, June 2 and 3, 1915, *For. Rel., Lansing Papers*, I, 418, 426. Charles Warren, assistant attorney-general, agreed with Lansing on the armed ship question. Lansing to Warren, June 7, 1915, Lansing Papers.

[141] *For. Rel., Lansing Papers*, I, 426.

[142] Lansing to Dr. E. M. Gallandot of Hartford, Conn., June 2, 1915, Lansing Papers.

[143] David F. Houston, *Eight Years with Wilson's Cabinet* (2 vols., Garden City, N.Y.: Doubleday, Page & Co., 1926), I, 137; Seymour, *Intimate Papers*, II, 5–6.

[144] Bryan to Wilson, June 2, 1915, *For. Rel., Lansing Papers*, I, 419–420.

[145] Bryan to Wilson, June 3, 1915, *For. Rel., Lansing Papers*, I, 422–426, 427–428.

[146] Lansing's Desk Diary, Lansing Papers.

[147] Lansing to Bryan, June 5, 1915, *For. Rel., Lansing Papers*, I, 438–439.

[148] Lansing to Bryan, enclosing the draft note, June 7, 1915, *For. Rel., Lansing*

Papers, I, 441–444; Lansing Memorandum on suggested changes in the draft note, June 6, 1915, D/S File 763.72/1864½, Archives. Lansing was assisted by L. H. Woolsey, the department's legal adviser.

[149] Bryan sent Wilson on June 4 the opinions of Senator Thomas S. Martin and Representative Henry D. Flood that, in their judgment, the Congress and the public were opposed to war over the *Lusitania.* The two Democrats desired a curb against travel on belligerent vessels.—*For. Rel., Lansing Papers,* I, 436–437.

[150] Wilson to Bryan, June 5 and 7, 1915, *For. Rel., Lansing Papers,* I, 438, 439.

[151] Lansing, "Difficulties of Neutrality," *Sat. Eve. Post,* April 18, 1931, 6–7.

[152] Lansing, *War Memoirs,* 30.

[153] See McMaster, *The United States in the World War,* I, 107–109; Rappaport, *British Press and Wilsonian Neutrality,* 41.

[154] Lansing to Gerard, June 9, 1915, *For. Rel., 1915 Supp.,* 436–438.

CHAPTER IV: LANSING ENTERS THE CABINET

[1] Baker, *Wilson, Life and Letters,* V, 167, emphasizes Wilson's dependence on Lansing by noting that on one day, September 17, 1914, the President wrote Lansing eight different letters on various neutrality problems.

[2] See the sketch of Lansing in *Current Opinion,* April, 1915, 239–240, quoting editorials of various newspapers on Lansing's functions within the State Department.

[3] Lansing to William Dulles, November 13, and to George V. S. Camp, November 14, 1914, Lansing Papers. In these letters Lansing defended Bryan as a hardworking, conscientious person, fully in touch with the foreign situation.

[4] Oswald Garrison Villard, then a Washington newspaper correspondent and an administration supporter, related in his memoirs an amusing story demonstrating Bryan's sensitivity toward his special relationship with Lansing. Bryan had great difficulty in his interviews with the press, fumbling for answers and constantly badgered by the slanted questions coming from the more hostile newspaper reporters. After one of these painful episodes, Bryan solicited aid from Villard, who after a few days' cogitation, advised the secretary to let Lansing handle the press. Bryan misunderstood Villard to mean that he should resign and rushed to the White House and demanded to know if Villard were reflecting Wilson's views. Villard finally managed to clear the matter.—Oswald Garrison Villard, *Fighting Years, Memoirs of a Liberal Editor* (New York: Harcourt, Brace & Co., 1939), 273–275.

[5] Entry of June 24, 1915, House Diary, Papers of Edward M. House, Historical Manuscripts Division, Yale University Library.

[6] Lansing to Bryan, June 9, 1915, Lansing Papers.

[7] Bryan to Lansing, June 28, 1915, Lansing Papers.

[8] Entry of June 13, 1915, House Diary.

[9] Edith Bolling Wilson, *My Memoir* (Indianapolis: Bobbs-Merrill, 1939), 63–64, relates that Wilson, while on a cruise on the *Mayflower,* told her that he was seriously considering Lansing for the position, because of Lansing's experience and his relations with John Watson Foster, whom Wilson respected greatly and hoped would help guide Lansing along the right path. Wilson was also influenced by Tumulty, his secretary, who favored Lansing because of the latter's pro-Allied sympathies. See John H. Blum, *Joe Tumulty and the Wilson Era* (Boston: Houghton Mifflin Co., 1951), 98.

[10] Kerney, *Political Education of Wilson,* 356–357.

[11] New York *Times,* June 16, 1915.

[12] Lansing believed, incorrectly, that House had desired the appointment of Walter Hines Page as secretary of state. House did write Page in June, 1915, that he pre-

ferred the latter's appointment; however, his Diary indicates that he never thought seriously of Page, and in a letter to Mrs. Lansing on April 19, 1931, he denied that he had ever favored Page for the post.—House Papers.

[13] Entry of June 14, 1915, House Diary.

[14] See above, entry of June 14, 1915, House Diary.

[15] House to Wilson, June 16, 1915, Wilson Papers. This message disproves the assertion that Lansing secured the office of secretary by currying favor with Colonel House. In addition to House's statement that he hardly knew Lansing, a study of the papers of both individuals indicates that there had been no real contact before July, 1915.

[16] Josephus Daniels, then secretary of the navy, states that the Cabinet favored Newton D. Baker or Frank L. Polk for the position. Daniels was a harsh critic of Lansing, accusing him of following "dollar diplomacy," with no "consecration to peace or to democracy." These reactions were largely the result of Daniels' close friendship with Bryan, and also reflected his resentment of the critical remarks Lansing later made in reference to Wilson at the Paris Peace Conference. See Daniels, *Wilson Era, Years of Peace*, 436–437, 441–442.

[17] See the accounts in McAdoo, *Crowded Years*, 338, and Houston, *Eight Years in Wilson's Cabinet*, I, 141. In a letter to Julius W. Pratt, June 24, 1928, Lansing commented that both McAdoo and Houston had desired the secretaryship of state, but that Wilson had cleverly "clipped their wings." Lansing believed that his later relations with Houston were affected by this incident, feeling that Houston, holding an inferior Cabinet post, retained much envy and jealousy.—Lansing Papers.

[18] Lansing, *War Memoirs*, 15–17.

[19] *Congressional Record*, 64th Cong., 1st sess., 238.

[20] Lansing's appointment as secretary of state received favorable press comment as a nonpolitical act that might well set a precedent for future administrations.— *Literary Digest*, June 26, 1915, 1545–1546; *The Nation*, July 1, 1915, 7–8. A New York *Times* editorial for June 25, 1915, praised the new Cabinet as a sharper appearing body with a "Lansing-Garrison-Lane face."

[21] James Brown Scott, "The Secretaryship of State and Mr. Lansing," *The Atlantic Monthly*, Vol. 116, October, 1915, 568–572.

[22] Lansing, *War Memoirs*, 368–369.

[23] Sketch of Jean Jules Jusserand, May, 1916, Sketch Book, Lansing Papers. Lansing took advantage of a month's absence from his official duties, caused by ill-health, to record his impressions of a number of the diplomats then in Washington.

[24] Jean Jules Jusserand, *Le Sentiment Amércain pendant la Guerre* (Paris: Payot, 1931), 39. Jusserand relates (pp. 45–46) an interesting story involving Lansing. The ambassador received word that Mlle. Jeanne de Bettignies had been condemned to death by the German authorities for aiding Allied prisoners-of-war to escape. Jusserand quickly sought from Lansing an appointment to see President Wilson, in order to secure an American appeal for mercy. Lansing's reaction was typical of his realistic approach, inquiring why there was so much concern over one woman when many men were being killed every day in the war. Upon Jusserand's passionate appeal, during which he drew parallels involving the heroism of Southern women during the Civil War, Lansing was touched and arranged the requested conference.

[25] Jusserand's wit and humor were well demonstrated by his remark made upon signing one of Bryan's peace treaties: "There! At last there will end for all times the ceaseless wars between France and the United States. What a happy hour!"— quoted by Lansing, Jusserand Sketch, Lansing Papers.

[26] Lansing to Jusserand, November 12, 1924, Lansing Papers.

[27] Sketch of Sir Cecil Spring-Rice, May, 1916, Sketch Book, Lansing Papers. Though Lansing was most contemptuous in his estimation of Spring-Rice, the British ambassador thought highly of Lansing, considering him most able, sympathetic, and charming in manners. See Spring-Rice to Sir Edward Grey, February 12, 1916, in Gwynn, *Letters of Spring-Rice*, II, 313–314.

[28] See Lansing to Bryan, March 11, 1915, *For. Rel., Lansing Papers*, I, 210–211.

[29] Entry of December 15, 1915, House Diary.

[30] Polk to Wilson, July 11, 1916, Wilson Papers.

[31] Lansing, *War Memoirs*, 170.

[32] Lansing, *War Memoirs*, 167–169.

[33] See House's account of a conversation with Page on September 25, 1916, in Seymour, *Intimate Papers*, II, 318–319.

[34] Sketch of Count V. Macchi di Cellere, May, 1916, Sketch Book, Lansing Papers.

[35] Sketch of George Bakhmeteff, May, 1916, Sketch Book, Lansing Papers.

[36] As quoted by Lansing, *ibid.*

[37] House was never thoroughly at ease with Bernstorff in the way that he was with Jusserand and Spring-Rice—Seymour, *Intimate Papers*, I, 338.

[38] Sketch of Count Johann von Bernstorff, May, 1916, Sketch Book, Lansing Papers.

[39] Johann von Bernstorff, *My Three Years in America* (New York: Chas. Scribners & Sons, 1920), 156–157. Bernstorff (p. 328) felt that it was useless to talk with Lansing since Wilson decided all important matters. Part of this impression was probably the result of Lansing's extreme distrust, manifested in a reluctance to discuss matters with the Ambassador.

[40] See below, pp. 122–123.

[41] Sketch of Dr. Constantin Theodor Dumba, May, 1916, Sketch Book, Lansing Papers.

[42] Dumba employed Archibald, an American citizen, to deliver dispatches to Vienna through the Allied lines. He was caught by the British authorities and his papers impounded.

[43] Lansing considered Zwiedinek a most likable although mediocre person. Sketch of Baron Erich Zwiedinek, May, 1916, Sketch Book, Lansing Papers.

[44] Lawrence, *The True Story of Woodrow Wilson*, 78. William Phillips, an assistant secretary under Lansing and a long-term career officer, has commented, "...I don't think Wilson ever really cared for him, although he respected him."— "The Reminiscences of William Phillips," MS., Oral History Research Office, Columbia University.

[45] Wilson had earlier practiced law, but had soon come to view the legal profession as boring and overly materialistic. See Arthur S. Link, *Wilson, the Road to the White House* (Princeton University Press, 1947), 6–7, 10.

[46] Hofstadter, *American Political Tradition*, 236.

[47] Entry of March 28, 1916, House Diary.

[48] Excerpt, House to Mrs. Lansing, April 19, 1931, House Papers.

[49] Robert Lansing, *The Peace Negotiations, a Personal Narrative* (Boston and New York: Houghton Mifflin Co., 1921), 38–43.

[50] See Frederick Bausman, *Facing Europe* (New York and London: Century Co., 1926), 203–205. Brand Whitlock comments that social relations between Mrs. Lansing and the second Mrs. Wilson were strained also.—Allan Nevins, ed., *The Letters and Journal of Brand Whitlock* (New York: D. Appleton-Century Co., 1936), II, 587.

[51] Lansing, "Difficulties of Neutrality," *Sat. Eve. Post*, April 18, 1931, 106.

[52] On August 6, 1915, a group of prominent pacifists, led by Jane Addams, Lillian D. Wald, Dr. Aletta Jacobs of Holland, and Emily Balch, presented to

Lansing a petition for an immediate peace mediation offer by the United States and proposed that an unofficial committee be established to facilitate the negotiations. Lansing rejected the suggestion as impractical and further informed the women that international morality was a delusion, that no nation could be trusted to keep its pledge whenever questions of survival were involved. The pacifists were shocked at Lansing's "unspeakably lower moral level" and left convinced that the Secretary was too pro-Ally to aid any peace efforts. Wilson approved of Lansing's rejection of the peace proposals.—See Villard, *Fighting Years,* 297–298; Baker, *Wilson, Life and Letters,* VI, 122–123; and Lansing to Wilson, August 18, 1915, *For. Rel., Lansing Papers,* I, 13–14.

[53] Baker, *Wilson, Life and Letters,* VI, 120.

[54] Lansing, "Difficulties of Neutrality," 106; *War Memoirs,* 349–350. Lansing modified his published opinions of Wilson, as his private notes differ considerably.

[55] "The Mentality of Woodrow Wilson," November 20, 1921, Confidential Memoranda, Lansing Papers. Wilson's biographer, Link, regards this as a good analysis of the president.—*Wilson and the Progressive Era,* 32.

[56] Link, *Wilson and the Progressive Era,* 32.

[57] "Interview with Colonel House at the Biltmore," October 11, 1920, Confidential Memoranda, Lansing Papers. Lansing credited House with many of the plans adopted by Wilson, especially Article X of the League of Nations Covenant.

[58] See Lane to George W. Lane, November 28, 1919, in A. W. Lane and L. H. Well, eds., *The Letters of Franklin K. Lane* (Boston and New York: Houghton Mifflin Co., 1922), 322.

[59] Notter, *Origins of the Foreign Policy of Woodrow Wilson,* 248–249, attributes the use of personal representatives to Wilson's earlier distrust of the holdover Republican appointees abroad and to his belief that informal observers were more efficient than career men in the foreign service.

[60] Entry of June 25, 1915, House Diary.

[61] George Sylvester Viereck, *The Strangest Friendship in History, Woodrow Wilson and Colonel House* (New York: Liveright, Inc., 1932), 78, observes that House opposed Wilson's tentative decision to replace Lansing in 1917 with Newton D. Baker because House feared that a new secretary might not be sympathetic with his unofficial role.

[62] House to Lansing, July 7, 1915, House Papers.

[63] House to Lansing, July 29, 1915, House Papers.

[64] Lansing to House, July 30, 1915, House Papers.

[65] Polk was appointed counselor August 26, 1915. Burleson and Tumulty had desired the appointment of A. Mitchell Palmer, but Lansing had rejected Palmer as too conceited; House agreed. Lansing really wanted John W. Davis, an old friend, but Wilson refused on the grounds that Davis was needed in the Justice Department, and in any case was too conservative. See Lansing to House, July 9, 26, and 30, and House to Lansing, July 30, 1915, House Papers.

[66] Lansing, *War Memoirs,* 362–363. Polk's wit and quickness of decision complemented Lansing's legal qualities. See William Phillips, *Ventures in Diplomacy* (Boston: the Beacon Press, 1952), 74.

[67] For example, Long wrote House on July 2, 1917, that there were several matters in the Department that he would like to talk over. Again, on March 23, 1917, Long wrote, "I am taking advantage of the intimation I have had that I might write to you frankly." Long attempted to aid House in disposing of the department's patronage.—Breckinridge Long Papers, Manuscripts Division, Library of Congress.

[68] Entry of October 13, 1915, House Diary.

[60] Entry of November 28, 1915, House Diary.

[70] Entry of March 28, 1916, House Diary.

[71] House to Lansing, May 30, 1916, House Papers.

[72] House to Charles Seymour, March 24, 1928, as quoted in Seymour, *Intimate Papers*, IV, 21–22.

CHAPTER V: THE LUSITANIA AND THE ARABIC

[1] "Embarrassment of Action in the *Arabic* Case," August 25, 1915, Confidential Memoranda, Lansing Papers.

[2] Lansing, *War Memoirs*, 24.

[3] Lansing, *War Memoirs*, 25.

[4] "Consideration and Outline of Policies," July 11, 1915, Confidential Memoranda, Lansing Papers.

[5] Lansing believed that the German government sought to keep Mexico in a "state of ferment and anarchy," in order to menace the United States and thereby distract her attention from the European War.—"The Conference in Regard to Mexico," October 10, 1915, Confidential Memoranda, Lansing Papers.

[6] Although this study is not directly concerned with the Latin American policy of the Wilson administration, it should be noted that this policy was one founded squarely on the accepted concepts of the national interest.—See Dexter Perkins, *Hands Off: A History of the Monroe Doctrine* (Boston: Little, Brown & Co., 1941), 266–271. Although Lansing was generally the one concerned with Latin America, since the president was occupied with domestic and European affairs, Wilson was cognizant of the general trend there, and he specifically approved the secretary's course on a number of vital issues. In regard to the Monroe Doctrine, Lansing had drafted a memorandum (June 11, 1914, D/S File 710. 11/185½, Archives) which frankly described the doctrine as a unilateral policy based on the superior power of the United States and dedicated primarily to its own national security; the counselor then asked if the doctrine should not be revised so as to prohibit not only European political penetration but financial and economic infiltrations as well. After becoming secretary, Lansing forwarded this memorandum to the president, once more urging the national interest and safety in regard to Latin America. Wilson accepted the paper as a guide, for its arguments ". . . seem to me unanswerable."— Wilson to Lansing, November 29, 1915, D/S File 710.11/189, Archives. Lansing also defended the occupation of Haiti in 1915 and the purchase of the Danish West Indies on the grounds of the national interest versus a German threat.—Lansing to Wilson, August 7, 1915, D/S File 838.00/1275c, Archives; and Lansing, "Drama of the Virgin Island Purchase," New Yor *Times*, magazine section, July 19, 1931. Also see Charles Callan Tansill, *The Purchase of the Danish West Indies* (Baltimore: Johns Hopkins Press, 1932), 474–483. Clearly, Wilson accepted the argument of the national interest in regard to Latin America.

[7] In general, the American press, although considering the German note of May 28 unsatisfactory, did not advocate a resort to war. Similarly, few newspapers viewed the June 9 American note as presaging hostilities.—*Literary Digest*, L (June 12 and June 19, 1915), 1383–1384, 1452–1453.

[8] Bernstorff, *My Three Years in America*, 160.

[9] Gerard to Lansing, July 5, 1915, *For. Rel., 1915 Supp.*, 461.

[10] Lansing to Gerard, July 6, 1915, *For. Rel., 1915 Supp.*, 462.

[11] Lansing to Wilson, July 7, 1915, *For. Rel., Lansing Papers*, I, 453.

[12] Wilson to Lansing, July 7, 1915, *For. Rel., Lansing Papers*, I, 453–454.

[13] Lansing to Gerard, July 8, 1915, *For. Rel., 1915 Supp.*, 462.

[14] Gerard to Lansing, July 8, 1915, in Savage, *Maritime Commerce*, II, 351–355.

[15] *Ibid.*

[16] Lansing to Gerard, July 14, 1915, D/S File 763.72/1940, Archives.

[17] Lansing to Wilson, July 12, 1915, *For. Rel., Lansing Papers,* I, 455.

[18] For example, Chandler P. Anderson, one of the department's legal advisers, sent Lansing on July 17 a memorandum which concluded that nothing short of fear of war would induce Germany to meet the American demands.—Memorandum by C. P. Anderson, dated July 13, 1915, Wilson Papers.

[19] Cone Johnson, Memorandum of July 14, 1915, D/S File 763.72/1968½, Archives, and Memorandum of July 16, 1915, *For. Rel., Lansing Papers,* I, 460–463.

[20] Lansing to Wilson, July 14, 1915, *For. Rel., Lansing Papers,* I, 457–458.

[21] Lansing, "Observations on the German Note of July 8," dated July 14, 1915, D/S File 763.72/1969½A, Archives. Lansing enclosed these notes in his letter to Wilson, cited above.

[22] *Ibid.*

[23] Wilson to Lansing, July 13, 1915, *For. Rel., Lansing Papers,* I, 455–456.

[24] Lansing to Wilson, July 15, 1915, *For. Rel., Lansing Papers,* I, 458–459.

[25] "Draft Reply to the German Note of July 8,"—July 16, 1915, D/S File 763.72/1940, Archives. The draft was sent to Wilson on July 19.

[26] Lansing's redraft of the American Note, July 19, 1915, D/S File 763.72/1940, Archives.

[27] Lansing to Wilson, July 21, 1915, *For. Rel., Lansing Papers,* I, 463–464.

[28] Wilson to Lansing, July 21, 1915, *For. Rel., Lansing Papers,* I, 464.

[29] For the text of the note to Gerard, see *For Rel., 1915 Supp.,* 480–482. A number of congratulatory telegrams on the note were sent to Lansing, including one from Harry Pratt Judson, president of the University of Chicago, on July 24.—Lansing Papers.

[30] Lansing, *War Memoirs,* 37–39. The Allies reacted bitterly to the threat which they believed implicit in the phrase "freedom of the seas." See Rappaport, *The British Press and Wilsonian Neutrality,* 49.

[31] Lansing, *War Memoirs,* 40–41; Bernstorff, *My Three Years in America,* 166–167.

[32] Presumably, Wilson intended "freedom of the seas" to mean the exemption of all private property from capture. See Seymour, *Intimate Papers,* I, 406–407.

[33] Lansing to Gerard, July 18, 1915, *For. Rel., 1915 Supp.,* 476–477.

[34] Bernstorff, *My Three Years in America,* 163–164.

[35] Lansing later asserted that only German "stupidity" in renewing the submarine war saved the situation for the Allies.—*War Memoirs,* 41.

[36] Lansing to Wilson, June 12, 1915, *For. Rel., Lansing Papers,* I, 299–300.

[37] Spring-Rice to Grey, July 22, 1915, *British and Foreign State Papers,* 1915, CIX, 826.

[38] *For. Rel., 1915 Supp.,* 472–474.

[39] Page wrote House on August 4, 1915, that the lawyers in the State Department were ruining America's only valuable friendship, that of Great Britain, and concluded that, "I sometimes wish there were not a lawyer in the world."—Hendrick, *W. H. Page,* II, 54–56.

[40] Grey to Page, July 23, 1915, *Command Papers.* Cd. 8233, 11–14; *For. Rel., 1915 Supp.,* 168–171.

[41] Wilson to Lansing, July 29, 1915, *For. Rel., Lansing Papers,* I, 302–303.

[42] Page to Lansing, August 13, 1915, Lansing Papers.

[43] Borchard and Lage, *Neutrality for the United States,* 206.

[44] Lansing to Spring-Rice, July 28, 1915, *For. Rel., 1915 Supp.,* 490; Lansing to Wilson, July 28, 1915, *For. Rel., Lansing Papers,* I, 301–302.

[45] See Baker, *Wilson, Life and Letters,* V, 377–378; Tansill, *America Goes to War,* 221–223.

[46] Wilson to Lansing, August 9, 1915, as printed by Baker, *Wilson, Life and Let-*

ters, V, 378. Lansing wrote House on July 30 that he hoped the british offer would quiet the cotton agitation in the southern states.—House Papers.

⁴⁷ Page to Lansing, August 24, 1915, *For. Rel., 1915 Supp.*, 174. Sir Edward Grey did not want to place cotton on the contraband list, but he was forced to by public opinion.

⁴⁸ For an account of the revocation of the loan ban policy, see Paul Birdsall, "Neutrality and Economic Pressures, 1914–1917," *Science and Society*, III (Spring, 1939), 217–228; Van Alstyne, "Private American Loans to the Allies," *Pac. Hist. Rev.*, II, 180–193, Tansill, *America Goes to War*, 103–105; Peterson, *Propaganda for War*, 99–102. W. P. G. Harding, *The Formative Period of the Federal Reserve System* (Boston: Houghton Mifflin, 1925), 41, presents little information on this problem.

⁴⁹ McAdoo to Lansing, August 23, 1915, *For. Rel., Lansing Papers*, I, 141–142; United States Senate, *Hearings on the Munitions Industry*, 74th Cong., 2d sess., 7865.

⁵⁰ Hamlin to Lansing, August 24, 1915, *For. Rel., Lansing Papers*, I, 143; Senate, *Hearings on the Munitions Industry*, 7864. John Bassett Moore wrote Benjamin Strong of the Federal Reserve Bank in New York City, on August 25, that though the munitions trade was legal, it was "confessedly unneutral," and consequently the Federal Reserve Banks, with governmental connections, should observe caution in handling financial matters involved in the war trade.—*Hearings*, 7775–7778.

⁵¹ *For. Rel., Lansing Papers*, I, 142–143. Forgan listed four alternative replies.

⁵² Lansing to Wilson, August 25, 1915, *For. Rel., Lansing Papers*, I, 143.

⁵³ Wilson to Lansing, August 26, 1915, *For. Rel., Lansing Papers*, I, 144.

⁵⁴ Lansing to Wilson, September 6, 1915, *For. Rel., Lansing Papers*, I, 144–147.

⁵⁵ *Ibid.*

⁵⁶ *Ibid.*

⁵⁷ Wilson to Lansing, September 7, 1915, *For. Rel., Lansing Papers*, I, 147; Baker, *Wilson, Life and Letters*, V, 381–382.

⁵⁸ For an account of the raising of the first Anglo-French loan, see Thomas W. Lamont, *Henry P. Davison; the Record of a Useful Life* (New York and London: Harper Bros., 1933), 186–200. The public stand of the government was reported by the New York *Times*, September 14, 1915, as "assurances had been received that if it were arranged as a straight credit arrangement, no objection would be offered by the State Department on the score of a possible violation of neutrality."

⁵⁹ McAdoo wrote Lansing September 11, 1915, that since the loans to be floated demanded a favorable public opinion, Great Britain could be persuaded to modify sharply the blockade and other objectionable practices.—Lansing Papers. The secretary, however, failed to exploit the opportunity.

⁶⁰ Van Alstyne, "Private American Loans to the Allies, 1914–1916," *Pac. Hist. Rev.*, II, 193.

⁶¹ Penfield to Lansing, July 2, 1915, *For. Rel., 1915 Supp.*, 790–793.

⁶² Lansing, *War Memoirs*, 55.

⁶³ Lansing to Wilson, July 8, 1915, *For. Rel., Lansing Papers*, I, 122–123.

⁶⁴ Lansing, *War Memoirs*, 56–57.

⁶⁵ Lansing, *War Memoirs*, 58–59.

⁶⁶ Wilson to Lansing, August 5, 1915, *For. Rel., Lansing Papers*, I, 125.

⁶⁷ Lansing to Wilson, August 6, 1915, *For. Rel., Lansing Papers*, I, 125–127.

⁶⁸ Wilson to Lansing, August 9, 1915, *For. Rel., Lansing Papers*, I, 127.

⁶⁹ Lansing to Penfield, August 12, 1915, *For. Rel., 1915 Supp.*, 794–798. Lansing later wrote that Wilson's habit of making verbal changes in the department's notes resulted in the popular misconception that most state papers were written personally by the president. Lansing felt that Wilson was not intellectually conceited in

making such changes, but rather sought the most careful expression possible.—*War Memoirs*, 57–58.

[70] Bryan to Lansing, August 16, 1915, *For. Rel., Lansing Papers*, I, 128.

[71] House to Lansing, August 17, 1915, *For. Rel., Lansing Papers*, I, 128.

[72] Baron Stephen Burian, *Austria in Dissolution* (New York: George H. Doran Co., 1925), 118.

[73] Millis, *Road to War*, 207–208, 214–215.

[74] Lansing, *War Memoirs*, 76–77.

[75] Entry of August 10, 1915, House Diary. Colonel House recorded that Wilson's order was not very complimentary to the two secretaries, but noted that McAdoo seemed agreeable about the entire affair.

[76] Tansill, *America Goes to War*, 355–357.

[77] Lansing, *War Memoirs*. 75–76.

[78] Lansing to McAdoo, August 14, and McAdoo to Lansing, August 18, 1915, *Hearings on the Munitions Industry*, 10139–10140. Funds were then being arranged through Federal Reserve Banks for loans to cotton growers, with the purpose of thus stabilizing the market price.

[79] Lansing to Wilson, August 20, 1915, *For. Rel., Lansing Papers*, I, 467–468.

[80] Wilson to Lansing, August 21, 1915, *For. Rel., Lansing Papers*, I, 468. House wrote Wilson on August 22 and recommended a break in diplomatic relations with Germany.—Seymour, *Intimate Papers*, II, 29–31.

[81] Lansing to Wilson, August 24, 1915, *For. Rel., Lansing Papers*, I, 470–471.

[82] The president replied that Lansing's letters closely corresponded to his own thoughts on the matter. Wilson to Lansing, August 26, 1915, *For. Rel., Lansing Papers*, I, 471.

[83] "Embarrassment of Action in the *Arabic* Case," August 25, 1915, Confidential Memoranda, Lansing Papers.

[84] Bernstorff to Lansing, August 24, 1915, *For. Rel., 1915 Supp.*, 524. Most of the *Arabic* negotiations were conducted in Washington, and Ambassador Gerard was largely ignored by the State Department. Gerard soon complained that Lansing did not bother even to keep him informed of developments.—Gerard to House, September 20, 1915, in Seymour, *Intimate Papers*, II, 42.

[85] Lansing to Gerard, August 10, 1915, in Savage, *Maritime Commerce*, II, 367–368.

[86] Bernstorff to the German foreign secretary, August 24, 1915, *For. Rel., 1915 Supp.*, 525.

[87] Lansing to Wilson, August 26, 1915, *For. Rel., Lansing Papers*, I, 471–473.

[88] Lansing, *War Memoirs*, 47.

[89] Bernstorff, *My Three Years in America*, 177–179.

[90] See General Erich George A. S. von Falkenhayn, *The German General Staff and its Decisions, 1914–1916* (New York: Dodd, Mead & Co., 1920), 177–178.

[91] Gerard to Lansing, August 25, 1915 (received August 26), *For. Rel., 1915 Supp.*, 526.

[92] Bernstorff to Lansing, September 1, 1915, *For. Rel., 1915 Supp.*, 530–531; Bernstorff, *My Three Years in America*, 177. Lansing suspected that Bernstorff had exceeded his instructions, and credited the ambassador with thus preventing deterioration of the situation.—*War Memoirs*, 48–49.

[93] Tansill, *America Goes to War*, 369–370.

[94] On September 8, Bernstorff sent Lansing a note claiming that the *Hesperian* probably hit a mine.—*For. Rel., Lansing Papers*, I, 476. Gerard reported, September 11, that the Foreign Office refused to discuss the sinking, as no American lives were lost.—*For. Rel., 1915 Supp.*, 545.

[95] Lansing's position was weakened by the *Baralong* incident of August 19. The

U-27 had halted the British vessel *Nicosian* and was allowing the crew and passengers to remove themselves to safety when the *Baralong* approached the scene, flying the American flag. The *Baralong*, one of the first of the Q-boats disguised as a merchantman, ran up the British flag at the last moment and proceeded to destroy the *U-27*. According to the affidavits of Americans on the *Nicosian*, the *Baralong* ruthlessly shot survivors of the *U-27* in the water. Lansing later protested this misuse of the American flag.—See *For. Rel., 1915 Supp.*, 576–577.

⁹⁶ Bernstorff to Lansing, September 8, 1915, *For. Rel., 1915 Supp.*, 545.

⁹⁷ Gerard to Lansing, September 7, 1915, *For. Rel., 1915 Supp.*, 539–540.

⁹⁸ Lansing to Wilson, September 11, 1915, *For. Rel., Lansing Papers*, I, 478–480.

⁹⁹ For a brief account, see Millis, *Road to War*, 215–216.

¹⁰⁰ Page to Lansing, September 1 and 3, 1915, *For Rel., 1915 Supp.*, 936–941.

¹⁰¹ Wilson to Lansing, September 3, 1915, *For. Rel., Lansing Papers*, I, 80.

¹⁰² Bernstorff, *My Three Years in America*, 198.

¹⁰³ Lansing to Wilson, September 7, 1915, *For. Rel., Lansing Papers*, I, 80–82. In an enclosed memorandum, Dumba defended the plans for strikes among Austro-Hungarian nationals employed in munitions plants as necessary to prevent these laborers from violating Austrian laws and because they were inhumanly exploited by their employers in an "unscrupulous sweating system." Dumba concluded with a request that the Department of Labor coöperate with his endeavor to relieve the misery of these workers!

¹⁰⁴ For an account of the Lansing-Dumba interview on September 7, see Lansing, *War Memoirs*, 64–66, and Constantin Dumba, *Memoirs of a Diplomat*, transl. by I. F. D. Morrow (Boston: Little, Brown & Co., 1932), 263–267. Dumba admitted that his activities, though not criminal, justified his recall; he only resented the peremptory manner in which the recall was made.

¹⁰⁵ Lansing to Penfield, September 8, 1915, *For. Rel., 1915 Supp.*, 933–934.

¹⁰⁶ Lansing defended his refusal to allow Dumba to cable Vienna an explanation of the affair on the grounds that ". . . it would have been unneutral to defeat the British authorities in their successful interception of his correspondence."—Lansing to Polk, September 20, 1915, Lansing Papers.

¹⁰⁷ House wrote Wilson on September 17, 1915, that Bernstorff believed the Dumba recall had convinced Berlin of the seriousness of the situation.—Seymour, *Intimate Papers*, II, 39–40.

¹⁰⁸ Lansing to Wilson, September 13, 1915, *For. Rel., Lansing Papers*, I, 480–482. Lansing also sent, at Bernstorff's request, a statement of facts concerning the *Arabic* to the German Foreign Office.— *For. Rel., 1915 Supp.*, 547–548.

¹⁰⁹ Bernstorff to Lansing, October 2, 1915, *For. Rel., Lansing Papers*, I, 483.

¹¹⁰ Lansing, "Memorandum of a Conversation with Bernstorff," October 5, 1915, *For. Rel., Lansing Papers*, I, 485–486.

¹¹¹ Bernstorff to Lansing, October 5, 1915, *For. Rel., 1915 Supp.*, 560.

¹¹² The *Frye* case was settled during these negotiations, on the basis that no American vessel should be destroyed unless it carried absolute contraband, and, in no case, without safety provisions for the crew and passengers. The United States asserted that the provisions of safety were not discharged by merely allowing escape in open lifeboats.—Lansing to Gerard, October 12, 1915, in Savage, *Maritime Commerce*, II, 388–390.

¹¹³Bernstorff reported to his Government that Wilson and the State Department were desirous of letting the *Lusitania* case drift.—Bernstorff, *My Three Years in America*, 191, 193.

¹¹⁴ When Bernstorff, in early September, originally gave the German pledge not to sink passenger liners without warning, Page reported that British leaders and the press viewed the American government's acceptance of the assurance as a sign of

weakness. Wilson and Lansing realized that the British government at least hoped that the submarine embroilment would preclude an American protest of the Allied blockade. Lansing concluded from Page's letter that Great Britain desired to have the United States "pull their chestnuts out of the fire."—Page to Lansing, September 8, 1915, in Savage, *Maritime Commerce*, II, 382–383; Lansing to Wilson, September 9, 1915, *For. Rel., Lansing Papers*, I, 476.

[115] See Bryan to Page, March 30, 1915, *For. Rel., 1915 Supp.*, 152–156.

[116] Turlington, *Neutrality, World War Period*, 18–20, 56–57, points out that if the presumption of enemy destination were applied to American goods, it certainly should have been applicable to British exports. Whereas American exports to the European neutrals were valued at, in millions of dollars, 165 in 1913, 151 in 1914, and 340 in 1915, British exports increased from 218 in 1913 to 323 in 1915. Thus while American exports to the northern neutrals were increasing, British exports were also expanding and partly at the price of restricting American trade. The British blockade was a commercial one, dedicated to supplanting Germany in the neutral trade. France, on the other hand, tended to agree with the State Department that the blockade should be strictly enforced, and was ready to sacrifice her own commercial interests in order to isolate Germany completely. See Guichard, *The Naval Blockade*, 68; Consett, *Triumph of Unarmed Forces*, 48–50.

[117] Tansill, *America Goes to War*, 518–519.

[118] House defended the note, in a stormy session with Spring-Rice, as a necessary move which would not ruin Anglo-American relations.—Seymour, *Intimate Papers*, II, 75–78.

[119] Lansing to Wilson, October 9, and Wilson to Lansing, October 21, 1915, *For. Rel., Lansing Papers*, I, 303, 304.

[120] Lansing to Wilson, October 21, 1915, *For. Rel., Lansing Papers*, I, 304–305. The secretary also wished to be free to press the forthcoming expulsion of Von Papen and several other members of the German embassy staff.

[121] Lansing to Page, October 21, 1915, *For. Rel., 1915 Supp.*, 578–601.

[122] As quoted in Baker, *Wilson, Life and Letters*, V, 384.

[123] Notter, *Origins of the Foreign Policy of Woodrow Wilson*, 450.

[124] House to Sir Edward Grey, October 17, 1915, in Seymour, *Intimate Papers*, II, 90–91.

[125] Page to House, November 12, 1915, in Hendrick, *W. H. Page*, II, 69–80.

[126] Rappaport, *British Press and Wilsonian Neutrality*, 72–73, points out that the British public was puzzled by the American inability to perceive the correctness of the Allied cause, and therefore they tended to conclude that Americans were more concerned with profits than with the inhumanity of German warfare.

[127] Grey to House, November 11, 1915, in Seymour, *Intimate Papers*, II, 79–80.

CHAPTER VI: PUBLIC OPINION AND THE SUBMARINE

[1] "Thoughts Suggested by the Rumor that Germany Intends to Renew Ruthless Submarine Warfare," January 9, 1916, Confidential Memoranda, Lansing Papers.

[2] Seymour, *American Diplomacy during the World War*, 109. Bernstorff, *My Three Years in America*, 213–214, misinterpreted Lansing's motives, which he thought were primarily concerned with a money indemnity.

[3] Tansill, *America Goes to War*, 382–383.

[4] Lansing to Wilson, November 2, 1915, *For. Rel., Lansing Papers*, I, 488–489.

[5] Lansing to Wilson, November 11, and Wilson to Lansing, November 17, 1915, *For. Rel., Lansing Papers*, I, 489–490.

[6] Lansing, Memorandum of an Interview with Bernstorff, November 17, 1915, *For. Rel., Lansing Papers*, I, 490–491.

[7] Bernstorff reported to his government, December 2, 1915, that though Lansing believed Congress might declare war, neither he nor Colonel House shared that fear. Bernstorff did feel that there was a rising tide of anti-German feeling in America and that the *Lusitania* case should be compromised in some way.—*My Three Years in America*, 215–216.

[8] Tansill, *America Goes to War*, 384–389. The German execution of the English nurse, Edith Cavell, accused of aiding the escape of Allied prisoners in Belgium, proved to be a sensational propaganda asset and it was used to brand Germany as inhumane and utterly ruthless. See Peterson, *Propaganda for War*, 61–62.

[9] Lansing wrote Wilson on November 17, 1915, that L. W. Nieman of the Milwaukee *Journal* reported that the Middle West was beginning to favor an entry into the war.—D/S File 763.72/2271½A, Archives.

[10] Entry of December 20, 1915, Lansing Desk Diary.

[11] Lansing to Wilson, November 19, 1915, *For. Rel., Lansing Papers*, I, 491–493.

[12] Wilson to Lansing, November 21, 1915, *For. Rel., Lansing Papers*, I, 493.

[13] Morrissey, *American Defense of Neutral Rights*, 120–121.

[14] Lansing, *War Memoirs*, 87–90. In an interview with the Austrian chargé, Baron Zwiedinek, Lansing stated that the act could only be by Germany, since it was too brutal for the "chivalrous and kindly" Austrians.

[15] Lansing to Wilson, December 3, 1915, *For. Rel., Lansing Papers*, I, 497–498.

[16] Wilson to Lansing, December 5, 1915, *For. Rel., Lansing Papers*, I, 498; Lansing to Penfield, December 6, 1915, *For. Rel., 1915 Supp.*, 623–625. Colonel House, who had recommended that diplomatic relations be severed, described the note as "Lansingesque" and although he agreed with its general tenor, felt that Wilson was too casual in letting the note go forward exactly as drafted by the secretary.—Entry of December 8, 1915, House Diary.

[17] Lansing, Memorandum of a Conversation with Zwiedinek, December 11, 1915, *For. Rel., Lansing Papers*, I, 93–94, and December 13, 1915, Wilson Papers.

[18] Lansing proposed in a letter to Wilson on November 20, 1915, that a central clearance agency be set up within the State Department to coördinate intelligence work.—*For. Rel., Lansing Papers*, I, 218–221. The jealousies of the several executive departments prevented adoption of his plan, although some coördination was achieved through regular meetings of the heads of the State, Navy, War, Justice, Treasury, and Commerce departments. The State Department established its own intelligence section in April, 1916, organized under Leland Harrison.—Lansing, *War Memoirs*, 84.

[19] Lansing to Wilson, November 29, 1915, *For. Rel., Lansing Papers*, I, 83–84. Von Nuber's recall was not requested, as Zwiedinek succeeded in persuading Lansing to overlook this particular case.—*War Memoirs*, 81–83.

[20] Wilson to Lansing, November 29, 1915, *For. Rel., Lansing Papers*, I, 84. Colonel House had advised the president, on November 21, to break relations with Austria and to dismiss the "obnoxious underlings" of the German embassy.—Seymour, *Intimate Papers*, II, 47.

[21] Wilson to Lansing, and Lansing to Wilson, December 2, 1915, *For. Rel., Lansing Papers*, I, 87–88.

[22] Lansing, Memorandum of a Conversation with Bernstorff, December 1, 1915, *For. Rel., Lansing Papers*, I, 86–87. On December 2, House wrote Lansing that Bernstorff deserved some consideration and help, to which Lansing replied that Bernstorff appeared ". . . more fearful of his own skin than the skins of his Military and Naval *Attaches*."—*ibid.*, I, 88–89.

[23] Bernstorff to Lansing, November 25, 1915, *For. Rel., Lansing Papers*, I, 496–497.

[24] Lansing to Bernstorff, December 15, and Bernstorff to Lansing, December 16,

204 *Notes to pages 112–115*

1915, *For. Rel., Lansing Papers*, I, 498. Bernstorff sought to transfer the negotiations to Colonel House.—see *For. Rel., Lansing Papers*, I, 494–496.

[25] Penfield to Lansing, December 15, 1915, *For. Rel., 1915 Supp.*, 638–639.

[26] Lansing to Wilson, December 17, 1915, *For. Rel., Lansing Papers*, I, 499–500; Lansing to Penfield, December 19, 1915, *For. Rel., 1915 Supp.*, 647–648.

[27] Lawrence, *The True Story of Woodrow Wilson*, 180 .

[28] Lansing, Memorandum of a Conversation with Zwiedinek, December 21, 1915, *For. Rel., Lansing Papers*, I, 503–504. Lansing was encouraged by a report from Gerard on December 24 that Germany would do much to prevent an American break with Austria. Gerard felt that the moment was propitious to force settlement on the *Lusitania*.—*For. Rel., 1915 Supp.*, 650.

[29] Penfield to Lansing, December 23, 1915, *For. Rel., Lansing Papers*, I, 505.

[30] Wilson to Lansing, December 27, 1915, *For. Rel., Lansing Papers*, I, 506–507.

[31] Lansing feared that if arbitration were accepted with Austria, Germany would demand it for settlement of the *Lusitania* case.—*War Memoirs*, 93–94.

[32] Lansing to Wilson, December 21, 1915, *For. Rel., Lansing Papers*, I, 221–222. Wilson replied, December 24, that he felt Stone was reflecting views other than his own.

[33] Lansing, *War Memoirs*, 92–93. Lansing was also concerned with the domestic political aspect of the situation presented by Stone, as his defection would leave the Republican leader, Senator Henry Cabot Lodge, in a commanding position.

[34] Lansing to Wilson, December 28, 1915, *For. Rel., Lansing Papers*, I, 507–508.

[35] Wilson to Lansing, December 29, 1915, *For. Rel., Lansing Papers*, I, 508–509. Evidently Lansing had previously assured the president that a break in diplomatic relations with Austria would not necessarily mean war, for Wilson tartly asked the secretary what new evidence had caused him to change his earlier opinion.

[36] Penfield to Lansing, December 29, 1915, *For. Rel., 1915 Supp.*, 655–658.

[37] Lansing, Memorandum of a Conversation with Bernstorff, December 31, 1915, *For. Rel., Lansing Papers*, I, 510–511.

[38] Lansing, *War Memoirs*, 94–97. The *Persia* mounted a 4.7" gun on the stern.

[39] Notter, *Origins of the Foreign Policy of Woodrow Wilson*, 464. In the week of December 6–13, ten resolutions were introduced in Congress to curtail or halt the traffic in munitions. Lansing sought and secured the aid of Senator Lodge, Republican leader in Congress, in mustering support to defeat the embargo proposals. Wilson later expressed his appreciation to Lodge for his aid in preventing a major congressional revolt.—Henry Cabot Lodge, *The Senate and the League of Nations* (New York: Charles Scribner's Sons, 1925), 65–69.

[40] Baker, *Wilson, Life and Letters*, VI, 156–157.

[41] Lansing, *War Memoirs*, 111–112.

[42] "Thoughts Suggested By The Rumor That Germany Intends To Renew Ruthless Submarine Warfare," January 9, 1916, Confidential Memoranda, Lansing Papers. Lansing recorded his views that the American people lacked the racial unity possessed by most countries, and were a heterogeneous mixture of peoples with few of the qualities of nationality. The only factor capable of unifying such a diverse people was, in his view, the political principles of democracy and law underlying the American system of government, and as Lansing felt that German absolutism threatened democracy everywhere, he hoped that the American people would soon realize that "... it is safer and surer and wiser for us to be one of many enemies than to be in the future alone against a victorious Germany."

[43] Lansing, *War Memoirs*, 101.

[44] Tansill, *America Goes to War*, 416–418, concludes that Lansing's explanation of the *modus vivendi* was a little too subtle.

[45] Morrissey, *American Defense of Neutral Rights*, 106–107, proceeds on the as-

sumption that Lansing was making a genuine effort to solve the submarine problem, and consequently she criticizes the secretary for oversimplification of the issue.

⁴⁶ Lansing, *War Memoirs*, 101, 109–110.

⁴⁷ Morrissey, *American Defense of Neutral Rights*, 201–202, points out that in the fall of 1914, before the armed ship question arose, German naval leaders decided that the submarine could not operate efficiently enough to halt English imports if the submarines were bound by the rules of cruiser warfare.

⁴⁸ Sir Archibald Hurd, *The Merchant Navy* (3 vols., London: John Murray, 1921–1929), III, 110–111. Hurd supplies a table demonstrating that in the period from January 1, 1916, to January 25, 1917, three hundred and ten armed vessels were attacked by submarines and whereas seventy-four were sunk, mostly by torpedo, two hundred and thirty-six escaped. Conversely, of three hundred and two unarmed vessels similarly attacked, two hundred and thirty-five were sunk, mostly by gunfire, and only sixty-seven escaped.

⁴⁹ By December 25, 1915, seven hundred and sixty-six British merchant vessels had been armed. This practice was steadily carried forward, with one thousand seven hundred and forty-nine armed by September 18, 1916.—Hurd, *Merchant Navy*, II, 237–240.

⁵⁰ Hurd, *Merchant Navy*, II, 243. The *Waimana* was detained until September 22, when she was allowed to proceed after removal of the gun.

⁵¹ Lansing to Wilson, September 12, 1915, *For. Rel., Lansing Papers*, I, 330–331. The Joint State-Navy Neutrality Board supported the secretary's position.—Tansill, *America Goes to War*, 412–413.

⁵² Wilson to Lansing, September 13, 1915, *For. Rel., Lansing Papers*, I, 331–332.

⁵³ Lansing wrote Wilson on August 30, 1915, in regard to the *Baralong* incident: "To me the conduct of the British Naval Authorities is shocking. . . ." The incident was protested as a misuse of the American flag, but to no avail. See *For. Rel., Lansing Papers*, I, 39; *For. Rel., 1915 Supp.*, 576–577, 604–606.

⁵⁴ Gerard to Lansing, December 10, 1915, *For. Rel., 1915 Supp.*, 652–654. Additional information on the number of British vessels which had fired on submarines was dispatched by Gerard on February 14, 1916.—United States Department of State, *Papers Relating to the Foreign Relations of the United States, 1916, Supplement* (Washington: G.P.O., 1929), 187–198.

⁵⁵ *Congressional Record*, 64th Cong., 1st sess., 495.

⁵⁶ Millis, *Road to War*, 255–256; Notter, *Foreign Policy of Woodrow Wilson*, 473.

⁵⁷ Lansing to Wilson, January 2, 1916, *For. Rel., Lansing Papers*, I, 332–333.

⁵⁸ Lansing to Wilson, January 7, 1916, *For. Rel., Lansing Papers*, I, 334–335.

⁵⁹ Wilson to Lansing, January 10, 1916, *For. Rel., Lansing Papers*, I, 335.

⁶⁰ Lansing to Wilson, January 17, 1916, D/S File 763.72/2355b, Archives.

⁶¹ Lansing to Wilson, January 17, 1916, *For. Rel., Lansing Papers*, I, 336.

⁶² Wilson to Lansing, January 17, 1916, *For. Rel., Lansing Papers*, I, 336.

⁶³ Lansing to Spring-Rice, January 18, 1916, *For. Rel., 1916 Supp.*, 146–148.

⁶⁴ Seymour, *Intimate Papers of Colonel House*, II, 210–214.

⁶⁵ Jusserand to Lansing, January 22, 1916, *For. Rel., 1916 Supp.*, 149–150.

⁶⁶ Page to Lansing, January 25, 1916, *For. Rel., 1916 Supp.*, 151–152.

⁶⁷ When the proposal became publicly known, the British press echoed this distrust of Germany.—Rappaport, *British Press and Wilsonian Neautrality*, 81–82.

⁶⁸ Bernstorff recognized that coercive measures against the Allies were impossible, and in testimony before a *Reichstag* committee, October 22 and November 14, 1919, he pointed out that the United States was dependent upon the British merchant marine.—Carnegie Endowment for International Peace, Division of International Law, *Official German Documents Relating to the World War* (2 vols., New York and London: Oxford University Press, 1923), I, 252–253; II, 736.

[69] Notter, *Origins of the Foreign Policy of Woodrow Wilson*, 473; Tansill, *America Goes to War*, 419.

[70] Lansing, Memorandum of a Conversation with Bernstorff, January 25, 1916, *For. Rel., Lansing Papers*, I, 523–525. Although Grey's reply had not yet arrived, Lansing had received Jusserand's unfavorable preliminary memorandum and realized that the Allies would reject his *modus vivendi*.

[71] Lansing to Wilson, January 27, 1916, *For. Rel., Lansing Papers*, I, 338.

[72] Seymour, *Intimate Papers*, II, 84–85.

[73] Seymour, *Intimate Papers*, II, 85; Notter, *Origins of the Foreign Policy of Woodrow Wilson*, 447. Wilson, however, told House in September of 1915 that he had never been sure that the United States would not have to enter the war, especially if Germany appeared likely to win.

[74] Entry of October 14, 1915, House Diary.

[75] Lansing to Wilson, November 24, 1915, *For. Rel., Lansing Papers*, I, 495–496. Baker, *Wilson, Life and Letters*, VI, 129, 133–134.

[76] House to Wilson, January 16, 1916, in Seymour, *Intimate Papers*, II, 133–134. In letters to Wilson on January 30 and February 3, House requested that a diplomatic break over the *Lusitania* case be postponed until his return to the United States, and expressed the fear that otherwise his agreement with Grey would be upset.—*ibid.*, II, 146–147. On the other hand, Lansing also complained of interference, writing Wilson on January 31 that House's meddling with the *Lusitania* negotiations showed "the danger of attempting to negotiate at two ends of the line."—*For. Rel., Lansing Papers*, I, 529–530.

[77] Seymour, *Intimate Papers*, II, 218–219.

[78] House to Lansing, February 5, 1916, D/S File 763.72/2418½, Archives. Lansing had cabled House on February 2 that he felt the proposed *modus vivendi* was a "fair and humane" solution of the submarine problem.—*For. Rel., Lansing Papers*, I, 339.

[79] House to Lansing, February 14, 1916, *For. Rel., Lansing Papers*, I, 342. House collected written arguments against the *modus vivendi* from Lord Bryce and other British leaders, and presented them to Wilson upon his return from Europe.—Seymour, *Intimate Papers*, II, 192, 211.

[80] House presented the memorandum to Wilson and Lansing on March 6, 1916.—Seymour, *Intimate Papers*, II, 199. Lansing later wrote that Wilson's modification of the agreement with Grey, which was changed to state that the United States would "probably" intervene if Germany refused to accept the settlement resulting from the projected peace conference, made the agreement valueless to the Allies.—Lansing, "When Wilson Failed as Peacemaker," *Saturday Evening Post*, June 20, 1931, 10.

[81] Entry of March 4, 1916, House Diary.

[82] Lansing to Wilson, January 7, and Lansing, Memorandum of a Conversation with Bernstorff, January 10, 1916, *For. Rel., Lansing Papers*, I, 515–516, 516–517. Bernstorff handed the secretary a memorandum by the German Foreign Office which stated that the German government expected the United States to take energetic measures toward the establishment of "freedom of the seas," in view of Germany's modification of submarine warfare to conform with American desires.

[83] Bernstorff to Lansing, January 22, 1916, *For. Rel., Lansing Papers*, I, 519–520.

[84] Lansing to Wilson, January 24, 1916, *For. Rel., Lansing Papers*, I, 521–522.

[85] Wilson to Lansing, January 24, 1916, *For. Rel., Lansing Papers*, I, 522.

[86] Lansing, Memorandum of a Conversation with Bernstorff, January 25, 1916, *For. Rel., Lansing Papers*, I, 523–525.

[87] Lansing, Memorandum of a Conversation with Bernstorff, January 26, 1916, *For. Rel., Lansing Papers*, I, 525.

[88] Lansing, *War Memoirs*, 112–113.

⁸⁹ Lansing, Memorandum of March 6, 1916, D/S File 763.72/2479½, Archives.

⁹⁰ Zwiedinek to the Austro-Hungarian Foreign Office, January 26, 1916, *For. Rel., Lansing Papers*, I, 337.

⁹¹ Lansing, Memorandum on Zwiedinek's Cable, January 26, 1916, *For. Rel., Lansing Papers*, I, 337.

⁹² Lansing, *War Memoirs*, 113–114. Lansing stated that Bernstorff even speculated as to Lansing's probable successor.

⁹³ Sketch of Baron Erich Zwiedinek, November, 1916, Sketch Book, Lansing Papers.

⁹⁴ The German Foreign Office to the German Embassy, February 6, 1916, *For. Rel., Lansing Papers*, I, 339.

⁹⁵ Lansing, Memorandum of a Conversation with Zwiedinek, February 9, 1916, *For. Rel., Lansing Papers*, 341–342. The chargé claimed that since the cable had been sent to the State Department and then dispatched after censorship, he had the right to assume that the cable's accuracy was approved by the department. Lansing, of course, denied this assertion and stated that the department only censored such messages for military information.—Zwiedinek to Lansing, February 24, and Lansing to Zwiedinek, February 25, 1916, D/S File 763.72/2415½, Archives.

⁹⁶ House wrote Wilson on March 12 that Bernstorff asserted that the German government had become involved in the armed-ship question at the instigation of the United States.—Seymour, *Intimate Papers*, II, 224–225. On March 14, Gerard reported that officials of the German government believed that Lansing had favored the German side of the controversy, until overruled by President Wilson.—*For. Rel., Lansing Papers*, I, 680–681. Arthur Zimmermann, then the German undersecretary for foreign affairs, testified before a *Reichstag* investigating committee on November 6, 1919, that he had concluded from Lansing's proposed *modus vivendi* that Germany could reach an understanding with the United States, and that at least the February 10 proclamation in regard to armed ships would not be taken as an excuse for severance of diplomatic relations.—*Official German Documents*, I, 496–497.

⁹⁷ Gerard to Lansing, February 10, 1916, enclosing the German Memorandum (dated February 8), *For. Rel., 1916 Supp.*, 163–166.

⁹⁸ On February 4, Bernstorff had submitted to Lansing a statement on the *Lusitania* case which met most of the American demands, and assumed liability for the American lives lost on the vessel. Although the statement did not clearly recognize the illegality of the sinking of the *Lusitania*, both Wilson and Lansing were willing to accept it as the best obtainable under the circumstances. The case was not formally closed, however, because of the February 10 proclamation on armed ships. After the armed-vessel question was removed by the forthcoming *Sussex* pledge, the *Lusitania* negotiations were not revived and remained in quiescence throughout the remaining months of American neutrality. See Lansing, *War Memoirs*, 156–157; Bernstorff, *My Three Years in America*, 220–223.

⁹⁹ Morrissey, *American Defense of Neutral Rights*, 109–110.

¹⁰⁰ McMaster, *The United States in the World War*, I, 242.

¹⁰¹ Bernstorff to Lansing, February 28, 1916, *For. Rel., 1916 Supp.*, 181–182.

¹⁰² Morrissey, *American Defense of Neutral Rights*, 110–111; Tansill, *America Goes to War*, 474–475.

¹⁰³ Annin, *Woodrow Wilson*, 217–219; Gratten, *Why We Fought*, 328. Lansing attributed the release of the text to the British Foreign Office or one of the Allied embassies in Washington. Evidently the secretary had been overly optimistic and had hoped that the proposal could be kept secret indefinitely, thereby enabling the State Department to act freely without public embarrassment.—Lansing, Memorandum of March 6, 1916, D/S File 763.72/2479½, Archives.

[104] On February 8, the German chancellor, Theobald von Bethmann-Hollweg, released a press statement on the *Lusitania* negotiations, in which he asserted that the United States was demanding too much of the German government (admission of liability for the *Lusitania*) and that though his government would not accept a humiliating settlement, it would strive to avoid war with the United States. Lansing replied, in a press interview on February 10, that the American government only desired a fair settlement and that such press releases as that by Bethmann-Hollweg merely increased the tension and gave the impression that Germany was trying to force the issue. *For. Rel., 1916 Supp.*, 161–162. During this same period, Lansing received reports from Gerard that high officials within the German Foreign Office had warned him that if the United States pushed Germany too far, the German government would seek an alliance with Japan and Russia, and would try to embroil the United States in conflict with Japan.—Gerard to Lansing, January 31 and February 11, 1916, *ibid.*, 155, 167.

[105] See Tansill, *America Goes to War*, 420. The New York *Times*, in an editorial on February 14, opposed any changes in the American policy of September, 1914, toward armed ships on the basis that such would destroy the value of the *Arabic* pledges and would allow Germany a free hand in the prosecution of submarine warfare.

[106] Lansing, *War Memoirs*, 116.

[107] Morrissey, *American Defense of Neutral Rights*, 111; Tansill, *America Goes to War*, 463–465.

[108] Senator Sterling introduced a resolution February 15 which opposed any change in the American policy toward armed ships.—*Cong. Rec.*, 64th Cong., 1st sess., 2759–2763. Senator Stone, chairman of the Foreign Relations Committee, then conferred with Lansing and planned the defense against Sterling's resolution. Stone to Lansing, February 15, 1916, Lansing Papers. Thereupon, Stone and Lodge clashed in debate on the issue, with Lodge defending the right of defensive armament in a long and somewhat irrelevant address.—*Cong. Rec.*, 2763–2766, 2768; see also, Henry Cabot Lodge, *War Addresses, 1915–1917* (Boston and New York: Houghton Mifflin Co., 1917), 85–114.

[109] Tansill, *America Goes to War*, 462; Millis, *Road to War*, 267–268.

[110] Tansill, *America Goes to War*, 465–467; Notter, *Origins of the Foreign Policy of Woodrow Wilson*, 488–490. Lansing recorded in his daily Desk Diary, on February 24, that Wilson had told Representatives Champ Clark, Henry D. Flood, and Claude Kitchin that he desired war with Germany.

[111] *For. Rel., 1916 Supp.*, 177–178.

[112] Entry of March 4, 1916, House Diary.

[113] Lansing to the Diplomatic Officers in Europe, February 16, 1916, *For. Rel., 1916 Supp.*, 170.

[114] Lansing to Flood, March 3, 1916, *For. Rel., Lansing Papers*, I, 343–347.

[115] See Morrissey, *American Defense of Neutral Rights*, 118–119. Appended to the memorandum which Lansing sent to Flood was a list of reference citations from authorities on international law, intended to support the administration's contention that a merchant vessel did have the right to arm defensively without becoming a ship of war. Among the citations was one by Chief Justice John Marshall on the *Nereide* case, arising out of the War of 1812. Lansing and the Joint State-Navy Neutrality Board quoted Marshall's decision as proof of the right of defensive armament. Borchard and Lage, *Neutrality for the United States*, 117–122, and Tansill, *America Goes to War*, 649, allege that this was a deliberate misrepresentation, since Marshall had ruled that the armed *Nereide* was "an open and declared belligerent," partaking fully of a belligerent character and the dangers pertaining thereto. Morrissey, *American Defense of Neutral Rights*, fn., 14–15, concludes that

Marshall has been misinterpreted and that he did not rule that the neutral character of neutrals traveling on armed belligerent merchantmen was forfeited by resistance offered by the ship, and that by his reference to "belligerent" character, Marshall only meant that a neutral on board an armed ship was subject to the danger of capture of the vessel and its removal to port for prize court proceedings.

[116] Spring-Rice to Lansing, March 23, 1916, *For. Rel., 1916 Supp.*, 211–212.

[117] Lansing to Spring-Rice, April 7, 1916, *For. Rel., 1916 Supp.*, 223–224.

[118] Lansing, Memorandum on the Status of Armed Merchant Vessels, March 25, 1916 (released on April 26), in Savage, *Maritime Commerce*, II, 487–492.

[119] The release of the memorandum was delayed in order to make easier Lansing's "retreat" from the January 18 position.

[120] See William Graves Sharp, *The War Memoirs of William Graves Sharp, American Ambassador to France, 1914–1919*, ed. by W. Dawson (London: Constable & Co., Ltd., 1931), 112, 124–125.

[121] Lansing to Wilson, March 27, 1916, *For. Rel., Lansing Papers*, I, 537–539.

[122] Baker, *Wilson, Life and Letters*, VI, 180; Seymour, *Intimate Papers*, II, 227.

[123] See Morrissey, *American Defense of Neutral Rights*, 126. The New York *Tribune* polled 81 senators and 318 members of the House of Representatives, and reported that only 4 felt that the *Sussex* attack justified a resort to war.

[124] Wilson to Lansing, March 30, 1916, *For. Rel., Lansing Papers*, I, 539.

[125] House recorded in his Diary, April 2, that no one, including himself, knew what Wilson intended to do and that Lansing was quite unhappy over the situation.— Seymour, *Intimate Papers*, II, 229.

[126] Lansing, *War Memoirs*, 135.

[127] Lansing, Draft Instructions to Gerard, handed to Wilson on April 6, 1916, *For. Rel., Lansing Papers*, I, 540–542.

[128] House Diary entry for April 5, 1916, in Seymour, *Intimate Papers*, II, 230, 231. House also tried to invoke the House-Grey plan for intervention, but Grey replied that the time was not yet opportune.

[129] Tansill, *America Goes to War*, 497–498.

[130] Lansing to Wilson, April 10, 1916, *For. Rel., Lansing Papers*, I, 542–543. Bernstorff called on Lansing on this same day and offered to help attempt to resolve the crisis, but the secretary only made noncommittal replies to the ambassador's overtures.—*For. Rel., Lansing Papers*, I, 544–545.

[131] The German secretary of state for foreign affairs to Ambassador Bernstorff, April 11, 1916 (received April 13), *For. Rel., Lansing Papers*, I, 545–546; Gerard to Lansing, April 11, 1916, *For. Rel., 1916 Supp.*, 227–229. Tansill, *America Goes to War*, 499, asserts that a careful check of the German Marine Archives shows that the German government was sincere in its belief that the *Sussex* had not been torpedoed.

[132] Lansing, *War Memoirs*, 137.

[133] Lansing to Wilson, April 12, 1916, *For. Rel., Lansing Papers*, I, 546–547.

[134] Lansing to Wilson, April 15, 1916, D/S File 763.72/2580A, Archives. Lansing also apparently tried to increase the presidential anger against Germany, writing Wilson on April 15 that a news dispatch indicated that the German government had decorated a submarine commander, one Lieutenant Steinbrinck, whom Lansing assumed to have been the commander of the craft which torpedoed the *Sussex*. Wilson was skeptical, and replied on April 17 that he did not know that the name of the submarine which attacked the *Sussex* had yet been ascertained.—*For. Rel., Lansing Papers*, I, 548–549, 551.

[135] Lansing to Gerard, April 18, 1916, *For. Rel., 1916 Supp.*, 232–236.

[136] Lansing, Memorandum of a Conversation with Bernstorff, April 20, 1916, *For. Rel., Lansing Papers*, I, 555–559.

[137] See Baker, *Wilson, Life and Letters*, VI, 191.

[138] Lansing to Wilson, April 24 and 25, 1916, *For. Rel., Lansing Papers*, I, 351–352, 561.

[139] For an account of Gerard's interview with Kaiser Wilhelm II, see James W. Gerard, *My Four Years in Germany* (New York: George H. Doran Co., 1917), 338–343.

[140] Gerard to Lansing, May 4, 1916, *For. Rel., 1916 Supp.*, 257–260.

[141] Lansing believed that Germany was motivated toward peace with America because of financial stringency, which perhaps could be repaired through loans raised in the United States, and because of the fear, prevalent among German commercial classes, of a postwar trade ostracism. Sketch of Count Johann von Bernstorff, May, 1916, Sketch Book, Lansing Papers.

[142] Lansing to Wilson, May 6, 1916, *For. Rel., Lansing Papers*, I, 563–564.

[143] *For. Rel., Lansing Papers*, I, 564–565.

[144] Seymour, *Intimate Papers*, II, 243.

[145] Lansing to Wilson, and Wilson to Lansing, May 8, 1916, *For. Rel. Lansing Papers*, I, 565–566; Lansing, *War Memoirs*, 143–144.

[146] Lansing to Gerard, May 8, 1916, *For. Rel., 1916 Supp.*, 263.

[147] *For. Rel., Lansing Papers*, I, 567.

[148] Lansing, *War Memoirs*, 142.

[149] Lansing did continue to try to "needle" the German government and Ambassador Bernstorff. Gerard reported on May 8 that the German government would punish the submarine officer responsible for the *Sussex* attack (*For. Rel., 1916 Supp.*, 265–266). Lansing thereafter repeatedly requested from Bernstorff specific details as to the "punishment," until at last the harassed ambassador complained to Colonel House that such "nagging" was unduly complicating official relations.—House to Wilson, May 14, 1916, Wilson Papers.

CHAPTER VII: RELATIONS WITH THE ALLIES

[1] "The President's Attitude Toward Great Britain and Its Dangers," September, 1916, Confidential Memoranda, Lansing Papers.

[2] See Tansill, *America Goes to War*, 548–549; Morrissey, *American Defense of Neutral Rights*, 138.

[3] Lansing, *War Memoirs*, 125.

[4] Lansing to Page, January 4, 1916, *For. Rel., 1916 Supp.*, 591–592. Lansing had consulted the State-Navy Neutrality Board, and the board on December 29 had held that the detention of a neutral vessel plying between neutrals, and not subject to the charge of violation of blockade, was illegal. The board especially condemned the British examination of mails bound from European neutrals to American ports.—Tansill, *America Goes to War*, 550–551.

[5] House to Wilson, January 7, 1916, Wilson Papers.

[6] Jusserand to Lansing (dated February 15), April 3, 1916, *For. Rel., 1916 Supp.*, 598–601.

[7] Page to Lansing, April 15, 1916, *For. Rel., 1916 Supp.*, 603.

[8] Lansing to Page, May 13, 1916, *For. Rel., 1916* Supp., 603–604.

[9] Lansing to Wilson, May 20, 1916, *For. Rel., Lansing Papers*, I, 308–309. Wilson replied on May 22 and approved the draft note. He commented that Lansing, who had been ill during the first part of May, had been "missed" at the recent Cabinet meeting.—*ibid.*, I, 309. The president's sympathy for the secretary's poor health was rather limited, however. Early in May, Wilson and House had planned to appoint Frank L. Polk, counselor of the state department, national chairman of the Democratic party. House advised Wilson that Lansing was too ill to spare Polk, but the president replied that Lansing's inconvenience was not as important as the needs of

the party. Nevertheless, because of the Colonel's repeated expressions of fear over the burden of work which would then fall on Lansing's shoulders, Wilson finally capitulated and turned instead to Vance McCormick.—Seymour, *Intimate Papers*, II, 349–351.

¹⁰ Lansing to Jusserand, May 24, 1916, *For. Rel., 1916 Supp.*, 604–608. Originally the State Department had planned to send the note only to Great Britain, but Grey, learning of this in advance, complained through Spring-Rice that the American government was being unfair in selecting cases that applied only to Great Britain, since the British government was acting in the name of all the Allies. Grey expressed the hope that the State Department was not following the German example of trying to divide the Allied Powers, and he added that a protest to Great Britain alone would further concentrate the hostility of the American public against the British government.—Seymour, *Intimate Papers*, II, 307–309.

¹¹ Morrissey, *American Defense of Neutral Rights*, 138.

¹² Jusserand to Lansing, October 12, 1916, *For. Rel., 1916 Supp.*, 624–628.

¹³ Lansing to Wilson, October 13, 1916, *For. Rel., Lansing Papers*, I, 321.

¹⁴ Lansing to Wilson, October 17; 1916, *For. Rel., Lansing Papers*, I, 321–322.

¹⁵ Wilson to Lansing, November 14, 1916, *For. Rel., Lansing Papers*, I, 325–326.

¹⁶ Page to Lansing, January 15, 1916, *For. Rel., Lansing Papers*, I, 305.

¹⁷ Lansing to Page, January 20, 1916, *For. Rel., Lansing Papers*, I, 305–307.

¹⁸ Page to Lansing, January 22, 1916, *For. Rel., Lansing Papers*, I, 306–307.

¹⁹ *Ibid.*

²⁰ Lansing to Wilson, January 24, 1916, *For. Rel., Lansing Papers*, I, 307–308.

²¹ Wilson to Lansing, January 24, 1916, *For. Rel., Lansing Papers*, I, 308. Lansing had felt that Page was reflecting the views of Colonel House, then in Europe, but Wilson replied that "... it is all Page."

²² For example, Sir Edward Grey was asked, in the House of Commons on October 28, 1915, if the modified declaration were not fettering the Navy, to which he replied that since the declaration had no international legality or force, the Navy was unhindered. Again, on March 9, 1916, Lord Robert Cecil had to defend the ministry against charges that the declaration was interfering with the blockade of Germany.—Great Britain, *The Parliamentary Debates*, Fifth Series, House of Commons, 1914–1917, Vol. 75, Col. 327–328, and Vol. 80, Col. 1812–1814.

²³ Page to Lansing, April 4, 1916, *For. Rel., 1916 Supp.*, 361. Article 19 prohibited the blockade of neutral ports.

²⁴ Lansing to Page, April 8, 1916, *For. Rel., 1916 Supp.*, 362.

²⁵ Lansing to Page, November 11, 1916, *For. Rel., 1916 Supp.*, 483.

²⁶ Spring-Rice to Lansing, April 24, 1916, *Command Papers*, Cd. 8234, 18–32, and *For. Rel., 1916 Supp.*, 368–382. Page had informed Lansing on April 19 that presentation of the note was being held because of the inopportuneness of the time, but that it would be presented whenever the Secretary indicated his preference.—*ibid.*, 364.

²⁷ Spring-Rice to Lansing, April 24, 1916, *Command Papers*, Cd. 8234, 18–32.

²⁸ See Tansill, *America Goes to War*, 528–529.

²⁹ Seymour, *Intimate Papers*, II, 284–285.

³⁰ Anderson to Lansing, January 10, 1916, Lansing Papers.

³¹ Notter, *Origins of the Foreign Policy of Woodrow Wilson*, 539.

³² Lansing to Wilson, June 23, 1916, *For. Rel., Lansing Papers*, I, 311–312.

³³ Sharp to Lansing, July 8, 1916, *For. Rel., 1916 Supp.*, 408; Lansing to Chargé Laughlin, September 18, 1916, *ibid.*, 446–447

³⁴ Lansing turned down several requests from New York state politicians that he consent to run as the Democratic candidate for governor and, similarly, he refused to accept the post of permanent chairman of the New York State Democratic Committee. Writing W. C. Osborn, the active state chairman, on February 12, he noted,

"The impression prevails that our foreign relations are entirely removed from partisanship of any sort. . . ."—Lansing Papers.

[35] Baker, *Wilson, Life and Letters*, VI, 244. Lansing on several occasions expressed his fears to Vance McCormick, Democratic national chairman, that this was a dangerous slogan.

[36] See the address by Elihu Root to the New York state convention, February 15, 1916, in Robert Bacon and James Brown Scott, eds., *Addresses on International Subjects by Elihu Root* (Cambridge: Harvard University Press, 1916), 427–447; and Lodge's address to the Harvard Republican Club, on October 23, 1916.—Lodge, *War Addresses*, 177–186.

[37] See Lansing to Bryan, January 9, 1915, *For. Rel., Lansing Papers*, I, 188–190.

[38] Lansing to Wilson, September 21, 1916, *For. Rel., Lansing Papers*, I, 569–570.

[39] Lansing to Wilson, September 22, 1916, *For. Rel., Lansing Papers*, I, 314–318.

[40] Wilson to Lansing, September 29, 1916, *For. Rel., Lansing Papers*, I, 570–571, 319. In regard to the *Lusitania*, Wilson cautioned Lansing that a move might enable Germany to supply German-American "mischief makers" with campaign materials.

[41] Lansing to Wilson, September 30 and October 2, 1916, *For. Rel., Lansing Papers*, I, 319–320, 571–572. Wilson had even hesitated to receive Ambassador Gerard, then on leave from his Berlin post, but Lansing persuaded him that failure to do so would stir up political trouble, the charge being that Wilson was too busy with politics to pay attention to an ambassador recently returned from one of the principal belligerents.—Lansing to Wilson, October 16, 1916, *ibid.*, I, 572–573.

[42] Lansing to Page, January 25, 1916, *For. Rel., 1916 Supp.*, 339.

[43] Page to Lansing, February 16, 1916, *For. Rel., 1916 Supp.*, 352–353.

[44] For a detailed discussion, see Thomas A. Bailey, "The United States and the Blacklist during the Great War," *Journal of Modern History*, VI (1934), 14–35.

[45] See Morrissey, *American Defense of Neutral Rights*, 144; Tansill, *America Goes to War*, 537; and Seymour, *American Diplomacy during the World War*, 74–79.

[46] The "hovering" of Allied warships just outside the three-mile limit, for the purpose of searching vessels as they left American ports, had been protested by the State Department on several occasions, notably December 16, 1915. *For. Rel., 1915 Supp.*, 879–880.

[47] The *China* case concerned the British removal of twenty-eight Germans, eight Austrians, and two Turkish nationals from the American vessel *China*, on February 18, 1916, while bound from Shanghai to Manila. Lansing lodged vigorous protests on the basis that the sovereignty of the United States had been violated, in a manner reminiscent of the Civil War *Trent* affair, and he demanded the immediate release of the captives. Public opinion was little concerned with the case, and Lansing was therefore free to concentrate on it for the sake of historical and legal precedent. Despite British protests that the seized men were enemy agents and military reservists, Lansing compelled their release. Even Ambassador Page displayed great energy in pressing the matter. See *For. Rel., 1916 Supp.*, 633–653; Thomas A. Bailey, "World War Analogues of the *Trent* Affair," *American Historical Review*, XXXVIII (1932–33), 286–290.

[48] Seymour, *Intimate Papers*, II, 313.

[49] Lansing's address was inserted in the *Congressional Record*, 64th Cong., 1st sess., Appendix 1170–1171, by William A. Cullop, representative from Indiana.

[50] Spring-Rice to Grey, June 9, 1916, in Gwynn, *Spring-Rice*, II, 336.

[51] Polk to Lansing, July 24, 1916, Polk Papers.

[52] Polk to Page, July 26, 1916, *For. Rel., 1916 Supp.*, 421–422.

[53] Lansing to Polk, July 31, 1916, Lansing Papers.

[54] See Seymour, *Intimate Papers*, II, 315. Wilson also chose to press a naval expansion program at this time.

⁵⁵ Lansing to Kitchin, August 17, 1916, *For. Rel., 1916 Supp.*, 432–434. Also see Bailey, "The United States and the Blacklist," *Jour. Mod. Hist.*, VI, 20; and Tansill, *America Goes to War*, 432–434. House recorded in his Diary, November 17, that he and Lansing had to do "team work" and guide the president along the right course.—Seymour, *Intimate Papers*, II, 327.

⁵⁶ Notter, *Origins of the Foreign Policy of Woodrow Wilson*, 546–547.

⁵⁷ Tansill, *America Goes to War*, 541–542.

⁵⁸ Redfield to Lansing, October 23, 1916, *For. Rel., 1916 Supp.*, 466–477.

⁵⁹ In late November, the Federal Reserve Board made a move to curb loans to the Allies, and a report was released November 26 which cautioned American banks against investments in unsecured Allied notes and loans.—Press Statement of the Federal Reserve Board, November 28, 1916, in Savage, *Maritime Commerce*, II, 535–537. Shortly thereafter, the comptroller of the currency planned to issue a statement which expressed pleasure at the limited amount of foreign currencies held in national banks, but by this time Wilson felt that the matter had gone too far, and with the aid of Lansing the statement was indefinitely delayed.—Tansill, *America Goes to War*, 122–124. Entries of December 4, 6, 1916, Lansing Desk Diary.

⁶⁰ Page to Lansing, October 11, 1916, *For. Rel., 1916 Supp.*, 455–456. Grey was also disturbed by the recent visit to America of the *Deutschland*, a merchant submarine, and he was especially irritated by the operations of the *U-53* off the American coast. Although British opinion blamed the United States for permitting the craft to enter American ports and waters, the State Department rejected the protests.—Lansing to Wilson, September 6, 1916, Wilson Papers; and Polk to House, October 19, 1916, in Seymour, *Intimate Papers*, II, 325–326.

⁶¹ Lansing to Page, November 24, 1916, *For. Rel., 1916 Supp.*, 485–486.

⁶² Bailey, "The United States and the Blacklist," *Jour. Mod. Hist.*, VI, 32–33.

⁶³ House to Wilson, October 20, 1916, in Seymour, *Intimate Papers*, II, 379.

⁶⁴ Seymour, *Intimate Papers*, II, 379–380; Lansing, *War Memoirs*, 165. Wilson took the precaution of sending Lansing a letter on the subject before the election, in order to avoid charges of a postelection chagrin and "grand-standing."

⁶⁵ House Diary entry for November 9, 1916, in Seymour, *Intimate Papers*, II, 382–383.

CHAPTER VIII: AMERICA ENTERS THE WAR

¹ "Certainty of War with Germany," January 28, 1917, Confidential Memoranda, Lansing Papers.

² Seymour, *Intimate Papers*, II, 411.

³ In May, 1916, the Spanish government proposed a joint effort at mediation, which the American government declined on the grounds the Allied Powers were not yet willing to entertain suggestions of a peace conference.—*For. Rel., 1916 Supp.*, 28–29, 46–47. In the same month, Wilson received a papal request that action on the *Sussex* crisis be postponed while an attempt was made to persuade the belligerents to reach a settlement. The American government postponed a reply until after the *Sussex* case was closed.—*For. Rel., Lansing Papers*, I, 15–16.

⁴ Buehrig views Wilson's policy as not lacking in acumen; faced by complex and novel problems, the president sought to pick his way carefully, gradually shifting from a policy based on defense of neutral rights, which he soon realized was an inadequate statement of the national interest, to a policy of mediation and collective security.—*Wilson and the Balance of Power*, 266.

⁵ "The President's Attitude toward Great Britain and Its Dangers," September, 1916, Confidential Memoranda, Lansing Papers. Lansing attributed much of Wilson's mediation plans to the ideas advanced by Colonel House.

⁶ Lansing, *War Memoirs*, 176–177.

⁷ "What Will the President Do?" December 3, 1916, Confidential Memoranda, Lansing Papers.

⁸ *Ibid.*

⁹ Gerard to Lansing, September 14, 1916, *For. Rel., Lansing Papers*, I, 569.

¹⁰ Gerard to Lansing, September 25, 1916, *For. Rel., 1916 Supp.*, 55; Bethmann-Hollweg to Bernstorff, October 9, 1916, *Official German Documents*, II, 986–987.

¹¹ Seymour, *Intimate Papers*, II, 404.

¹² Baker, *Wilson, Life and Letters*, VI, 387–388; Lansing, "When Wilson Failed as Peacemaker," *Saturday Evening Post*, June 20, 1931, 11. Lansing also, at the Colonel's request, helped dissuade Wilson from again sending House to Europe on a peace mission.

¹³ Lansing, *War Memoirs*, 178.

¹⁴ Lansing to Wilson, December 8, 1916, *For. Rel., Lansing Papers*, I, 575–576.

¹⁵ Lansing to Wilson, December 10, 1916, in Lansing, *War Memoirs*, 179–180; Baker, *Wilson, Life and Letters*, VI, 396.

¹⁶ Chargé Joseph C. Grew to Lansing, December 12, 1916, *For. Rel., 1916 Supp.*, 85–86.

¹⁷ Lansing, *War Memoirs*, 182–184; Houston, *Eight Years with Wilson*, I, 219. Josephus Daniels, *The Wilson Era: Years of War and After, 1917–1921* (Chapel Hill: University of North Carolina Press, 1946), 24, writes that within the Cabinet, Lansing, McAdoo, Lane, Redfield, and Houston stood for early entry into the war, without awaiting a German violation of the submarine pledges.

¹⁸ Lansing to the American Representatives in the Allied Capitals, December 16, 1916, *For. Rel., 1916 Supp.*, 94–95.

¹⁹ Lansing, *War Memoirs*, 184.

²⁰ Lansing to the American Representatives in the Belligerent Capitals, December 18, 1916, *For. Rel., 1916 Supp.*, 97–99. At the confidential press conference, held December 20, Lansing gave out news of the dispatch of the December 18 mediation proposal. Two reporters violated the secrecy rule and informed certain Wall Street stock speculators of the news in advance of the general release, and these men exploited the tip to make a handsome profit on the stock market. Charges were raised that Lansing had given Bernard Baruch advance information on the mediation note, and a congressional investigation resulted. Lansing maintained a dignified silence, except to deny that he had met Baruch, with whom the secretary was not acquainted at that time. The charges of improper conduct, with which Thomas W. Lawson was associated, were found to be unsubstantiated and the committee completely exonerated Lansing and other accused officials.—See Lansing, *War Memoirs*, 319–320; Blum, *Tumulty and the Wilson Era*, 122–128.

²¹ Page to Lansing, December 22, 1916, *For. Rel., 1916 Supp.*, 108–109. See Rappaport, *The British Press and Wilsonian Neutrality*, 109–112, for an account of the reaction of the British press.

²² *For. Rel., 1916 Supp.*, 106–107 (sent as a circular to diplomatic officers abroad).

²³ Lansing, *War Memoirs*, 186–190.

²⁴ Lansing to Edward N. Smith, January 21, 1917, Lansing Papers.

²⁵ Ambassador Spring-Rice told the secretary, on January 13, that his press statement had "saved the situation."—Lansing, *War Memoirs*, 190. Also see Baker, *Wilson, Life and Letters*, VI, 404–406; E. E. Robinson and V. J. West, *The Foreign Policy of Woodrow Wilson, 1913–1917* (New York: Macmillan Co., 1917), 132–133. The New York *Times*, in an editorial December 22, concluded that Lansing's statement showed that the nation was near war with the Central Powers, and that this fact had largely motivated Wilson's mediation note.

²⁶ E. Bolling Wilson, *My Memoir*, 122–123.

²⁷ Lansing, "When Wilson Failed as Peacemaker," *Saturday Evening Post*, June 20, 1931, 124. Lansing wrote that some "stock-dealing friends" of Wilson put pres-

sure on the president and Tumulty for a press retraction, since the original statement had caused wild gyrations on the stock market. House recorded the event in his Diary for December 21, and noted that although Lansing should have consulted Wilson in advance of the first press statement, it should have been allowed to stand as no harm was done.—House Diary.

[28] Peterson, *Propaganda for War*, 297–298.

[29] Tansill, *America Goes to War*, 623, points out that Wilson had "neglected" Colonel House in regard to the mediation note, and he had instead submitted the final drafts to Lansing for approval.

[30] Lansing to the American Representatives in the Belligerent Capitals, December 24, 1916, *For. Rel., 1916 Supp.*, 112.

[31] Zimmermann to Bernstorff, December 26, 1916, *Official German Documents*, II, 1005.

[32] Gerard to Lansing, December 26, 1916, *For. Rel., 1916 Supp.*, 117–118.

[33] Sharp to Lansing, January 10, 1916, United States Department of State, *Papers Relating to the Foreign Relations of the United States, 1917, Supplement No. 1* (Washington: G.P.O., 1931), 6–9. On December 29, the Allies, formally rejected the German peace overture of December 12.—*For. Rel., 1916 Supp.*, 123–125.

[34] House Diary Entry for January 11, 1917, in Seymour, *Intimate Papers*, II, 416.

[35] *Ibid.*; E. Bolling Wilson, *My Memoir*, 126–127.

[36] Lansing, *War Memoirs*, 193–194; Lansing, "When Wilson Failed as Peacemaker," *Saturday Evening Post*, June 20, 1931, 125–126. Ambassador Page also protested inclusion of the phrase.

[37] Lansing, *War Memoirs*, 194.

[38] *For. Rel., 1917 Supp. 1*, 24–29.

[39] Lansing, *War Memoirs*, 196.

[40] *Official German Documents*, II, 1320–1321.

[41] Elkus to Lansing, January 8, and Gerard to Lansing, January 11, 1917, *For. Rel., 1917 Supp. 1*, 81–82, 88.

[42] Bernstorff to Lansing, January 10, 1917, *For. Rel., 1917 Supp. 1*, 82–87. Bernstorff had received the memorandum on January 4. In his report to Zimmermann, he commented that it was useless to discuss the memorandum with Lansing, "since Wilson decides *everything*."—*Official German Documents*, II, 1017.

[43] Lansing to Wilson, January 12, 1917, Wilson Papers.

[44] Lansing to Wilson, December 21, 1916, Wilson Papers. On January 15, 1917, Lansing sent Wilson a list of twenty-one recent sinkings, which included several American vessels; the list included those sunk with warning.

[45] "Note on the Probable Renewal of Submarine Warfare," January 24, 1917, Confidential Memoranda, Lansing Papers. Lansing recounted that a member of the German embassy had recently been "overheard" expressing great alarm that a friend had just sailed for Europe.

[46] "Certainty of War with Germany," January 28, 1917, Confidential Memoranda, Lansing Papers.

[47] Lansing to Wilson, January 17, 1917, *For. Rel., Lansing Papers*, I, 580. For Page's letter of January 5, see *For. Rel., 1917 Supp.*, 1, 546.

[48] Tansill, *America Goes to War*, 633–635. While the armed-ship question was under consideration, Ambassador Bernstorff was negotiating with Colonel House on the matter of war aims. Lansing was more or less ignorant of these developments because of Wilson's neglect to keep the secretary fully informed. On January 24, House brought the secretary up to date and informed him that Bernstorff desired a quick signing of a "Bryan peace-treaty," presumably to prevent the United States from going to war over the forthcoming announcement of unrestricted submarine warfare.—House Papers.

⁴⁹ Wilson to Lansing, January 24, 1917, *For. Rel., Lansing Papers*, I, 581.

⁵⁰ Wilson to Lansing, January 31, 1917, *For. Rel., Lansing Papers*, I, 581.

⁵¹ Lansing did contemplate classifying armed vessels carrying gun crews belonging to the British Navy or its reserve units as one of the criteria pertaining to ships of war. When he so informed Ambassador Spring-Rice, the latter lost control of his emotions and berated the secretary for allegedly attempting to deprive merchant vessels of their defenses against the "ruthless" submarine. In contradistinction, Ambassador Jusserand received the information calmly and agreed with Lansing that a way could be easily found to satisfy such a policy, perhaps by merely having the ship companies, instead of the Allied governments, pay the salaries of the gun crews.—"Memorandum of an Interview with the British Ambassador," January 18, and "Memorandum of an Interview with the French Ambassador," January 22, 1917, Confidential Memoranda, Lansing Papers.

⁵² Memorandum on Armed Merchantmen, January 30, 1917, *For. Rel., Lansing Papers*, I, 584–591.

⁵³ Lansing to Wilson, January 31, 1917, *For. Rel., Lansing Papers*, I, 582–584.

⁵⁴ *For. Rel., Lansing Papers*, I, fn., 582.

⁵⁵ Lansing to Wilson, January 31, 1917, *For. Rel., Lansing Papers*, I, 581–582.

⁵⁶ Bernstorff to Lansing, January 31, 1917, *For. Rel., 1917 Supp. 1*, 96–102.

⁵⁷ Bernstorff to House, January 31, 1917, *For. Rel., 1917 Supp. 1*, 34–36. Lansing felt that the Allied Powers never would have accepted such terms.—*War Memoirs*, 197–198.

⁵⁸ Lansing, *War Memoirs*, 222; Bernstorff, *My Three Years in America*, 379–380.

⁵⁹ "Memorandum of the Severance of Diplomatic Relations with Germany," February 4, 1917, Confidential Memoranda, Lansing Papers.

⁶⁰ *Ibid.* At the Cabinet meeting of February 2, Wilson again referred to the "yellow" danger and the possibility that an American entry into the war might enable Japan, perhaps through an alliance with Russia, to dominate China.—Houston, *Eight Years with Wilson*, I, 229. Lansing was also cognizant of such threats but believed that the best way to meet them was by ensuring an Allied victory.

⁶¹ Seymour, *Intimate Papers*, II, 439; Appointment Book, Lansing Papers.

⁶² "Memorandum of the Severance of Diplomatic Relations with Germany," February 4, 1917, Confidential Memoranda, Lansing Papers. Before going to the White House for this conference, Senator Stone suggested to Lansing that the belligerents be requested to agree to a ten-day armistice. Lansing, who viewed this proposal as merely a stalling device, rejected it as of no practical value.

⁶³ Lansing to Wilson, February 2, 1917, *For. Rel., Lansing Papers*, I, 591–592.

⁶⁴ *Ibid.*

⁶⁵ Franklin K. Lane to George W. Lane, February 9, 1917, in Lane and Wall, *Letters of Franklin K. Lane*, 233–234.

⁶⁶ "Memorandum of the Severance of Diplomatic Relations with Germany," February 4, 1917, Confidential Memoranda, Lansing Papers.

⁶⁷ *Ibid.*

⁶⁸ *Ibid.*

⁶⁹ Lansing to Bernstorff, February 3, 1917, *For. Rel., 1917 Supp. 1*, 106–108. Lansing, despite his distrust and dislike for Bernstorff, believed that the ambassador had done his best to avert war and had warned Berlin of the full implications of submarine warfare. Consequently, Lansing wrote Bernstorff, on the eve of his departure, that he was "...not unmindful of the efforts which you have made to prevent the break which has occurred...."—Lansing to Bernstorff, February 13, 1917, Lansing Papers. Also see Bernstorff, *My Three Years in America*, 393.

⁷⁰ Lansing to Edward N. Smith, February 27, 1917, Lansing Papers.

⁷¹ Lansing, *War Memoirs*, 219.

[72] Lansing, *War Memoirs*, 307.

[73] Lansing to Wilson, February 5, and March 26, 1917, *For. Rel., Lansing Papers*, I, 593, 631–632. Lansing feared German activities in these areas, which would menace the Panama Canal.

[74] Memorandum, dated February 1, 1917, Lansing Papers.

[75] See Thomas A. Bailey, *The Policy of the United States toward the Neutrals, 1917–1918* (Baltimore: Johns Hopkins Press, 1942), 20–26.

[76] Lansing, *War Memoirs*, 198–201; Notter, *Origins of the Foreign Policy of Woodrow Wilson*, 619–621; Baker, *Wilson, Life and Letters*, VI, 464–465.

[77] *For. Rel., Lansing Papers*, I, 19–20.

[78] Lansing, *Peace Negotiations*, 16–17.

[79] Lansing's Comments on Wilson's "Bases of Peace," February 7, 1917, *For. Rel., Lansing Papers*, I, 20–22. The memorandum, although not identified as to author, has corrections in Lansing's handwriting. In his *War Memoirs*, 200–201, Lansing states that the document was his and was forwarded to the president.

[80] *For. Rel., Lansing Papers*, I, 20–22.

[81] Lansing, *War Memoirs*, 201–202.

[82] Another "peace" move failed at the same time. Ambassador Bernstorff, before his departure, handed the Swiss minister a memorandum which proposed a resumption of negotiations between the United States and Germany, providing that the submarine blockade was allowed to continue. The United States refused to enter any discussion until the *Sussex* pledge was renewed. See *For. Rel., Lansing Papers*, I, 597–599; and *For. Rel., 1917 Supp. 1*, 126, 129, 139–141.

[83] For a brief account, see Notter, *Origins of the Foreign Policy of Woodrow Wilson*, 622–624.

[84] Lansing, *War Memoirs*, 247–248.

[85] Lansing to Penfield, February 4, 1917, *For. Rel., 1917 Supp. 1*, 112–113.

[86] Lansing to Page, February 8, and Page to Lansing, February 11, 1917, *For. Rel., 1917 Supp. 1*, 40–41; 41–44. Lloyd George, the British prime minister, gave the Allied reply to Ambassador Page.

[87] Page to Lansing, February 21, and Penfield to Lansing, February 28, 1917, *For. Rel., 1917 Supp. 1*, 56, 62–63.

[88] "Memorandum of an Interview with Count Tarnow Tarnowski, the ambassador-designate of Austria-Hungary," March 29, 1917, Confidential Memoranda, Lansing Papers.

[89] Zwiedinek to Lansing, April 9, 1917, *For. Rel., 1917 Supp. 1*, 594–595. In a final interview with Tarnowski, Lansing tried to impress upon him that America would enable the Allies to win the war and thus the Allies, not Germany, would determine the peace. The secretary also remarked that Poland would be restored to independence, and that the German city of Danzig would either be turned over to the new Poland or else be declared a free port.—"Memorandum of My Last Interview with Count Tarnowski before his departure from Washington," May 1, 1917, Confidential Memoranda, Lansing Papers.

[90] Lansing to Wilson, February 13, 1917, *For. Rel., Lansing Papers*, I, 604.

[91] Blum, *Tumulty and the Wilson Era*, 130–131; Lansing, *War Memoirs*, 224–225. The British government offered to arm American vessels.—Lansing to Wilson, February 14, 1917, in Savage, *Maritime Commerce*, II, 563–564.

[92] Lansing, Memoranda on Arming Merchant Vessels, February 21 and March 6, 1917, D/S File 763.72/3468½ and 3468½A, Archives.

[93] Baker, *Wilson, Life and Letters*, VI, 472. For the text of the address, see Savage, *Maritime Commerce*, II, 568–569. At a Cabinet meeting in late February, Secretary Lane remarked that, according to reports, the wives of American consular officials leaving Germany were stripped and given acid baths in order to de-

tect any secret writing on their flesh. Allegedly, Lansing reported that these obviously wild rumors were true. See Lane and Wall, *Letters of Franklin K. Lane*, 239–240; and Daniels, *Wilson Era, Years of War*, 20.

[94] See Millis, *Road to War*, 410.

[95] Page to Lansing, February 24, 1917, *For. Rel., 1917 Supp. 1*, 147–148.

[96] "Memorandum on the Message of Zimmermann to the German Minister to Mexico," March 4, 1917, Confidential Memoranda, Lansing Papers. The British desired to conceal the fact that they had "cracked" the German cipher, as they hoped to continue to intercept and translate German code messages.

[97] Millis, *Road to War*, 407–408.

[98] Lansing, *War Memoirs*, 231–232.

[99] Lansing to Edward N. Smith, March 3, 1917, Lansing Papers.

[100] Lansing to Wilson, March 6, 1917, Wilson Papers.

[101] Lansing to Wilson, March 8, 1917, *For. Rel., Lansing Papers*, I, 616–618.

[102] Savage, *Maritime Commerce*, II, 581. This action was based on a statute of 1797.

[103] "Note on War with Germany," March 19, 1917, Confidential Memoranda, Lansing Papers. For an interesting treatment of the transitional phase to war, which emphasizes the role of the *Laconia* sinking and the Zimmermann telegram, see Samuel K. Spencer, Jr., *Decision for War, 1917* (Rindge, N.H.: Richard R. Smith, 1953). Spencer views the sinking of the British liner *Laconia* on February 25, 1917, as the German "overt act" awaited by Wilson, and the move to arm merchant vessels as the type of response envisioned by the president when relations with Germany had been severed.—pp. 36–37, 49–50. In comment, to Lansing the "overt act" came later, and the expected response was to be a war entry.

[104] Page to Lansing, March 5, 1917, in Savage, *Maritime Commerce*, II, 570–571.

[105] Lansing, *War Memoirs*, 233–234.

[106] Lansing to House, March 19, 1917, *For. Rel., Lansing Papers*, I, 628–629.

[107] House to Lansing, March 20, 1917, *For. Rel., Lansing Papers*, I, 629–630.

[108] Lansing to Wilson, March 19, 1917, *For. Rel., Lansing Papers*, I, 626–628.

[109] *Ibid.*

[110] Houston, *Eight Years with Wilson*, I, 241–244.

[111] "Memorandum of the Cabinet Meeting," March 20, 1917, Confidential Memoranda, Lansing Papers.

[112] *Ibid.*

[113] House Diary Entry for April 2, 1917, in Seymour, *Intimate Papers*, II, 467–468; Lansing, *War Memoirs*, 238.

[114] For the War Address of April 2, 1917, see *For. Rel., 1917 Supp. 1*, 195–203.

[115] House to Lansing, April 5, 1917, *For. Rel., Lansing Papers*, I, 638.

[116] Lansing to House, April 4, 1917, *For. Rel., Lansing Papers*, I, 636.

[117] Savage, *Maritime Commerce*, II, 596–597.

[118] Lansing to Edward N. Smith, April 7, 1917, Lansing Papers.

[119] "Memorandum on Our Declaration of War Against Germany," April 7, 1917, Confidential Memoranda, Lansing Papers. Lansing here indicated that he already was thinking not of a limited participation in the war but rather of a full involvement in the struggle.

CHAPTER IX: CONCLUSIONS

[1] See Buehrig, *Wilson and the Balance of Power*, 83, 103–104.

[2] Sketch of Count Johann von Bernstorff, May, 1916, Sketch Book, Lansing Papers.

[3] See Link, *Wilson and the Progressive Era*, 277, 279–281.

[4] Buehrig, *Wilson and the Balance of Power*, 168–169, 266, 272–275.

BIBLIOGRAPHY

BIBLIOGRAPHY

MANUSCRIPTS

PRIVATE PAPERS

(All are in the Library of Congress, Manuscripts Division, unless otherwise noted.)

William Jennings Bryan. The letter books are the most valuable, although much of the correspondence therein, pertaining to the functions of the State Department, has been printed in Volume I, *For. Rel., Lansing Papers.*

Josephus Daniels. This collection has not been entirely opened, with the Diary and selected correspondence closed to scholars. Of the remaining materials, a few were pertinent to this study. (1952.)

Edward Mandell House—Yale University Library. The files on the House-Lansing correspondence and the private diaries were most valuable; much of this material has not been published.

Robert Lansing, 1911–1928. Includes 62 volumes of correspondence, daily Desk Diary books, and Confidential Memoranda. Upon Lansing's death, the State De-partment removed a valuable selection of diplomatic documents from this collection, but the remainder is of great value, particularly the private memoranda.

Breckinridge Long. These papers have not yet been completely processed, and most of the collection relates to the period of Lansing's career after 1917. Long was Third Assistant Secretary of State.

Woodrow Wilson. 1,183 boxes, arranged in nine series. Most valuable, contains material as yet unexploited.

In addition, the following collections were consulted which have some bearing on this study:

Chandler Parsons Anderson
Newton D. Baker (those sections available in 1954)
John Watson Foster
Leland Harrison
Frank L. Polk (House Collection, Yale University Library)
Elihu Root
William Howard Taft

OFFICIAL DOCUMENTS

United States Department of State. Diplomatic Correspondence, 1914–1920. Instructions, dispatches, miscellaneous letters, and interdepartmental memoranda which are in the Foreign Affairs Section of the National Archives.

PRINTED DOCUMENTS

GERMANY

Carnegie Endowment for International Peace, Division of International Law. *Official German Documents Relating to the World War* (New York and London: Oxford University Press, 1923). 2 vols. A valuable compilation, including testimony before the *Reichstag* concerning the outbreak of hostilities with the United States.

GREAT BRITAIN

British and Foreign State Papers, 1914–1920 (London: His Majesty's Stationery Office, 1918–1923). Vols. 108–113. Contain the major diplomatic exchanges with the United States.

Correspondence Between His Majesty's Government and the United States Respecting the Rights of Belligerents, Command Papers (London, His Majesty's Stationery Office, 1915–16). Cd. 7816, 8233, 8234.

The Parliamentary Debates, House of Commons. Fifth Series, 1914–17.

UNITED STATES

Congressional Record, 1914–1917.

Department of State. *American and British Claims Arbitration, under the Special Agreement concluded between the United States and Great Britain, August 18, 1910: Report of Fred K. Nielsen* (Washington: G.P.O., 1926). 638 pp.

Department of State. *Papers Relating to the Foreign Relations of the United States, 1914, 1915, 1916, 1917, Supplements* (Washington: G.P.O., 1928–31). A selection of the most important material pertaining to relations with the European belligerents during the period of American neutrality.

Department of State. *Papers Relating to the Foreign Relations of the United States; The Lansing Papers, 1914–1920* (Washington: G.P.O., 1940). 2 vols. These documents were removed from Lansing's collection after his death in 1928 and are a valuable selection covering the major events during the neutrality period (vol. I) and the war participation (vol. II).

Congress. Senate. *Hearings Before the Special Senate Committee on the Investigation of the Munitions Industry,* 74th Cong., 2d sess. Contains documents relating to Lansing's role in the approval of credits and loans to the belligerents.

Savage, Carlton, ed. *Policy of the United States toward Maritime Commerce in War* (Washington: G.P.O., 1936). 2 vols. A valuable collection of selected documents pertaining to neutral rights, mostly from the World War I period.

LETTERS, DIARIES, MEMOIRS, AND AUTOBIOGRAPHIES

Bacon, Robert, and James Brown Scott, eds. *Addresses on International Subjects by Elihu Root* (Harvard University Press, 1916). 463 pp.

Baker, Ray Stannard. *Woodrow Wilson: Life and Letters* (Garden City, New York: Doubleday, Doran & Co., 1935–39). 8 vols.

Baker, Ray Stannard, and William E. Dodd, eds. *The Public Papers of Woodrow Wilson* (New York: Harper & Bros., 1925–26). 6 vols.

Bernstorff, Count Johann von. *My Three Years in America* (New York: Chas. Scribner's Sons, 1920). 428 pp.

———. *Memoirs of Count Bernstorff,* transl. from German (New York: Random House, 1936). 383 pp.

Bethmann-Hollweg, Theobald von. *Reflections on the World War,* transl. by George Young (London: Butterworth, Ltd., 1920). 172 pp.

Bryan, William Jennings and M. B. *Memoirs of William Jennings Bryan* (Philadelphia: John C. Winston Co., 1925). 560 pp.

Burian, Baron Stephen. *Austria in Dissolution* (New York: George H. Doran Co., 1925). 455 pp.

Daniels, Josephus. *The Life of Woodrow Wilson, 1856–1924* (Will H. Johnston, 1924). 381 pp.

———. *The Wilson Era: Years of Peace, 1910–1917* (Chapel Hill: University of North Carolina Press, 1944). 615 pp.

———. *The Wilson Era: Years of War and After, 1917–1921* (Chapel Hill: University of North Carolina Press, 1946). 654 pp.

Dumba, Constantin. *Memoirs of a Diplomat*, transl. by I. F. D. Morrow (Boston: Little, Brown & Co., 1932). 347 pp.

Falkenhayn, General Erich Georg A. S. von. *The German General Staff and its Decisions, 1914–1916* (New York: Dodd, Mead & Co., 1920). 332 pp.

Foster, John Watson. *Diplomatic Memoirs* (Boston and New York: Houghton Mifflin Co., 1909). 2 vols.

Gerard, James W. *My Four Years in Germany* (New York: George H. Doran Co., 1917). 448 pp.

Grew, Joseph C. *Turbulent Era, A Diplomatic Record of Forty Years, 1904–1945* (Boston: Houghton Mifflin Co., 1952). 2 vols.

Grey, Viscount of Fallodon. *Twenty-Five Years, 1892–1916* (New York: Frederick A. Stokes Co., 1937). 2 vols. in one.

Gwynn, Stephen, ed. *The Letters and Friendships of Sir Cecil Spring-Rice* (Boston: Houghton Mifflin Co., 1929). 2 vols.

Harding, William P. G. *The Formative Period of the Federal Reserve System* (Boston: Houghton Mifflin Co., 1925). 320 pp.

Hendrick, Burton J., ed. *The Life and Letters of Walter H. Page* (Garden City, New York: Doubleday, Page & Co., 1926). 3 vols.

Houston, David F. *Eight Years with Wilson's Cabinet* (Garden City, New York: Doubleday, Page & Co., 1926). 2 vols.

Hull, Cordell. *The Memoirs of Cordell Hull* (New York: Macmillan Co., 1948). 2 vols.

Ishii, Kikujiro. *Diplomatic Commentaries*, ed. by Wm. R. Langdom (Baltimore: Johns Hopkins University Press, 1936). 351 pp.

Jusserand, Jean Jules. *Le Sentiment Amércain pendant la Guerre* (Paris: Payot, 1931). 157 pp.

Lane, A. W., and L. H. Wall, eds. *The Letters of Franklin K. Lane* (Boston and New York: Houghton Mifflin Co., 1922). 473 pp.

Lansing, Robert. *War Memoirs of Robert Lansing, Secretary of State* (Indianapolis: Bobbs-Merrill, 1935). 383 pp. Published after his death, and based upon his private memoranda and correspondence, 1915–1917. No reference is made to his role in regard to loans and credits to the Allies, and very little material on his career as counselor of the State Department.

———. *The Peace Negotiations, A Personal Narrative* (Boston & New York: Houghton Mifflin Co., 1921). 328 pp. Lansing's apologia for his role at the Paris Peace Conference.

———. "The North Atlantic Fisheries Arbitration," *American Journal of International Law*, V (1911), 1–31.

———. "The Difficulties of Neutrality," *Saturday Evening Post*, April 18, 1931, 6–7.

———. "When Wilson Failed as Peacemaker." *Saturday Evening Post*, June 20, 1931, 10–11.

Lodge, Henry Cabot. *War Addresses, 1915–1917* (Boston and New York: Houghton Mifflin Co., 1917). 303 pp.

———. *The Senate and the League of Nations* (New York: Charles Scribner's Sons, 1925). 424 pp.

McAdoo, William G[ibbs]. *Crowded Years, the Reminiscences of William G. McAdoo* (Boston and New York: Houghton Mifflin Co., 1931). 542 pp.

Nevins, Allan, ed. *The Letters and Journal of Brand Whitlock* (New York: Appleton-Century Co., 1936). 2 vols.

Orlando, Vittorio Emanuele. "Wilson and Lansing," *Saturday Evening Post*, March 23, 1929, 6–7.

Phillips, William. "The Reminiscences of William Phillips," Ms., Oral History Research Office, Columbia University.

———. *Ventures in Diplomacy* (Boston: The Beacon Press, 1952). 477 pp.

Redfield, William Cox. *With Congress and Cabinet.* (Garden City, New York: Doubleday, Page & Co., 1924). 307 pp.

Scott, James Brown, ed. *President Wilson's Foreign Policy, Messages, Addresses and Papers* (New York and London: Oxford University Press, 1918). 424 pp.

Seymour, Charles, ed. *The Intimate Papers of Colonel House* (Boston and New York: Houghton Mifflin Co., 1926–28). 4 vols.

Sharp, William Graves. *The War Memoirs of William Graves Sharp, American Ambassador to France, 1914–1919*, ed. by W. Dawson (London: Constable & Co., Ltd., 1931). 431 pp.

Straus, Oscar S. *Under Four Administrations; from Cleveland to Taft* (Boston and New York: Houghton Mifflin Co., 1922). 456 pp.

Tumulty, Joseph P. *Woodrow Wilson as I Know Him* (Garden City, New York: Doubleday, Page & Co., 1921). 553 pp.

Villard, Oswald Garrison. *Fighting Years, Memoirs of a Liberal Editor* (New York: Harcourt, Brace & Co., 1939). 543 pp.

Wilson, Edith Bolling. *My Memoir* (Indianapolis: Bobbs-Merrill, 1939). 386 pp.

NEWSPAPERS AND PERIODICALS

Current Opinion.
The Literary Digest.
New Republic.
New York *Times.*
The Outlook.

BOOKS AND ARTICLES

Annin, Robert Edwards. *Woodrow Wilson, a Character Study* (New York: Dodd, Mead & Co., 1924). 404 pp.

Arnett, A. M. *Claude Kitchin and the Wilson War Policies* (Boston: Little, Brown & Co., 1937). 341 pp.

Atwater, Elton. *American Regulation of Arms Exports* (Washington: Carnegie Endowment for International Peace, Division of International Law, Monograph No. 4, 1941). 287 pp.

Bailey, Thomas A. "World War Analogues of the *Trent* Affair," *American Historical Review*, XXXVIII (1932–33), 286–290.

———. "The United States and the Blacklist during the Great War," *Journal of Modern History*, VI (1934), 14–35.

———. "The Sinking of the Lusitania," *American Historical Review*, XLI (1935), 54–73.

———. *The Policy of the United States toward the Neutrals, 1917–1918* (Baltimore: Johns Hopkins University Press, 1942). 520 pp.

———. *A Diplomatic History of the American People* (New York: Appleton-Century-Crofts, 1950, 4th ed.). 986 pp.

Bausman, Frederick. *Facing Europe* (New York and London: Century Co., 1926). 330 pp.

Beard, Charles A. *The Devil Theory of War; an Inquiry into the Nature of History and the Possibility of Keeping Out of War* (New York: Vanguard Press, 1936). 124 pp.

———. "New Light on Bryan and the Wilson War Policies," *The New Republic*, Vol. 87 (June 17, 1936), 177–178.

Birdsall, Paul. "Neutrality and Economic Pressures, 1914–1917," *Science and Society*, III (Spring, 1939). 217–228.

Blum, John M. *Joe Tumulty and the Wilson Era* (Boston: Houghton Mifflin Co., 1951). 337 pp.

Borchard, Edwin M., and W. P. Lage. *Neutrality for the United States* (New Haven: Yale University Press, 1940, 2d ed.). 461 pp.

Briggs, Herbert W. *The Doctrine of Continuous Voyage* (Baltimore: Johns Hopkins University Press, 1926). 226 pp.

Buehrig, Edward H. *Woodrow Wilson and the Balance of Power* (Indiana University Press, 1955). 325 pp.

Callahan, James M. *American Foreign Policy in Mexican Relations* (New York: Macmillan Co., 1932). 644 pp.

Child, Clifton James. "German-American Attempts to Prevent the Exportation of Munitions of War, 1914–1915," *Mississippi Valley Historical Review*, XXV (1938–39), 351–368.

———. *The German-Americans in Politics, 1914–1917* (Madison: University of Wisconsin Press, 1939). 193 pp.

Consett, M. W. W. P., and O. H. Daniel. *The Triumph of Unarmed Forces, 1914–1918* (London: Williams & Norgate, 1923). 344 pp.

Crighton, J. C. "The *Wilhelmina:* An Adventure in the Assertion and Exercise of American Trading Rights during the World War," *American Journal of International Law*, XXXIV (1940), 74–88.

Curti, Merle E. *Bryan and World Peace*, in *Smith College Studies in History*, Nos. 3 and 4, 1931, Vol. 16, pp. 113–262.

Davis, Forest. *The Atlantic System, the Story of Anglo-American Control of the Seas* (London: George Allen & Unwin Ltd., 1943). 328 pp.

"Editorial Comment on the Appointment of Mr. Robert Lansing as Counselor of the Department of State," *American Journal of International Law*, VIII (1914), 336–338.

Einstein, Lewis. "The United States and Anglo-German Rivalry," *The National Review*, LX (January, 1913), 736–750. Actually signed by "Washington."

Foster, H. Schuyler, Jr. "How America Became Belligerent; A Quantitative Study of War News, 1914–1917," *American Journal of Sociology*, XL (January, 1935), 464–475.

Fuller, Joseph V. "The Genesis of the Munitions Traffic," *Journal of Modern History*, VI (1934), 280–293.

——. "William Jennings Bryan," in Samuel Flagg Bemis, ed., *The American Secretaries of State and Their Diplomacy* (10 vols., New York: Alfred A. Knopf, 1929), X, 4–44. Signed "Anonymous."

Garner, James Wilford. *International Law and the World War* (London and New York: Longmans, Green & Co., 1920). 2 vols.

——. "Violations of Maritime Law by the Allied Powers during the World War," *American Journal of International Law*, XXV (1931), 26–49.

Grattan, C. Hartley. *Why We Fought* (New York: Vanguard Press, 1929). 453 pp.

Guichard, Louis. *The Naval Blockade*, transl. by C. R. Turner (New York: D. Appleton & Co., 1930). 321 pp.

Hackett, Charles W. *The Mexican Revolution and the United States, 1910–1926* (Boston: World Peace Foundation, 1926), IX, 339–446.

Hibben, Paxton, and C. Hartley Grattan. *The Peerless Leader, William Jennings Bryan* (New York: Farrar & Rinehart, 1929). 446 pp.

Hill, Charles E. "John Watson Foster," *The Dictionary of American Biography* (31 vols., ed. by Dumas Malone, 1933), VI, 551–2.

Hofstadter, Richard. *The American Political Tradition and the Men Who Made It* (New York: Alfred A. Knopf, 1949). 378 pp.

Howden-Smith, Arthur D. *Mr. House of Texas* (New York & London: Funk & Wagnalls Co., 1940). 381 pp.

Hurd, Sir Archibald. *The Merchant Navy* (London: John Murray, 1921–29). 3 vols.

Hyde, Charles C. *International Law Chiefly as Interpreted and Applied by the United States* (Boston: Little, Brown & Co., 1922). 2 vols.

Jessup, Philip C. *Elihu Root* (New York: Dodd, Mead & Co., 1938). 2 vols.

Kennan, George F. *American Diplomacy, 1900–1950* (University of Chicago Press, 1951). 155 pp.

Kenworthy, J. M., and George Young. *Freedom of the Seas* (London: Hutchinson & Co., 1928). 283 pp.

Kerney, James. *The Political Education of Woodrow Wilson* (New York and London: Century Co., 1926). 503 pp.

Lamont, Thomas W. *Henry P. Davison, the Record of a Useful Life* (New York and London: Harper Bros., 1933). 373 pp.

Lane, David F. "Robert Lansing as His Friends Know Him," *Colliers*, November 13, 1915, 22–24.

Lansing, Robert. *Notes on Sovereignty from the Standpoint of the State and the World* (Washington: Carnegie Endowment for International Peace, 1921). 94 pp.

——. "Drama of the Virgin Islands Purchase," July 19, 1931, Magazine Section, New York *Times*.

Lawrence, David. *The True Story of Woodrow Wilson* (New York: George H. Doran Co., 1924). 368 pp.

Leopold, Richard W. *Elihu Root and the Conservative Tradition* (Boston: Little, Brown & Co., 1954). 222 pp.

———. "The Problem of Intervention, 1917: an Historical Retrospect," *World Politics*, II (April, 1950), 405–425.

Link, Arthur S. *Wilson, the Road to the White House* (Princeton, New Jersey: Princeton University Press, 1947). 570 pp.

———. *Woodrow Wilson and the Progressive Era, 1910–1917* (New York: Harper & Bros., 1954). 331 pp.

Lippmann, Walter. *The Stakes of Diplomacy* (New York: Henry Holt & Co., 1915, 1917). 235 pp.

———. *United States Foreign Policy: Shield of the Republic* (Boston: Little, Brown & Co., 1943). 177 pp.

McMaster, John Bach. *The United States in the World War* (New York and London: D. Appleton & Co., 1918). 2 vols.

Mahan, A. T. *The Interest of America in International Conditions* (Boston: Little, Brown & Co., 1910 and 1915). 212 pp.

Millis, Walter. *Road to War: America, 1914–1917* (Boston: Houghton Mifflin Co., 1935). 466 pp.

Moore, John Bassett. *A Digest of International Law* (Washington: G.P.O., 1906). 8 vols.

———. "America's Neutrality Policy," New York *Times*, May 16, 1937, Magazine Section, 1.

Morrissey, Alice M. *The American Defense of Neutral Rights, 1914–1917* (Cambridge, Mass.: Harvard University Press, 1939). 230 pp.

Nearing, Scott, and Joseph Freeman. *Dollar Diplomacy, A Study in American Imperialism* (New York: Ruebsch & The Viking Press, 1925). 353 pp.

Notter, Harley. *The Origins of the Foreign Policy of Woodrow Wilson* (Baltimore: Johns Hopkins University Press, 1937). 695 pp.

Osgood, Robert Endicott. *Ideals and Self-Interest in America's Foreign Policy; The Great Transformation of the Twentieth Century* (University of Chicago Press, 1953). 491 pp.

Owsley, Frank L. "America and Freedom of the Seas, 1861–1865," in Avery Craven, ed., *Essays in Honor of William E. Dodd* (University of Chicago Press, 1935), 194–256.

Parkes, Henry Bamford. *A History of Mexico* (Boston: Houghton Mifflin Co., 1950–, rev. ed.). 446 pp.

Paxson, Frederic L. *American Democracy and the World War, Pre-War Years, 1913–1917* (Boston: Houghton Mifflin Co., 1936). 427 pp.

Perkins, Dexter. *America and Two Wars* (Boston: Little, Brown & Co., 1944). 213 pp.

———. *Hands Off: A History of the Monroe Doctrine* (Boston: Little, Brown & Co., 1941). 455 pp.

Peterson, Horace C. *Propaganda for War, the Campaign against 'American Neutrality, 1914–1917* (University of Oklahoma Press, 1939). 357 pp.

Phillips, Ethel C. "American Participation in Belligerent Commercial Controls, 1914–1917," *American Journal of International Law*, XXVII (1933), 675–693.

Pratt, Julius W. "Robert Lansing," in Samuel Flagg Bemis, ed., *The American Secretaries of State and Their Diplomacy* (10 vols., New York: Alfred A. Knopf, 1929), X, 47–175. Pratt had limited access to the Lansing Papers.

————. "Robert Lansing," *The Dictionary of American Biography* (31 vols., ed. by Dumas Malone, 1933), X, 609–611.

Rappaport, Armin. *The British Press and Wilsonian Neutrality* (Stanford University Press, 1951). 162 pp.

Robinson, E. E., and V. J. West. *The Foreign Policy of Woodrow Wilson, 1913–1917* (New York: Macmillan Co., 1917). 428 pp.

Scott, James Brown. "Robert Lansing, Counselor for the Department of State," *The American Review of Reviews*, LI (April, 1915), 424–427.

————. "The Secretaryship of State and Mr. Lansing," *The Atlantic Monthly*, CXVI (October, 1915), 568–572.

Seymour, Charles. *American Diplomacy During the World War* (Baltimore: Johns Hopkins University Press, 1934). 417 pp.

————. *American Neutrality, 1914–1917; Essays on the Causes of American Intervention in the World War* (New Haven: Yale University Press, 1935). 187 pp.

Spencer, Samuel K., Jr. *Decision for War, 1917;* the *Laconia* Sinking and the Zimmermann Telegram as Key Factors in the Public Reaction against Germany (Rindge, New Hampshire: Richard R. Smith Publisher, Inc., 1953). 109 pp.

Squires, James Duane. *British Propaganda at Home and in the United States from 1914 to 1917* (Cambridge, Mass.: Harvard University Press, 1935). 113 pp.

Stuart, Graham A. *American Diplomatic and Consular Practice* (New York and London: Appleton-Century Co., 1936). 560 pp.

————. *Latin America and the United States* (New York and London: Appleton-Century Co., 1943—4th ed.). 509 pp.

Syrett, H. C. "The Business Press and American Neutrality, 1914–1917," *Mississippi Valley Historical Review*, XXXII (1945), 215–230.

Tansill, Charles Callan. *America Goes to War* (Boston: Little, Brown & Co., 1938). 731 pp.

————. *The Purchase of the Danish West Indies* (Baltimore: Johns Hopkins Press, 1932). 548 pp.

Trevelyan, George Macaulay. *Grey of Fallodon* (London, New York and Toronto: Longmans, Green & Co., 1937). 393 pp.

Turlington, Edgar. *Neutrality, The World War Period*, Vol. III in Philip C. Jessup, *et al.*, eds., *Neutrality, Its History, Economics and Law* (4 vols., New York: Columbia University Press, 1936). 267 pp.

Vagts, Alfred. "Hopes and Fears of an American-German War, 1870–1915," *Political Science Quarterly* (1939–1940), Vol. 54, pp. 514–535, and Vol. 55, pp. 56–76.

Van Alstyne, Richard W. "Private American Loans to the Allies, 1914–1916," *Pacific Historical Review*, II (1933), 180–193.

————. "The Policy of the United States regarding the Declaration of London at the Outbreak of the Great War," *Journal of Modern History*, VII (1935), 434–447.

————. *American Diplomacy in Action* (Stanford University Press, 1947). 836 pp.

Viereck, George Sylvester. *The Strangest Friendship in History, Woodrow Wilson and Colonel House* (New York: Liveright, Inc., 1932). 375 pp.

Vinacke, Harold M. *A History of the Far East in Modern Times* (New York: F. S. Crofts & Co., 1941, 4th ed.). 643 pp.

Werner, M. R. *Bryan* (New York: Harcourt, Brace & Co., 1929). 374 pp.

Williams, Mary Wilhelmine. *Anglo-American Isthmian Diplomacy, 1815–1914* (Washington: American Historical Association, 1916). 356 pp.

Wise, Jennings C. *Woodrow Wilson, Disciple of Revolution* (New York: Paisley Press, 1938). 674 pp.

Wittke, Carl. *German-Americans and the World War* (Columbus, Ohio: Ohio Historical Collections, vol. 5, 1936). 223 pp.

INDEX

INDEX

Adams, George Burton, 179
Addams, Jane, Pacifist group shocked by Lansing, 195–196
Adriatic, 182
Alaska Boundary Tribunal, 1
Albert, Dr. Heinrich, 109; briefcase, 95, 97–98; not expelled, 111
Amherst College, 43
Ancona, 107, 113, 121; sunk, 110
Anderson, Chandler P., 2, 198; Anglo-American arbitrations, 175; *Falaba*, 190; British-Danish agreement, 138
Anglo-American arbitrations (Special Agreement of August, 1910), 1, 3, 175
Arabia, 149
Arabic, 76, 85, 107, 108, 109, 110, 115, 116, 131, 170, 200, 201; sunk 98–99; pledges 101, 103
Archibald, James F. J., 111, 195; Dumba's expulsion, 76–77, 102
Argentina, 14, 39
armed belligerent merchantmen, 19, 41, 57, 58, 182–183; problem of, 30–31; September, 1914, circular, 31; and the submarine, 31–32; *Lusitania*, 64, 65, 66, 88; *Hesperian*, 101; *Persia*, 113; Lansing's submarine-armed ship plan, 114–117, 204–205; new German policy, 123; circular of March, 1916, 127, 130; German memorandum of January, 1917, 153; and American reaction, 153–156
arms embargo: opposed by Lansing, 32–33; and neutrality, 33–34; Münsterberg letter, 37–39; Bryan-Stone letter, 39–40
Austria-Hungary: Dumba's recall, 76–77, 102; protests munitions trade, 95; and Lansing's reply, 95–97; *Ancona* crisis, 110, 113, 203, 204; denies responsibility for *Persia*, 113; and Lansing's submarine-armed ship proposal, 122–123; American efforts to detach from war, 161–162

Baker, Newton D., 194; considered by Wilson as Lansing's replacement, 78, 196
Bakhmeteff, George: Russian credit needs, 35; relations with Lansing, 75
Balfour, Sir Arthur James, 151–152

Baralong incident, 116, 200, 205
Baruch, Bernard, 214
Beer, George Louis, 179
Belgium, 18, 19, 44, 138, 140
Bering Sea Fur Seal arbitrations, 1
Berlin, 49
Bernstorff, Count Johann von, 119, 140, 151, 157, 192, 205, 206, 215; protests munitions trade, 39, 58–59; distrusted by Lansing, 75–76, 195; public opinion, 85; advises concessions, 89–90; cotton offer, 92; *Arabic* crisis, 100, 101, 103, 200; Archibald affair, 102, 201; and revived *Lusitania* negotiations, 109–110, 113, 121, 202–203, 204, 207; expulsion of von Papen and Boy-Ed, 111–112, 203; intrigues against Lansing, 122–123, 207; new armed-ship policy, 124; *Sussex*, 129–130, 209, 210; armed-ship memorandum, 153; announces unrestricted U-boat warfare, 156; receives passports, 158, 216; final peace effort, 217
Berwindvale, 127
Bethmann-Hollweg, Theobald von, 208
Bey, Rustem, 59, 190–191
blacklist, British controversy with America, 139, 141–143
Blaine, James G., 1
blockade, 42, 43, 51, 52, 54, 55, 56, 59, 63, 64, 77, 132, 152, 202; Britain's March 11, 1915, order-in-council, 53; cotton issue, 91–92; American protest of October 21, 1915, 104–105; Allied blockade well established by 1916, 135, 136; repeal of modified Declaration of London, 137, 138–139
Boy-Ed, Karl, 111
Brazil, 14
Bryan, William Jennings, 2, 3, 4, 6, 16, 31, 42, 44, 46, 47, 50, 54, 55, 59, 105, 176, 182, 194 215; and spoils-system, 3; chaos in State Department, 5; Nicaraguan treaty, 10–11; Declaration of London, 23; ban on belligerent loans, 34–35; short term credits, 36; letter to Senator Stone, 39–40; December 26, 1914, protest note, 47; efforts for submarine-foodstuffs arrangement, 52; opposed to strong note on *Falaba*, 57–58; objects to travel on belligerent

at outbreak of war, 19; opposes early mediation, 19; establishes Joint State-Navy Neutrality Board, 20; proclamation of neutrality, 20–21; negotiations on the Declaration of London, 22–30; criticisms of Page, 28; influence on Wilson, 30; 1914 armed-ship circular, 30–32; views on contraband trade, 32–33; Bryan ban on belligerent loans, 34; approves short-term credits, 35–36, 184; refutes Münsterberg letter, 36–39; Bryan-Stone letter, 39–40; "belligerent necessity," 43–44; policy of conciliation toward Allies, 44, 185–186; working arrangements on commerce, 46, 187; December 26, 1914, note to Allies, 46–47; rejects British reply of January 7, 1915, 47–48; transfer of ships, 48–49; frames "strict accountability" policy, 50–51, 188; suspects German "bargain," 51–52; predicts war with Germany, 52–53; reaction to Allied blockade, 53–55; for strong policy on the *Falaba* sinking, 56–59; rejects Bernstorff's arms trade protest, 59; reaction to the *Lusitania*, 60–61, 191; drafts strict note on *Lusitania*, 62; revises Wilson's draft, 62–63; against warning citizens, 63, 192; rejects German defense of *Lusitania* sinking, 65; signs second *Lusitania* note, 67; urges Bryan not to resign, 66–67; relations with Bryan, 68–70, 193; appointed Secretary of State, 70–72, 193, 194; relations with foreign envoys, 72–73; attracted by Jusserand, 73, 194; critical of Spring-Rice and Page, 73–75; irritated by di Cellere, 75; shocked by Bakhmeteff, 75; distrust of Bernstorff, 75–76, 195, 216; dislike of Dumba, 76–77; realism versus Wilson's intuition, 77–79; clashes with Wilson, 78–79; opposes formal mediation, 79; Wilson's lack of creative ideas, 80, 196; relations with House, 80–82; policy outlined in mid-1915, 83–84; rejects compromise offer on *Lusitania*, 85–89; concerned with American opinion, 87–88; Wilson's "freedom of the seas," 89; warns Bernstorff, 89–90; annoyance at British trade interferences, 90–91; repeal of Bryan loan ban, 93–95, 199; reply

to Austrian munitions trade protest, 95–97, 199–200; handles Dr. Albert affair, 98, 200; stern policy on the *Arabic*, 99; gives Bernstorff an "ultimatum," 100; dissatisfied with Bernstorff's pledge, 101; secures new *Arabic* pledges, 103, 200; forces recall of Dumba, 102, 201; and October 21, 1915, protest to Britain, 104–105; revives *Lusitania* negotiations, 108–110, 112, 206, 207, 208; feels war near, 108, 109–110; handles *Ancona* crisis, 110–111, 112–113, 203, 204; expulsion of von Papen and Boy-Ed, 111; disturbed by Senator Stone, 113; seeks submarine-armed ship *modus vivendi*, 114–118, 204–205; disappointed by British reaction, 119; House's reaction, 119–121, 206; House-Grey mediation scheme, 120, 206; Bernstorff "intrigue," 122–123, 206; congressional "revolt," 125–126, 207; retreats from *modus vivendi*, 126–127; *Sussex* crisis, 127–131, 209; restates American position toward belligerents, 131; fears drastic action against Allies, 132; Allied censorship of mails, 133–135; Page's analysis of America's interests, 136–137, 211; blockade issue, 135–139; fear of postwar Allied trade preference system, 138, 210; role in 1916 election, 139–141, 143, 144, 211, 212, 213; British blacklist, 141, 142–143; retaliatory legislation, 142–143; opposed 1916 mediation moves, 146–149; damages Wilson's peace move, 150–151, 214, 215; "peace without victory" address, 151–152; rejects German armed-ship memorandum of 1917, 153; feels *Sussex* pledge violated, 153; nearness of war, 154, 215; restatement of armed-ship policy, 155–156, 216; disabling of German ships, 156; urges Wilson to break with Germany, 156–158; ready for war, 159, 214; opposes effort for neutral front, 159–160; on Wilson's "Bases of Peace," 160–161; tries to detach Austria from war, 161–162, 217; arming American merchantmen, 162, 163; the Zimmermann telegram, 162–163; on overt act, 163; urges declaration of war, 164, 165; overjoyed at war message, 165; role

Lansing, Robert (*cont.*)
in neutrality period evaluated, 167–171; *War Memoirs*, 186; on American nationality, 204; health, 210–211
Latin America, 94, 160, 197
Lawson, Thomas W., 214
League to Enforce Peace, 78
League of Nations, 175, 196; Wilson's ideas criticized by Lansing, 78, 147–148, 160–161
Lloyd-George, David, 217
loans to belligerents, 19, 41, 103, 105, 167; Bryan ban, 34; short-term credits, 35–36; Bryan-Stone letter, 39–40, 185; ban repeal, 92–95, 199; and unrestricted submarine warfare, 152
Lodge, Henry Cabot, 204; Lansing's *modus vivendi*, 125, 208; 1916 election, 140
Long, Breckinridge, 81, 196
Lusitania, 60, 85, 87, 103, 104, 137, 170, 191, 192, 212; sunk 60–61; contraband goods, 62; first American note, 62–63; German defense, 64–65; second American note, 66; German compromise rejected, 85–86; third American note, 88–89; later negotiations, 89–90, 108–109, 112, 113, 119, 120, 121–122, 123, 201, 206, 207, 208; and 1916 election, 140–141

McAdoo, William Gibbs: Ship Purchasing bill, 48, 188; Lansing's appointment as secretary, 71–72, 177, 194; repeal of loan ban, 93, 94, 199; Dr. Albert affair, 98, 200; mediation, 149; for break with Germany, 158, 214; treasury manifests, 187
McCormick, Vance, 211, 212
McLemore, Atkins Jefferson, and Gore-McLemore resolution, 125–126
McRoberts, Samuel, 35, 184
Madero, Francisco, 12
Mahan, A. T., 179
mails, censorship, 133–135, 139, 141
Malone, Dudley Field, 62
Manchester Engineer, 127
Marina, 149
Martin, Thomas S., 193
Mayo, Admiral Henry T., 12, 13
mediation, 18, 19, 52, 79, 106, 119, 120, 121, 144, 213; Lansing opposes, 79, 146–148; and 1916 election, 145–146;

German 1916 note, 149; Wilson requests terms, 149, 150, 151; "peace without victory," 151–152; Wilson's final efforts, 159–162
Merion, 182
Mexico, 3, 11–12, 38, 177; Tampico affair, 12–16; Lansing's fears, 84, 197
Miller, David Hunter, 187
mines, use of, 49, 52
Monroe Doctrine, Lansing's restatement, 197
Moore, John Bassett, 3–4, 5, 70, 199
Morgan, J. P., and Company, 34–35, 36, 93–95 *passim*
Münsterberg, Hugo, 36–37, 40

Nation, 5
National City Bank of New York, 35, 36
naval stores, 45
Nereide case, cited by Lansing, 208–209
Netherlands, 25, 31; overseas trust, 46
neutral zone, considered by Lansing, 185
neutrality, definition, 185
Niagara Falls, and Mexican Conference, 14
Nicaragua, 10–11, 13, 178
Nicosian, *U-27*, and *Baralong* incident, 116, 200–201
Nieman, L. W., 203
North Atlantic Fisheries and Fur Seals Conference, in 1911, 1, 175

O'Gorman, James A., 3
Oliver, James H., 20
Orlando, Vittorio, 6
Osborn, W. C. 211
Outlook, 176

Page, Walter Hines, 23, 25, 27, 45, 47, 54, 137, 179, 186, 193, 195, 201–202, 211, 212; pro-Ally, 26; working arrangements on commerce, 26, 46; Declaration of London, 28–29; blockade, 54, 55; Lansing's opinion of, 73–75; irritated by "nagging" protests, 91, 198; reaction to October 21, 1915, protest, 106; and submarine-armed ship *modus vivendi*, 118, 119; mails issue, 134; blockade solution, 135–136; blacklist, 143; British reactions to Wilson's peace moves, 149; armed-ship policy change, 155, 211; Austria, 161;